PERSIAN COOKING
A Table of Exotic Delights

PERSIAN COOKING

A Table of Exotic Delights

Nesta Ramazani

QUADRANGLE

The New York Times Book Company

Book design: Tere LoPrete

Drawings by Leita Mitchell

Color photographs by Edwin Roseberry

Library of Congress Cataloging in Publication Data

Ramazani, Nesta, 1932–
    Persian cooking.

    1. Cookery, Iranian.   I. Title.
TX724.5.17R35 1974   641.5′955   73–90182
ISBN 0–8129–0430–3

To those nearest and dearest to me
Ruhi, Vaheed, David, Jahan, and Sima

Contents

Foreword	*ix*
Persia and Its Food	*xiii*
Appetizers	1
Soups *(Ab-Goosht, Ash, va Soup)*	9
Stuffed Vegetables *(Dolmeh)*	41
Persian Souffles *(Kookoo)*	53
Yogurt Dishes *(Borani)*	67
Vegetables *(Sabzijat)*	79
Salads *(Salad)*	91
Rice and Rice Dishes *(Pollo* and *Chello)*	103
Stewed Meat and Rice *(Khoresht)*	133
Stews, Casseroles, and Other Entrées *(Khorak)*	159
Kabab	195
Game Birds *(Kapk* and *Gharghavol)*	203
Bread *(Nan)*	211
Cookies, Pastries, and Confections *(Shirini)*	217
Puddings, Gelatin, and Other Desserts *(Desser)*	237
Sherbets (Cold Sweet Drinks) *(Sharbat)*	249
Pickles *(Torshi)*	255
Shopper's Guide	273
Glossary of Persian-English Foods	280
Index	285

(ILLUSTRATIONS FOLLOW PAGE 202)

Foreword

I was inspired to write this book on Persian culinary arts during a return visit to my homeland after having lived in the United States for 16 years. By that time, I had already acquired considerable experience preparing Persian meals for my Persian husband in our American kitchen. I had learned to streamline and simplify our meals in keeping with the more rapid tempo of American life. I had come to regret, fervently, my lack of interest in the kitchen when I was a young girl growing up in Iran but I improvised, as best I could, and experimented.

Then, by a stroke of good fortune, my husband, four children, and I were able to return to Iran for a year. Our friends and relatives feasted and feted us with traditional hospitality and generosity. I was unable to resist either their invitations or their insistence on second and third helpings. Throughout that year I not only dined sumptuously, but poked into kitchens, and extracted many a gastronomic secret from many an accomplished cook. I was genuinely impressed with the extraordinary culinary competence of most Iranian women—their art and dedication in preparing even the simplest meals, as well as their genius and imagination when entertaining. And I observed that it was not only housewives who were superb cooks; professional women with full-time jobs and large families were also continuing the ancient tradition of preparing elaborate meals without resorting to shortcuts.

Another factor that truly amazed me was the modesty of the kitchens from which these superb culinary accomplishments emerged. No electric ovens, no gadgets or time-saving devices, very little counter space, and barely adequate stoves. Yet somehow, through sheer dedication and love of cooking, gastronomic feasts were concocted in these meager surroundings that dazzled the eye and titillated the palate.

While traveling one day during our visit to Iran, we passed an encampment of migrant "gypsy" workers at the foot of Mount Demavend. I was fascinated to see how the women made their own daily bread—using little more equipment than a flat board and a long, thin stick for a rolling pin, their deft hands rolling out the dough with the thin stick, turning it over, rolling it out, almost faster than the eye could follow. The round, flat sheets of dough were then slapped against the hot lining of a home-made oven— a large hole dug in the ground, its sides heated with a thistle fire. There the dough adhered until crisp, when it was lifted out with a makeshift wooden prong. The flavor was delectable.

Meanwhile, a tantalizing fragrance arose from a small, black, iron pot hanging over a wood fire; it contained *ab goosht,* the staple soup of Iranian people. I marveled at what tasty foods these women managed to produce with only the most rudimentary equipment and very few ingredients.

Arthur Arnold, in his book *Through Persia by Caravan,* published in the late nineteenth century, described a similar experience.

> Kazem soon produced a saucepan—our only tureen—half full of nearly boiling soup. Chicken and rice came next, and Kazem to my surprise, declared that he had cutlets of mutton 'quite ready,' and an omelet 'to follow.' He had accomplished all this, including potatoes, with nothing but three big stones for his fire-place.
> (Arthur Arnold, *Through Persia by Caravan.* New York: Harper & Row, Publishers, 1877.)

During my memorable year there, all of my prejudices in favor of Persian food were reaffirmed—Persian food is delicious, varied, nutritious, and imaginative. This cuisine has evolved over many centuries and is the result of the cumulative experience of generations of cooks. It offers something for the gourmet in search of some new epicurean delight as well as something for every palate, and every budget. Here is food to feed the poor or to serve kings. Here is a culinary art so highly developed that the most lowly vegetable can tast divine, every meal can be a gastronomic treat, and every housewife can be a creative artist.

How unfortunate, I thought, that Persian cuisine is so little known in the West. I have yet to meet a European or American who does not enjoy Persian food when introduced to it. The food is neither highly spiced nor hot; it is usually delicately seasoned with herbs rather than spices and therefore palatable to Western tastes, even though different and unfamiliar. My personal observations convinced me that many a Western cook would be happy to prepare an ancient Persian feast, if only he or she knew how.

Since I am half English and half Iranian, am bilingual, and have spent half my life in Iran and half in the United States, I felt that I might be uniquely qualified to present the vast and varied delights of Persian cooking to Americans. This meant not only collecting recipes, but devising exact measurements. This was not an easy task, as the Persian housewife cooks "by ear" and seasons "to taste" with a "handful" of this and a "dash" of that, and has not the faintest notion of what the inside of a cookbook looks like.

My many friends and relatives in Iran were extremely gracious in sharing with me the secrets of their kitchens, as well as in describing their particular methods of preparing certain dishes. Without their assistance and cooperation, I could never have compiled such a comprehensive selection of recipes. Where I had no personal guidance, I referred to numerous Iranian women's magazines kindly supplied by my friend, Homa Taymurian, and to the excellent book by Rosa Montazemi, *Honar-e Ashpazi*. Mrs. Pari Ata'i, who directs a cooking school in Tehran, kindly gave me a demonstration lesson on several Persian dishes. Although the friends and relatives who helped me in this endeavor are too numerous to mention here, I would like to take this opportunity to thank them all for their kindness and cooperation; I would like especially to thank Mrs. Mehri Miraftab, whose warmth and generosity were memorable.

And finally, I want to thank my husband for encouraging me to undertake this endeavor.

I hope this book will introduce you to a new world of epicurean delights.

Persia and Its Food

From the earliest times Persians have been known for their hospitality, whether that of the tribesman offering rest and refreshment to a weary traveler, or that of the urbane city dweller offering a sumptuous repast to his guests. Tradition requires that guests or visitors be served only the finest food available, and always in the most bountiful manner possible.

Accounts of early travelers to Iran indicate that the dishes served have not changed appreciably over the centuries. The following is a description of how a Shah was entertained by a common physician. It was related by James J. Morier in 1824 in *The Adventures of Haji Baba of Isphahan.*

> Here were displayed all the refinements of cookery: rice, in various shapes, smoked upon the board; first the chilau, as white as snow; then the pilau, with a piece of boiled lamb, smothered in the rice; then another pilau, with a baked fowl in it; a fourth, coloured with saffron, mixed up with dried peas; and at length, the king of Persian dishes, the narinj pilau, made with slips of orange-peel, spices of all sorts, almonds, and sugar:
>
> Salmon and herring from the Caspian Sea were seen among the dishes, and trout from the river Zengi, near Erivan; then in china basins and bowls of different sizes were the ragouts, which consisted of hash made of a fowl boiled to rags, stewed up with rice, sweet herbs, and onions; a stew in which was a lamb's marrow-bone with some loose flesh about it, and boiled in its own juice; small gourds crammed with forcemeat and done in butter; a fowl stewed to rags, with a brown sauce of prunes; a large omelette about two inches thick; a cup full of the essence of meat mixed up with rags of lamb, almonds, prunes, and tamarinds, which was

poured upon the top of the chilau; a plate of poached eggs fried in sugar and butter; a dish of badenjans, slit in the middle and boiled in grease; a stew of venison.

After these came the roasts. A lamb was served up hot from the spit, the tail of which, like marrow, was curled up over its back. Partridges, and what is looked upon as the rarest delicacy in Persia, two capk dereh, partridges of the valley, were procured on the occasion. Pheasants from Mazanderan were there also, as well as some of the choicest bits of the wild ass and antelope.

The display and the abundance of delicacies surprised everyone; and they were piled up in such profusion around the king that he seemed almost to form a part of the heap.

(James J. Morier, *The Adventures of Haja Baba of Isphahan.* The Heritage Press, New York, 1947. [This work first appeared in 1824].)

Such a feast is still to be seen today on state occasions, at weddings, or other festivities in the homes of the well-to-do.

Abundance at any table is a tradition very much alive today. The modern Iranian hostess will prepare several main courses, all of which are placed on the table at the same time, giving the guests a variety of dishes from which to choose. Again, the dishes are similar to those described in this early nineteenth-century account:

When a person of rank gives his friends entertainment a piece of chintz or printed calico is spread in front of the felt carpets, on which they are seated. On this cloth, before each person, is laid a cake of bread, which serves the purpose of a plate. The dishes are brought in on large metal trays,—one of which is generally set down between every two or three individuals,—and contains pillaus, stews, sweetmeats, and other delicacies; while bowls of sweet and sour sherbets, with long-handled spoons of peartree wood swimming in them, are placed within their reach. If the feast be very sumptuous, the dainties appear in great profusion, and are sometimes heaped one upon another. The cookery is excellent of its kind. Persians, like other orientals, eat with their fingers; and the meat is cut into convenient mouthfuls, or stewed down so as to be easily torn to pieces.

(James Baillie Fraser, Esq., *Persia,* Harper & Bros., 1834.)

According to tradition the host repeatedly offers the food and the guest refuses it the first two or three times. This practice is still observed today. (When my husband and I first came to the United

States, we went home hungry after our first few social occasions, as we kept politely, we thought, refusing the food when it was first offered. Our empty stomachs quickly taught us to drop our Iranian customs, and to accept what was offered the first time.)

In a country such as Iran where there are many extremes of climate, strewn as it is with high rugged mountains, and immense desert regions, the hospitality of the villager or nomad can be a vital matter to a traveler crossing vast expanses of inhospitable terrain. Gertrude Bell, writing of her experiences in the early twentieth century, described the warm hospitality extended by an absolute stranger when she and her companion were parched and weary after traveling through an extensive stretch of arid land:

> He set before us on a sheet of bread a roast chicken, an onion, some salt, a round ball of cheese, and some bunches of grapes, then, seeing that we hesitated as to the proper mode of attacking the chicken, he took it in his fingers, delicately pulled apart wings, legs and breast, and motioned us again to eat. Never did roast chicken taste so delicious!
> (Gertrude Bell, *Persian Pictures*, Ernest Benn Ltd., London, 1928.)

Similar hospitality would be encountered today by travelers in Iran, particularly in remote areas where geographical isolation has fostered a historical continuity and preservation of traditions.

In many rural areas, in remote villages, and among certain tribespeople the old mode of eating persists. The food is served on a cloth on the floor, the family sits cross-legged around the cloth, and the food is eaten with fingers. To eat graciously and delicately with one's fingers is quite an art; it requires infinite poise and expertise to scoop up the food with the fingers of the right hand, compress it into a ball, and not allow a morsel to drop on the way to the mouth.

Most city dwellers eat at tables, and use implements. The cake of bread no longer serves as a plate, but is served on the side in a smaller form. The menus, however, are surprisingly similar to the ones described above, perhaps less elaborate, with not quite so much variety at once, but very much in the same tradition. The recipes for many of these dishes appear in this book.

Most of these dishes are traditionally prepared in private homes by the women who usually do the cooking. (Professional cooks, however, are invariably men.) Very few of the wide range of

Persian foods can be found in restaurants; their menus are almost invariably restricted to just three or four Persian dishes.

Any expected or unexpected visitor to a Persian home is always immediately offered refreshment appropriate to the time of day, and even in places of business, little glasses of tea served with hard lumps of sugar are first offered and quaffed before the business at hand is transacted.

Iran is a land of varied topography and extremes of climate, ranging from snow-capped mountains to vast stretches of wilderness, from sub-freezing temperatures to burning heat. It can generally be described as a high plateau strewn with mountains which gradually level off into arid deserts. Beyond the great Elborz mountain range, stretching like a vast wall across the north of the country, is the Caspian Sea coast, differing from the rest of the country in its heavy rainfall, and verdant forests. This is the region that produces the famous *domsiah* rice, prized by Iranians, and also citrus fruits, including oranges, tangerines, lemons, and limes. In the far south, on the plains of Khuzistan, and in oasis villages along the length of the Persian Gulf, the warm climate is well suited to the cultivation of the date palm. Wheat is grown in every section of the country except for the Caspian coast.

Much of the agricultural productivity of the land depends upon various irrigation systems, some of them dating from the first century A.D. One irrigation system widely used in Iran over the centuries is that of underground channels, called *qanats*. These channels run deep under the ground for distances of up to twenty miles. The system seems to be unique to Iran.

Mulberry trees, olive trees, cotton, tobacco, and tea are only a few of the agricultural products of Iran. The land is blessed, also, with a variety of luscious fruits and nuts. The peach and the apricot were first grown here, as well as the English walnut and the pistachio. Fresh and dried fruits and nuts are widely used in many dishes, such as plum soup, *shirin pollo*, and *fesenjoon*. Iranian pomegranates are succulent and tasty; when ripe they burst open to display their ruby-like seeds.

Sir Thomas Herbert, in the early seventeenth century, described his pleasure when he suddenly came upon the house and garden of Shah Abbas after having journeyed for days through parched and desolate land.

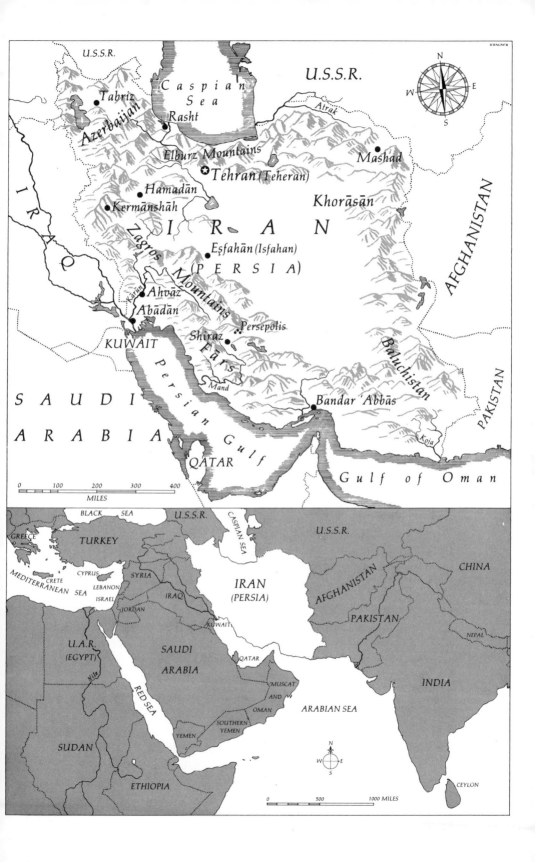

For five hundred paces it every way gives a series of all sorts of Persian fruits and flowers, Pomgranads, Peaches, Apricocks, Plums, Apples, Peares, Cherries, Chestnuts, Damask, red and white Roses, and other flowers innumerable.

(Sir Thomas Herbert, *Some Yeares Travels into Africa and Asia the Great. Especially Describing the Famous Empires of Persia and Industant.* London, 1638. Printed by R. Bip. for Jacob, Bloome & Richard Bishop.)

Fruits in season are served between meals as a refreshment; they are piled high on enormous platters or bowls, and are sweet and tree-ripened. Cucumbers in Persia are slender, firm, and crisp, and are often served as a fruit.

Fruits are also taken along by women and young children to the *hamam*, the public bath. Because the bath is usually a long, drawn-out affair, especially for the women, who make a social occasion of it, they often pack up some refreshments to take along to fortify themselves. After steaming for hours, being massaged, and scrubbed clean, they usually feel relaxed, thirsty, slightly faint from the heat, and greatly in need of sustenance. At that point they open the *boghchehs*, the provisions wrapped in a large cloth, and enjoy pomegranates, oranges, peaches, or other succulent fruits. This tradition, although gradually dying out in some cities, goes back many years, as attested to by John Fryer, who traveled in Persia from 1672 to 1681. He related:

When they retire to put on their Cloaths there awaits them a Collation of Fruits, Sweetmeats, and variety of Perfumes, as Rosewater, Rackeet, and the like, with all befitting Attendants, beside the usual Servitors, to administer either Coho [coffee], Tea, Tobacco, or Brandy, if faint.

(John Fryer, *A New Account of East India and Persia. Being 9 Years' Travels, 1672–1681.*)

As large areas of Iran are mountainous it is natural that sheep and goats are raised in abundance. Lamb is the favorite meat of the Iranians, and much of their cuisine reflects that preference. They have evolved, over the centuries, many varied ways of preparing lamb. The species of sheep raised in Iran is largely the fat-tailed sheep, a type having a large, pendulous tail wherein all the fat is stored. Consequently, the flesh of the animal is not marbleized with fat, but is rather lean, and has a delicate flavor. Again, Mr. Fryer:

The Sheep it brings forth are prodigiously large, trailing Tails after them, of the Weight, some of them, of Thirty Pound, full of Fat.

Sheep and goats sustain the nomadic life of the tribespeople of Iran, furnishing them with milk, butter, and cheese, and their wool is used for weaving the famous Persian carpets.

An animal must be slaughtered according to the ritual of *dhaka'a*, whereby its throat is slit, including the trachea and the oesophagus, thus avoiding any prolonged suffering. Preferably the victim should be laid upon its left side facing in the direction of the holy city of Mecca. At the moment of slaughter the name of God is invoked. The eating of pork is proscribed by the Muslim religion. Therefore, the reader will note there are no pork recipes in this book, as pork is not eaten by the Muslim population of Iran.

Iranians consider many foods to be health foods. Yogurt is believed to be a cure for many ailments, especially stomach upsets; indeed, a number of nutritionists today back up this claim, asserting that yogurt contains healthful bacteria that are an aid to good digestion. In most Persian homes it is served daily as an accompaniment to the main meal. It can be made out of the milk of sheep, goats, or cows.

Sir John Chardin, in his *Voyages en Perse,* related stories of the restorative powers of the *germek,* a type of melon. He saw people eating as much as 10 pounds of these small melons a day in the belief that they purged the body and refreshed the blood. He told the story of two doctors who arrived in Isphahan, saw the plentiful supplies of melons piled up in ships and stalls, and said: "Let us leave; there will be no work for us to do here. The people have here the remedy for all ills."

Long before refrigeration came to Iran, the populace had its own ingenious method of storing fruits such as melons in subterranean cellars, assuring a bountiful supply throughout the year.

Iranian grapes are renowned for their quality. There are at least 30 varieties, some of which are dried as raisins. According to Sir John Chardin: "The fairest Grape in Persia [is] of a Gold Colour, transparent and as big as a small olive." The best grapes of all are believed to be cultivated by the Zoroastrians in Negefabad, near Isphahan, presumably because their religion does not forbid them to drink wine.

In spite of the prohibition on drinking of alcoholic beverages for those of the Muslim religion, Iranians have long been skilled in the art of wine-making. "They also make the strongest Wine in the World, and the most luscious," according to Chardin. And, of course, there is the testimony of Omar Khayyam in *The Rubaiyat:*

> A book of verses underneath the bough
> A jug of wine, a loaf of bread and thou
> Beside me singing in the wilderness.
> Ah! wilderness were Paradise enow.

Inscription on a Seventeenth-Century Persian Bowl
in the Royal Ontario Museum

May this bowl be ever filled with God's blessings,
    And always stand among friendly folk.
Your thanks are due to God's grace;
    May his mercy be on the owner of the food.

This bowl, which contains rubies,
    Its rim is like the ruby's edge;
From its song comes happy peace, expansion of the soul.
    From the soul of the generous one is his gift,
    like food will it be.

Appetizers

Because Iran is a Muslim country, and the religion forbids the drinking of alcoholic beverages, the cuisine does not have cocktail appetizers. However, there are a number of Persian dishes that, in their original form or slightly modified, do lend themselves to being served as hors d'oeuvres or appetizers, although, admittedly, that was not their original purpose.

Drained Yogurt with Herbs

(Mast-e Kisei)

Yogurt may be thickened in the traditional Persian way by pouring it into a cheesecloth, pulling the ends together and tying them, and then hanging it overnight over a sink or bowl. All the liquid will slowly drain off, leaving the yogurt thick and creamy.

Yogurt thus thickened can be used in almost any way that you would use sour cream or cream cheese for appetizers. Yogurt has the advantage of being more piquant and considerably lower in calories than either sour cream or cream cheese.

Try mixing thickened yogurt with chopped fresh dill weed and/ or any of the following: parsley, mint, tarragon, chives, scallions. It is also delicious mixed with finely grated or chopped cucumbers, a dash of chopped mint, salt, and pepper. Or you could mix it with a package of dehydrated onion soup. If you like garlic, mince a clove of garlic and mix it into the yogurt.

To make your own yogurt, see Yogurt (*Mast*), page 70.

Feta Cheese Appetizers

(Hors d'oeuvre-e Panir)

Although in the United States feta cheese is an imported luxury, in Iran it is quite commonplace. It is always served with thin, flat bread—either as a meal, with fruit, or as a side dish on more elaborate tables. If you like it salty, use it as it comes from the jar or can; but if you prefer a blander taste, soak it for a few hours in plain water.

Feta cheese may be spread plain on crackers or, for a fancier appetizer, try mixing it with chopped fresh dill weed, and/or any of the following: chopped parsley, chopped chives, mint, tarragon. It may be crumbled with a fork and mixed with sour cream and any of the above herbs, or with cream cheese and herbs. Or try mixing it with cream cheese and soy sauce.

For hot, feta cheese appetizers, crumble it with a fork and mix it with chopped herbs or a package of dehydrated onion soup and a little sour cream or milk. Use this as a filling for tiny turnovers, using your favorite pastry recipe, a pie crust dough, or strudel dough. The turnovers may be prepared in any size or shape, squares, crescents, half-moons, or rolls. If using pastry or pie crust dough, bake them in the oven until brown. If using strudel dough, drop them into hot oil and deep-fry until golden brown.

Zucchini Hors d'Oeuvre

(Hors d'oeuvre-e Kadoo)

3 *large onions, grated*	¼ *cup lemon juice*
½ *cup salad oil*	1 *teaspoon salt*
1 *pound zucchini*	¼ *teaspoon pepper*
2 *tablespoons vinegar*	1 *cup water*
2 *teaspoons salt*	
1 *pound tomatoes (or 1*	
large can tomatoes)	

Sauté the onions in the salad oil until golden brown. Remove the zucchini stems with a sharp knife and slice. Place the zucchini slices in a bowl, cover with water; add vinegar and salt and soak for 30 minutes. Drain off the salted water, and add the zucchini to the sautéed onions. Slice the tomatoes and add.

Add the lemon juice, salt, pepper, and 1 cup of water. (If using canned tomatoes, omit the water.) Cover and simmer until tender (about 30 minutes). Mash with a potato masher; for a smoother dip, put through an electric blender. Serve as a spread or a dip.

Eggplant Hors d'Oeuvre

(Hors d'oeuvre-e Bademjan)

1 medium eggplant	½ package dehydrated
2 large onions, chopped	onion soup
or grated	dash of tabasco or
½ cup salad oil	worcestershire sauce
3–4 cloves garlic	1 teaspoon salt
4 cups yogurt	½ teaspoon pepper
1 tablespoon tomato	
sauce	

Peel the eggplant. Cut it into 5 or 6 pieces and drop them into boiling, salted water. Cover and simmer gently until tender (about 15 to 20 minutes). Drain well and cool. Either mash well, or put through an electric blender.

Sauté the onions in salad oil until golden brown. Grate the garlic, add it to the onions, and sauté. Add the eggplant. Beat the yogurt with an egg beater, and stir it into the eggplant. Stir in the tomato sauce, dehydrated onion soup, tabasco or worcestershire sauce, salt, and pepper. Serve either well chilled or warm as a dip or spread.

Cardoon Hors d'Oeuvre

(Hors d'oeuvre-e Kangar)

Cardoons, also known as prickly artichokes, grow in arid, desert country. In Persia they are considered quite a delicacy.

3 pounds cardoons	1 tablespoon tomato paste
1 large onion, grated	salt and pepper to taste
¼ cup butter or shortening	½ cup sour cream
3 tablespoons flour	

Cut the cardoons into small pieces, removing the thorny ends. Boil in salted water until tender. Drain, retaining the liquid (approximately 1 cup). Sauté the onion in butter or shortening until golden brown. Reduce the heat, stir in the flour, using a wire whisk to prevent lumping. Stir in the cooking liquid and the tomato paste. Add salt and pepper.

Stir and cook until the mixture thickens. Mash the cardoons or put them through an electric blender, and stir in. Spoon the sour cream into the mixture without stirring. Allow the heat of the cardoons to warm the sour cream for a few minutes, then stir it in. Serve warm or well chilled as a spread or dip.

Stuffed Grape Leaves

(Dolmeh-ye Barg-e Mo)

These make an excellent hors d'oeuvre. See page 45 for the recipe.

Caviar Appetizers

The finest caviar in the world comes from the Caspian Sea. When I was a young girl and caviar was cheap in Iran, I remember that my mother would sometimes send the maid out to buy a fresh supply of caviar, plenty of hot bread, butter, and lemons when she didn't feel like cooking a meal herself. We would have a feast fit for a king: we would spread the caviar thickly on buttered bread and squeeze fresh lemon juice over the top. Now the supply of sturgeon is somewhat depleted; caviar is expensive, even at its source of supply, and ordinary people can't afford to make a meal out of it anymore.

For a very special treat, place some Iranian caviar on Melba toast or other cracker that has been spread with mayonnaise or sour cream. Dot with mayonnaise, green pepper, or pimiento. Sprinkle a little lemon juice on top.

Caviar should always be kept refrigerated.

Yogurt and Cucumbers

(Mast-o-Khiar)

Please see the recipe on page 71. This dish makes an excellent dip.

Lentil Puree

(Pooreh-ye Adas)

Please see the recipe on page 84. This dish may be served as a dip or spread.

Soups

(AB GOOSHT, ASH, VA SOUP)

At meales they are the merriest men that may be: no people in the world have better stomacks, drinke more, or more affect voracity: yet are harmlessly merry; a mixture of meat, and drink, and mirth, excellently becoming them.

(Sir Thomas Herbert, *Some Yeares Travels into Africa and Asia the Great. Especially Describing the Famous Empires of Persia and Industant,* London, 1638.)

On a cold winter's day, while longing for a pot of hot soup, have you ever wished that you could toss together a few ingredients and come up with something tantalizing, tasty, inexpensive, and nourishing? Persian cuisine has the answer for you: an infinite variety of exquisite soups—thick and thin—made from the most homely kitchen staples.

There are three basic types of soup, each of which lends itself to infinite variety and creativity. The meat-based soup is called *ab goosht;* the vegetable-based soup is called *ash* (although this may also contain meat); the last type is simply called *soup,* and it resembles a French thin soup but has a uniquely Persian touch. The ingredients for each of these types are readily available in the United States.

Ab goosht is an ordinary, everyday dish of the Iranian masses; it contains little meat but provides a source of complete protein by utilizing different kinds of beans. It is an economical dish that can be stretched and stretched, yet is tasty enough to be eaten frequently by the well-to-do as well. When unexpected guests drop by for dinner, as they often do in Iran, the hostess will just ask the cook to add some water to the *ab goosht: ab-e ab goosht ra ziad kon,* and she knows that all will be well!

Once you have tried a few of these soups, you might like to work out your own variations.

If the length of time required for cooking these soups dismays you, relax! When a recipe says "simmer for 3 hours," it doesn't mean that you have to hover over the soup pot; usually you can toss together the ingredients, go away, and let the pot simmer by itself. However, if you haven't started the soup early enough and don't have 3 hours before dinner, you can always use a pressure cooker, usually with excellent results. Nowadays pressure cookers can be found in even the most traditional Iranian homes!

Lamb Shank Soup I

(Ab-Goosht)

(SERVES 6–8)

This is the basic recipe for simple *ab-goosht*.

3 *quarts water*	1 *package dehydrated*
2 *lamb shanks*	*onion soup*
½ *cup dried navy beans*	2 *teaspoons salt*
½ *cup dried chick-peas*	2 *teaspoons turmeric*
1 *can (15-ounce)*	¼ *teaspoon pepper*
tomatoes	2–3 *large potatoes*
2 *large onions, sliced*	

Bring the water to a boil in a large pot. Add all the ingredients except the potatoes; lower the heat, cover, and simmer for 2 hours. Peel the potatoes, quarter, and add to the soup. Cover again and simmer 30 minutes longer, or until the potatoes are done.

If desired, the meat, beans, chick-peas, and potatoes may be removed from the soup; the meat boned; and all these ingredients mashed to a pulp, known as *goosht-e koobideh* (forcemeat). This may be served separately with hot bread.

Lamb Shank Soup II

(Ab-Goosht-e Dizi)

(SERVES 6–8)

Anyone who has been to a Persian bazaar has seen the spectacular heavy copper pots traditionally used by Persian housewives. They vary in size from small to very large, are lined inside with pewter or tin, and are all of uniform shape. Because they are so heavy, foods cooked in them are especially tasty. They are superlative for preparing *ab-goosht* of different kinds. The following soup takes its name from these heavy copper pots—*dizi*.

Lacking a Persian copper pot, use the heaviest pot you have.

5–6 *quarts water*	⅓ *cup yellow split peas*
1 *can broth or*	6 *dried Persian limes or*
bouillon (beef or	6 *teaspoons powdered*
chicken)	*Persian lime*
1 *pound breast of lamb*	1 *large onion, sliced*
1 *pound lamb shanks*	3 *teaspoons salt*
2 *tablespoons tomato*	¼ *teaspoon pepper*
paste	2 *large potatoes*

Bring the water to a boil. Add the broth, meat, tomato paste, yellow split peas, Persian lime, onion, salt, and pepper. Reduce the heat, cover, and allow to simmer until the meat is tender (about 1½ hours, or 20 minutes in a pressure cooker).

Add the potatoes. When the potatoes (20 minutes, or 8 minutes in a pressure cooker) are done, remove the meat and potatoes from the soup. Bone the meat, and pound the meat and potatoes with a mortar and pestle until they form a thick paste. Return this meat paste to the soup and serve, or serve the paste separately with bread, as a spread.

Cranberry October Bean Soup

(Ab-Goosht-e Loobia Chiti)

(SERVES 6–8)

Prepare Lamb Shank Soup I as directed, substituting for the chick-peas and navy beans the following:

¼ *cup dried cranberry*	½ *cup dried lentils*
October beans	¼ *cup yellow split peas*
¼ *cup dried kidney beans*	*(optional)*

Yellow split peas cook faster than any of the other legumes, so they should be added for the last hour of cooking.

Lamb Shank Soup with Persian Limes

(Ab-Goosht-e Limoo Amani)

(SERVES 6–8)

Persian lime adds a marvelous, tart flavor to many soups and stews. It can be used whole or crushed to a powder. To prepare, remove the hard ends of the dried lime with a sharp knife, pound with a mortar and pestle, and remove the seeds.

Prepare Lamb Shank Soup I as directed, adding 2 dried Persian limes, either whole or powdered.

Lamb Shank Soup with Sour Grape Juice

(Ab-Goosht-e Ab-Ghooreh)

(SERVES 6–8)

Prepare Lamb Shank Soup I as directed, adding 1 cup of sour grape juice.

Quince Soup I

(Ab-Goosht-e Beh)

(SERVES 6–8)

Prepare Lamb Shank Soup I as directed. Substitute for the potatoes 1 large quince, peeled, cored, and cut into 1-inch cubes or into thin slices.

Quince Soup II
(Ab-Goosht-e Beh)

(SERVES 6–8)

2 large onions, sliced	¾ cup navy beans
3 tablespoons butter or shortening	1 tablespoon tomato paste
1 teaspoon turmeric	4 dried Persian limes (or 4 tablespoons lemon juice)
2–3 lamb shanks	
4–5 quarts water	2 quinces
3–4 teaspoons salt	1 cup dried apricots (optional)
¼ teaspoon pepper	
¼ teaspoon nutmeg	
1 package dehydrated onion soup	

Brown the onions in the butter or shortening in a large pot. Add the turmeric, stirring it into the onions. Add the meat, water, salt, pepper, beans, and nutmeg. Dissolve the dehydrated onion soup in ½ cup warm water and add. Bring to a boil, lower the heat, cover, and simmer gently for 1 hour.

Dilute the tomato paste in 2 tablespoons of warm water and add to the soup. Crush the Persian limes to a coarse powder, remove the seeds, and add the powder to the soup. Peel the quinces, cut in half, core, cut into cubes or slices, and add to the soup. For a sweet-sour taste, add dried apricots. Cover again, and simmer 30 minutes or longer.

Eggplant and Lentil Soup
(Ab-Goosht-e Bademjan va Adas)

(SERVES 10–12)

1 large onion, sliced	2–3 tablespoons tomato paste diluted in
¼ cup shortening	¼ cup warm water
3–4 lamb shanks	1 package dehydrated onion soup
4–6 quarts water	
1 can bouillon	2 medium eggplants
1 teaspoon salt	¾ cup lentils
¼ teaspoon pepper	

Sauté the onion in the shortening until golden brown. Add the lamb shanks and brown all over. Cover with water. Add the bouillon, salt, pepper, and diluted tomato paste. Dissolve the onion soup in ½ cup warm water and add. Cover and simmer gently for 2 hours.

Meanwhile, peel the eggplants, slice lengthwise, sprinkle with salt, and set aside to "perspire" for 20 minutes. Blot dry and add to soup. Add the lentils. Cover and simmer another 30 minutes. This soup is a complete meal in itself. Serve with hot bread.

Sour Cherry and Apple Soup

(Ab-Goosht-e Sib va Albaloo)

(SERVES 6–8)

This is a sweet-sour soup, exotic and tantalizing.
Dried sour cherries may be used instead of fresh ones. These should be soaked 4–6 hours before adding to the soup. They will be difficult to pit, and might be best left unpitted. To learn where dried sour cherries can be purchased, please refer to the Shopper's Guide.

6 quarts water	1 large onion, sliced
2 lamb shanks	4 cooking apples
1 can bouillon (beef or chicken)	¼ cup pitted sour cherries
¾ cup yellow split peas	1 tablespoon lemon juice
2–3 teaspoons salt	1 tablespoon sugar
¼ teaspoon pepper	

Bring the water to a boil in an enamel or porcelain pot. Add the meat, bouillon, yellow split peas, salt, pepper, and onion. Cover and simmer for 1½ hours. Peel and core the apples and cut into pieces; add them to the soup together with the cherries. Add the lemon juice and sugar. Cover and simmer for another 30 minutes, or until done. If this is too tart, add more sugar.

Persian Soup

(Ab-Goosht-e Boz Bash)

(SERVES 6–8)

2–3 lamb shanks	2 bunches leeks,
3–4 quarts water	chopped
1 cup red kidney	2 bunches parsley,
beans (or black-eyed	chopped
peas)	a few sprigs fresh
1 large onion, sliced	fenugreek, chopped
3 teaspoons salt	(optional)
¼ teaspoon pepper	2 tablespoons butter
1 teaspoon turmeric	or margarine
4 dried Persian limes	5–6 potatoes
(or 4 tablespoons	
lemon juice)	

Place the meat in a pot together with the water, beans, onion, salt, pepper, and turmeric. Bring to a boil, lower the heat, cover, and simmer gently for 1 hour. Remove the seeds from the Persian limes by crushing them open with a mortar and pestle. Pound the limes to a powder and add them to the soup. (If using lemon juice instead, add it at this time).

Sauté the leeks, parsley, and fenugreek lightly in butter or margarine; add them to the soup. Cover again, and continue simmering until the meat is very tender (about 1 hour more). For the last 15 to 20 minutes of cooking, add the potatoes, peeled and cut into quarters.

As with all *ab-goosht*, the beans, meat, and potatoes may be removed and mashed into a tasty forcemeat, which is then served with the soup and hot bread.

Yellow Split Pea Soup

(Ab-Goosht-e Lapeh)

(SERVES ABOUT 6)

2 large onions, sliced	4 quarts water
3 tablespoons butter	3 teaspoons salt
or shortening	¼ teaspoon pepper
1 cup yellow split peas	4 dried Persian limes
2–3 lamb shanks	3–4 potatoes (optional)
1 teaspoon turmeric	

Sauté the onions in the butter or shortening in a large pot. Add the yellow split peas and sauté briefly. Add the meat and sauté until brown. Stir in the turmeric. Add the water, salt, and pepper. Bring to a boil, cover, and simmer gently for 1 hour.

Crush the Persian limes with a pestle and remove the seeds; add the limes to the soup and continue simmering for 30 minutes longer. If desired, 3 or 4 potatoes, peeled, halved or quartered, may be added for the last 30 minutes of cooking.

Just before serving, the meat and potatoes may be removed, the meat boned, and these ingredients pounded to a pulp. It can be served with bread as a spread. The meat paste is called *goosht-e koobideh.*

Mint and Parsley Soup with Green Plums

(Ab-Goosht-e Na'na va Ja'fari)

(SERVES ABOUT 6)

2 large onions, sliced	¼ teaspoon pepper
4–5 tablespoons butter	1 pound fresh parsley
or shortening	5 sprigs fresh mint
2 lamb shanks	1 pound green plums
1 teaspoon turmeric	1 cup yellow split peas
3–4 quarts water	4–5 potatoes (optional)
2–3 teaspoons salt	

Sauté the onions in half of the butter or shortening until golden brown. Add the meat and sauté briefly. Stir in the turmeric. Add the water, salt, and pepper; bring to a boil, cover, and simmer gently for 1 hour.

Chop the parsley and mint. Sauté them lightly in the rest of the butter or shortening, and add to the soup. Add the green plums and yellow split peas, cover, and simmer for 30 minutes or more. If desired, 4 or 5 potatoes, peeled, halved or quartered, may be added for the last 30 minutes of cooking.

Wheat Soup I

(Ab-Goosht-e Gandom)

(SERVES 6–8)

2 large onions, sliced	1 cup white navy beans
3 tablespoons butter	4–5 tablespoons
or shortening	whole wheat berries
3 lamb shanks	1 tablespoon tomato
4 quarts water	paste
3–4 teaspoons salt	¼ teaspoon oregano
¼ teaspoon pepper	¼ teaspoon nutmeg
1 teaspoon turmeric	4–5 potatoes

Brown the onions in the butter or shortening in a large pot. Add the meat, water, salt, pepper, turmeric, and beans. Bring to a boil, lower the heat, cover, and simmer gently for 1 hour. Crush the dried Persian limes in a mortar and pestle, removing the seeds. Add the limes to the soup. Add the wheat, tomato paste, oregano, and nutmeg.

Peel the potatoes, halve or quarter them, and add to the soup. Cover and simmer 45 minutes longer. If desired, the meat, potatoes, and beans may be removed from the soup, the meat boned, and these ingredients mashed or put through a meat grinder or food mill. They may be served separately with bread or returned to the soup. Chicken may be substituted for the lamb shanks, if desired. Use 3 large legs or breasts, using the same procedure as above.

Wheat Soup II

(Halim)

(SERVES ABOUT 6)

2 lamb shanks	1 cup dried chick-peas
3 quarts water	2 cups whole wheat
2 large onions, sliced	berries
2–3 teaspoons salt	2 cups water
¼ teaspoon pepper	1 teaspoon cinnamon
¼ teaspoon turmeric	1 tablespoon butter

Place the meat in a large pot, and cover it with 8 cups of water. Bring it to a boil and lower the heat. Add the onions, salt, pepper, tumeric, and chick-peas. Cover and simmer for 1 hour. Soak the wheat berries in 2 cups of water, while the soup is cooking. Add it to the soup and simmer, covered, for 1 more hour. Remove the lamb shanks from the soup; bone the meat and pound it to a pulp. Return it to the soup. Just before serving, sauté the cinnamon in butter, and sprinkle it over the top.

Chicken or turkey (2 to 3 pounds) may be substituted for lamb shanks in this recipe. Cook as above; then bone the poultry and pound to a pulp; return it to the soup. Strips of chicken or turkey breast may be set aside to add on top of the soup just before serving.

Eggplant Soup

(Halim Bademjan)

(SERVES 6–8)

1 large onion, sliced	1 tablespoon turmeric
2 tablespoons butter or	2 tablespoons salt
shortening	¼ teaspoon pepper
4 quarts water	1 large eggplant
1 lamb shank	½ cup butter or
¼ cup dried chick-peas	shortening
(or kidney beans)	1–2 cups yogurt
½ cup navy beans	(or sour cream)
½ cup lentils	½ teaspoon cinnamon
1 cup rice	
1 package dehydrated	
onion soup	

Brown the onion in the butter or shortening in a large pot. Add the water, meat, chick-peas, navy beans, lentils, rice, dehydrated onion soup, turmeric, salt, and pepper. Bring to a boil. Cover and simmer until the meat is tender (about 1½ hours).

Peel and slice the eggplant; sauté in butter or shortening until brown on both sides. Add to the soup, cover, and continue simmering for another 30 minutes. Remove the meat and eggplant from the soup, pound well into a thick paste, and return to the soup.

Spoon a few tablespoons of the hot soup into the yogurt or sour cream to warm it; then stir the yogurt or sour cream into the soup. Just before serving, sprinkle the cinnamon over the top.

Rice and Spinach Soup

(Ash)

(SERVES 6–8)

2 large onions, sliced or chopped	3–4 quarts water
2 tablespoons butter	1 cup rice
1 bunch parsley, chopped	1 package dehydrated onion soup
1 pound spinach, chopped	½ cup lentils
2 bunches scallions or leeks, chopped	¼ cup kidney beans (optional)
a few sprigs Chinese parsley, chopped	2 teaspoons salt
	¼ teaspoon pepper
	½ cup yellow split peas
	3–4 tablespoons lemon juice

Sauté the onions in the butter until golden brown. Add the parsley, spinach, scallions or leeks, and Chinese parsley. Add the water, rice, dehydrated onion soup, lentils, kidney beans, salt, and pepper. Cover, bring to a boil, lower the heat, and simmer for 30 minutes. Add the yellow split peas and continue to simmer another 30 to 45 minutes. Stir in the lemon juice just before serving.

Yogurt Soup

(Ashe-e Mast)

(SERVES 6–8)

1 large onion, sliced	½ cup lentils
2 tablespoons butter or shortening	1 cup rice
	2 tablespoons salt
½ pound shoulder of lamb or lamb shank	1 teaspoon turmeric
	¼ teaspoon pepper
¼ cup dried chick-peas	3–4 quarts water
¼ cup white navy beans	2–3 cups yogurt

Sauté the onion in the butter or shortening in a large pot until brown. Add the meat and brown. Add all the other ingredients (except the yogurt), cover, and simmer for 1½ hours. Remove the meat from the soup; bone and pound it to a pulp; return it to the soup. Stir a few spoonfuls of hot soup into the yogurt in order to warm it; then add the yogurt to the soup, stirring gently.

Bean Soup with Meat

(Ashe-e Gooshti)

(SERVES 4–6)

1 large onion, sliced	½ cup lentils
1–2 tablespoons butter	¼ cup navy beans
1 bunch fresh parsley, chopped	¼ cup dried chick-peas
	½ tablespoon turmeric
½ pound fresh beet greens (or spinach), chopped	¼ teaspoon pepper
	2 tablespoons salt
	1 cup rice
¼ pound leeks, chopped	2–3 quarts water
1 lamb shank	

Brown the onion in the butter in a large pot. Add all the other ingredients. Cover and simmer until the meat is tender (about 1½ to 2 hours). Remove the meat from the soup; bone it and pound it to a pulp; return it to the pot.

Meatball Soup
(Ash-e Sak)

(SERVES 6–8)

1 large onion, sliced
1 tablespoon butter or
shortening
1 pound fresh spinach,
chopped
2–3 leeks, chopped
3 quarts water
(or more)
1 tablespoon turmeric
3 teaspoons salt
¼ teaspoon pepper
¾ cup yellow split peas
1 small onion, grated
1 package instant
dry broth

1 teaspoon turmeric
¼ teaspoon pepper
½ pound lean ground
beef
2 tablespoons butter
1 cup rice flour
½ cup cold water
1 cup sour grape juice
(or ⅔ cup lemon
juice)
¼ cup ground walnuts
(optional)

Sauté the onion in the butter or shortening until brown. Add the spinach, parsley, and leeks to the onions. Add the water, turmeric, salt, pepper, and yellow split peas. Cover and simmer for 30 minutes. Meanwhile, combine the grated onion, instant dry broth, turmeric, pepper, and ground beef. Mix together well with the hands and shape into tiny meatballs, about the size of small cherries. Brown these meatballs in butter. Drop them into the soup, cover again, and continue simmering for another 30 minutes.

Using a wire whisk, mix together the rice flour and cold water, making a smooth paste. Pour this paste slowly into the soup, stirring constantly. Add the sour grape or lemon juice. Simmer a few more minutes. The soup may be served plain or with yogurt. If adding yogurt, first spoon a few tablespoons of the hot soup into the yogurt to warm it, then stir the yogurt into the soup. Ground walnuts may be sprinkled over the top just before serving.

Another possibility would be to beat 3 or 4 eggs and pour them gradually into the soup, stirring continuously, a few minutes before serving.

Prune Soup
(Ash-e Aloo)

(SERVES 6–8)

1 large onion, sliced	1 pound fresh
2 tablespoons butter	spinach or beet
or shortening	greens, chopped
4 quarts water	a few sprigs coriander
1 cup rice	(Chinese parsley),
1 tablespoon turmeric	chopped (optional)
2 tablespoons salt	10–15 pitted prunes
¼ teaspoon pepper	(or Bokhara plums)
½ cup yellow split	1 tablespoon sugar
peas	a few sprigs fresh
2–3 leeks or scallions	mint, or
1 bunch parsley,	1 tablespoon dried
chopped	mint
	1 tablespoon butter

Brown the onion in the butter or shortening in a large pot. Add the water, rice, turmeric, salt, pepper, yellow split peas, leeks or scallions, parsley, spinach, and coriander. Bring to a boil, lower the heat, cover, and simmer for 30 minutes. Add the prunes or plums and sugar, and simmer another 30 minutes. Sauté the chopped mint in butter and sprinkle it over the top just before serving.

If desired, this soup may be prepared with a whole chicken. If so, the total cooking time would be 1½ hours. If desired, the chicken may be removed before serving, cooled and boned, then returned to the soup. Alternatively, tiny meatballs can be dropped into the soup during the last 30 minutes of cooking.

Pomegranate Soup

(Ash-e Anar)

(SERVES 6–8)

1 large onion, chopped
 or sliced
2 tablespoons butter
4 quarts water
½ cup lentils
¼ cup yellow split peas
1 cup rice
1 tablespoon oregano
3–4 tablespoons salt
¼ teaspoon pepper
1 bunch parsley,
 chopped
1 bunch leeks or
 scallions, chopped

½ pound fresh spinach,
 chopped
a few sprigs coriander,
 chopped (optional)
2 cups pomegranate
 juice, or 3–4
 tablespoons
 pomegranate syrup
a few sprigs fresh mint,
 chopped, or 1
 tablespoon dried mint
2 tablespoons butter

Brown the onion in the butter until golden brown. Add water, lentils, yellow split peas, rice, and seasonings. Cover and simmer for 15 minutes. Add the parsley, leeks or scallions, and coriander, together with the pomegranate juice. Simmer another 30 minutes or longer. Sauté the mint in butter; sprinkle over the soup just before serving.

If desired, small meatballs, seasoned with onion, turmeric, salt, and pepper, may be dropped into the soup for the last 30 minutes of cooking.

Tomato Soup

(Ash-e Gojeh Farangi)

(SERVES 6–8)

Follow the instructions for Pomegranate Soup (Ash-e Anar), substituting 2 cans of tomatoes and 2 tablespoons of tomato paste for the pomegranate juice or syrup, and eliminating the oregano. Add ¼ teaspoon of nutmeg and ⅛ teaspoon of cinnamon.

Currant Soup

(Ash-e Zereshk)

(SERVES 6–8)

Follow the instructions for Pomegranate Soup *(Ash-e Anar)*, adding 1 cup of currants to the soup just before serving.

Squash Soup

(Ash-e Kadoo)

(SERVES 6–8)

2 large onions, sliced	3–4 tablespoons sugar
2 tablespoons butter or shortening	¼ teaspoon pepper
1 cup rice	¾ pounds yellow summer squash
3 quarts water	1 tablespoon dried mint (optional)
1 cup lentils	1 tablespoon butter (optional)
½ cup lemon juice	
3–4 teaspoons salt	

Sauté the onions in the butter or shortening until golden brown. Add the rice, water, lentils, lemon juice, salt, sugar, and pepper. Cover and simmer for 30 minutes. Cut the squash into chunks and drop into the soup, cover, and simmer for another 30 minutes or longer. The ingredients should be soft and pulpy, making a thick soup.

If desired, tiny meatballs may be dropped into this soup during the last 30 minutes. For decoration, sautéed dried mint may be sprinkled on top just before serving.

Barley Soup

(Ash-e Jo)

(SERVES 6–8)

¼ pound dried kidney beans	2 pounds mixed greens (such as spinach, parsley, leeks, fresh coriander, fresh dill weed), chopped
¼ pound dried chick-peas	
½ pound lentils	
3–4 quarts water	
3–4 teaspoons salt	
¼ teaspoon pepper	2 cups diluted whey (or yogurt or sour cream)
1 teaspoon turmeric	
2 large onions, chopped	
2 tablespoons butter	1 tablespoon dried mint (optional)
1 pound lamb shank (optional)	
½ cup rice	1 tablespoon butter (optional)
1 cup barley	

Soak the kidney beans and chick-peas in water for several hours. Place these together with the lentils in a large pot. Add the water, salt and pepper, and turmeric. Sauté the onions in butter, and add, together with the meat, to the soup. Cover and simmer gently for 1 hour. Add the rice and barley to the soup; cover and simmer gently for another 30 minutes. Add the chopped greens to the soup, cover, and continue simmering for 30 minutes more.

Remove the meat from the pot and bone it. Pound it to a pulp and return it to the soup. Simmer until very thick. Remove the soup from the heat and add diluted whey (or yogurt or sour cream), warming it gently first with some hot soup. If desired, sprinkle sautéed dried mint over the top of the soup just before serving.

Mung Bean Soup

(Ash-e Mash)

(SERVES 6–8)

2 tablespoons shortening	⅛ teaspoon cinnamon
2 large onions, sliced	1 cup cold water
1 tablespoon turmeric	½ cup pinto beans
4 quarts water	1 cup rice
½ pound dried mung beans	10 small, whole, pearl onions, peeled
2 tablespoons salt	1 meat bone (optional)

In a large pot, melt the shortening and brown the onions. Stir in the turmeric. Add the water, mung beans, salt, and cinnamon. Bring to a boil and simmer, covered, for 1 hour. Pour in 1 cup of cold water. This will crack open the mung beans and bring the skins to the surface. Skim off the skins, if desired. Add the rice, pinto beans, small onions, and meat bone. Cover and simmer for 1 hour more, or longer.

Chick-Pea and Herb Soup

(Ash-e Shol Ghalamcar)

(SERVES 8–10)

½ pound chick-peas	½ pound lentils
½ pound beans (navy, kidney, or pinto)	3 teaspoons salt
2 large onions, chopped or sliced	½ teaspoon pepper
2 tablespoons butter or shortening	1½ cups rice
1 teaspoon turmeric	3 pounds mixed greens (such as leeks, scallions, fresh parsley, fresh dill weed, spinach, fresh coriander), chopped
2 pounds lamb shank	

Soak chick-peas and beans for several hours. Sauté the onions in the butter or shortening until golden brown. Add the turmeric. Add the meat, soaked beans, lentils, salt, pepper, and enough water to cover. Simmer gently, covered, for 1 hour. Add the rice and chopped greens. Cook another 30 minutes, stirring occasionally.

Legume and Noodle Soup

(Ash-e Reshteh)

(SERVES 8–10)

¼ cup dried chick-peas (or kidney beans)
¼ cup dried navy beans
¼ cup pinto (or cranberry October) beans
2 large onions, sliced
2 tablespoons butter or shortening
1 teaspoon turmeric
4 quarts water
2 tablespoons salt
¼ teaspoon pepper
2 packages instant dry broth
¼ pound fresh parsley, chopped
½ pound fresh spinach, chopped
¼ pound leeks, chopped
½ cup lentils
½ pound Chinese Udon noodles, or spaetzle egg noodles
2 tablespoons water
2 tablespoons flour
½ cup yogurt, sour cream or liquid whey
a few sprigs fresh mint, chopped, or 1 tablespoon dried mint
1 tablespoon butter

Presoak the chick-peas, navy beans, and pinto beans for 3 to 4 hours. Brown the onions in the butter or shortening in a large pot. Stir in the turmeric. Add the water, chick-peas, navy beans and pinto beans. Add the salt, pepper, and instant dry broth. Bring to a boil. Lower the heat, cover, and simmer gently for 30 minutes.

Add the parsley, spinach, and leeks to the soup. Add the lentils. Cover and simmer gently for 20 minutes. Add the noodles and continue simmering another 10 minutes. Stir 2 tablespoons of water into the flour, making a paste, and add it to soup. Warm the yogurt, sour cream, or whey by stirring a few spoonfuls of the hot soup into it; then add it to the soup. Just before serving, sauté the mint in butter, and sprinkle it over the top.

Wedding Soup

(Soup-e Aroosi)

(SERVES 6–8)

This dish, of Turkish origin, is popular among the Turkish-speaking peoples of Iranian Azerbaijan.

1 large onion, sliced	2 tablespoons salt
½ cup butter or	¼ teaspoon pepper
shortening	2 eggs
1–2 lamb shanks	1 tablespoon lemon juice
3–4 quarts water	1 tablespoon yogurt
1 can beef broth or bouillon	

Sauté the onion in the butter or shortening until golden brown. Add the lamb shanks and sauté until brown. Cover with water. Add the beef broth. Cover and simmer gently until tender (about 2 hours). Add the salt and pepper. Beat together the eggs, lemon juice, and yogurt. Add to the soup just before serving.

Cold Soup

(Soup-e Sard)

(SERVES ABOUT 6)

8 cups yogurt	1 cup cucumbers,
2 cups milk	grated or chopped
¼ cup heavy cream	4 teaspoons salt
½ cup fresh dill weed,	¼ teaspoon pepper
chopped	

Place the yogurt in a clean cheesecloth, pull the ends together, tie with a string, and hang up over a bowl or sink. Allow the liquid to drain overnight. The next morning beat the thickened yogurt well, add all the other ingredients, stir, and chill in the refrigerator until ready to serve. If desired, ¼ cup of dried currants or raisins and/or ¼ cup chopped walnuts may be added.

Scallion Soup

(Soup-e Piazcheh)

(SERVES ABOUT 6)

½ pound turnips, peeled and diced	20 scallions, chopped
¼ cup butter or shortening	salt and pepper to taste
5 cups broth (canned chicken)	2 egg yolks
1 pound potatoes, peeled and diced	1 cup heavy cream

Sauté the turnips lightly in the butter or shortening. Add the broth and the potatoes. Cover and simmer over a low heat until well done (about 30 minutes). Pour the soup into a colander, reserving all the liquid. Discard the potatoes and turnips if a thin soup is desired; or mash these vegetables well and return them to the soup if a thicker one is preferred.

Add the scallions to the soup. Add the salt and pepper, and simmer 10 minutes more. Beat the egg yolks and stir a few tablespoons of hot soup into them; then add the egg mixture to the soup. Stir in the cream. Serve hot.

Spinach Soup with Chinese Parsley

(Soup-e Sak)

(SERVES 6–8)

2 pounds spinach	⅓ cup butter
1 pound fresh Chinese parsley (coriander)	3 egg yolks
1 large onion, chopped	⅔ cup rice flour
4 cups broth, canned chicken or beef	salt and pepper to taste
	1 cup sour grape juice (or lemon juice)

Clean the spinach and Chinese parsley. Rinse, drain until dry, and chop coarsely. Sauté the onion in the butter until golden brown. Stir in the chopped spinach and Chinese parsley. Add the broth and 2 cups of water. Simmer gently, covered, until tender (about 20 minutes).

In a small bowl, add ½ cup water to the rice flour, stirring with a wire whisk to avoid lumps. Spoon ½ cup of the hot soup into this mixture, stirring constantly. Add this white sauce to the soup. Add the salt, pepper, and sour grape juice. Beat the egg yolks well. Remove the soup from the heat and allow to stand for a few minutes. Stir in the beaten egg yolks just before serving.

Lentil Soup I

(Soup-e Adas)

(SERVES 6–8)

This recipe comes from the province of Kerman.

2 cups lentils	salt and pepper to taste
8–10 cups water	4 packages instant
2 tablespoons salt	dry chicken or beef
2 large onions, grated	broth
¼ cup butter or	2 eggs
shortening	2–4 tablespoons lemon
2 tablespoons flour	(or orange) juice

Put the lentils into a large pot of boiling water and add 2 tablespoons of salt. Cover and cook gently until tender (about 30 minutes). Drain and reserve the cooking water. Puree the lentils by putting them through a food mill or electric blender.

Sauté the onions in the butter until golden brown. Sprinkle the flour over the onions, stirring constantly with a wire whisk. Add the lentil puree, cooking water, salt, pepper, and instant dry broth. Bring to a boil, turn the heat low, and simmer gently for 20 minutes. Beat the eggs with the lemon (or orange) juice, add to the soup, simmer briefly, and serve piping hot.

Lentil Soup II

(Soup-e Adas)

(SERVES ABOUT 6)

4 cups lentils	2 tablespoons flour
8 cups water	8 packages instant dry
1 large onion, sliced	broth or bouillon cubes
4 tablespoons butter	¼ teaspoon pepper

Soak the lentils in cold water for 2 hours. Bring to a boil, and add the onion. Cover and simmer gently until the lentils are tender. Drain, reserving the cooking water. Put the lentils and onion through a food mill; return to the soup.

Over a low heat, melt the butter in a saucepan; sprinkle the flour over it and stir, using a wire whisk. Add a few tablespoons of the hot soup, stir, and then add this mixture to the soup. Add the granulated broth and pepper. Continue simmering for a few minutes until the soup thickens. Water may be added if a thinner soup is desired.

This soup may also be prepared without putting the lentils and onion through a food mill. The resulting soup will not be quite so smooth, but it will still be tasty.

Green Plum Soup

(Eshgeneh-ye Gojeh)

(SERVES 6–8)

2 pounds green plums	2–3 tablespoons sugar
8 cups water	1 tablespoon dried mint
2 large onions, grated	(optional)
¼ cup butter or	1 tablespoon butter
or shortening	(optional)
1 tablespoon flour	½ teaspoon saffron
2 eggs, separated	(optional)

Wash and stem the plums. Place them in a kettle of boiling water and boil gently until tender. Save the cooking water. Remove the plums from the water and put them through a food mill so that the skins and pits will be removed, leaving the pulp.

Sauté the onions in butter or shortening until golden brown. Sprinkle the flour over the onions and stir with a wire whisk to avoid lumps. Stir in gradually ½ cup of hot water in which the plums were cooked. Gradually add more of the cooking water, about 4 cups in all. Add the plum pulp and simmer. Drop the whole egg yolks into the hot soup, letting them harden. Beat the egg whites until stiff and add them to the soup just before serving; then add the sugar.

The hardened egg yolks may either be left whole, or removed from the soup, chopped fine, and sprinkled over the top just before serving. Sautéed dried mint sprinkled over the soup just before serving will add a nice taste. This soup may also be flavored with ½ teaspoon of saffron.

Sour Cherry Soup

(Eshgeneh-ye Albaloo)

(SERVES 6–8)

1 large onion, grated	3 eggs, separated
½ cup butter or shortening	2 tablespoons water
½ cup white flour	2 tablespoons sugar
4–6 cups water	salt and pepper to taste
2 pounds sour cherries, pitted	1 tablespoon dried mint
	1 tablespoon butter

Sauté the onion in the butter or shortening in an enamel pan. Reduce the heat, stir in the flour a little at a time using a wire whisk to avoid lumps. Gradually add the water, stirring constantly. Add the cherries. Cover and simmer until the cherries are tender (about 15 minutes). Drop the whole egg yolks into the boiling soup, allowing them to harden. Beat the egg whites until fluffy, and add 2 tablespoons of water. A few minutes before serving, stir the egg whites into the soup. Add the sugar, salt, and pepper. Immediately before serving, sauté the dried mint briefly in butter and sprinkle over the top.

Dried sour cherries may be substituted for the fresh ones. They should be soaked 4–6 hours in cold water. They will be difficult to pit, so it might be best to leave them unpitted. Please consult Shopper's Guide for the addresses of stores where dried sour cherries may be purchased.

Cardoon Soup

(Soup-e Kangar)

(SERVES ABOUT 8)

1 large onion, chopped or grated	5 packages instant dry chicken or beef broth
¼ cup butter or shortening	4 tablespoons lemon juice
2 pounds cardoons	2 teaspoons salt
4 tablespoons flour	¼ teaspoon pepper
8 cups water	2 egg yolks

Sauté the onion in the butter or shortening until golden brown. Wash the cardoons and blot dry on paper towels. Remove the prickly parts, and chop into small pieces. Add to the onion and stir briefly. Sprinkle the flour onto the cardoons, stirring constantly.

Stir in the water; add the instant dry broth, lemon juice, salt, and pepper. Cover and simmer until the cardoons are tender (about 45 minutes). Beat the egg yolks; pour a little of the hot soup over them, beating constantly. Pour the egg yolks into the soup just before serving.

Green Plum Soup with Meat and Herbs

(Soup-e Gojeh)

(SERVES 6–8)

½ pound ground beef	¼ cup rice flour
½ teaspoon salt	1 large onion, grated
¼ teaspoon pepper	4 tablespoons butter
1 pound mixed herbs (leeks, parsley, tarragon, a few sprigs mint), finely chopped	4–6 cups water
	4 packages instant dry broth
	1 pound green, tart plums

Combine the beef, salt, pepper, 3 tablespoons of the chopped herbs, and 1 tablespoon of the rice flour. Knead well with the hands and shape into tiny meatballs about the size of cherries. Sauté the onion in butter until golden brown. Sprinkle the remaining rice flour over the onion, stirring with a wire whisk to avoid lumps.

Stir in the water gradually and add the granulated broth. Bring to a boil. Add the chopped herbs. Drop the meatballs into the soup and simmer gently for 30 minutes. Add the plums. Simmer 15 to 20 minutes longer and serve. Or you may boil the plums separately; put the through a food mill, removing the skins and pits; and add the pulp to the soup before serving.

Rice Flour Soup

(Soup-e Ard-e Berenj)

(SERVES 4–6)

4 tablespoons butter	2 tablespoons rice
½ cup rice flour	2 egg yolks
6 cups broth (canned, homemade, or diluted granulated mix)	¼ cup lemon juice
	½ teaspoon salt
	¼ teaspoon pepper
1 cup milk	

Melt the butter in a large pot over a low heat. Using a wire whisk, stir in the rice flour. Add the broth gradually, stirring constantly. Add the milk and rice. Cover and simmer gently about 30 minutes. Beat the egg yolks and lemon juice together, and add them to the soup. Add the salt and pepper. Simmer a few minutes more and serve.

Cauliflower Soup

(Soup-e Gol Kalam)

(SERVES 6–8)

1 head cauliflower	1 tablespoon potato flour (or all-purpose flour)
8 cups water	
1 large onion, chopped	
2–3 tablespoons butter	½ cup milk
1 teaspoon salt	1 egg yolk
¼ teaspoon pepper	½ cup cream
1 can chicken broth	1 tablespoon parsley, chopped
2–3 potatoes	

Remove the leaves and stem from the cauliflower. Place in a pot, together with the water, and boil, covered, for 10 minutes. Drain and reserve the liquid. Cut the cauliflower into small pieces, saving a few flowers to decorate the soup. Sauté the onion in the butter until golden brown. Add the cauliflower pieces, the cooking water, salt, pepper, and chicken broth.

Peel the potatoes, dice, and add. Cover and simmer until the potatoes are tender. With a wire whisk, stir the potato flour into the milk and add it to the soup. Beat the egg yolk in a small bowl; spoon a little hot soup into it and then add it to the soup. Add the cream and parsley. Simmer a few minutes longer and serve. Decorate the soup by floating a few raw cauliflower buds on top.

"Coy" Soup

(Soup-e Naz)

(SERVES 4–6)

Whoever heard of soup being coy? No matter—coyness is a highly valued trait in an Iranian woman, so the expression may be considered a compliment. Try this soup and see if it deserves such high praise.

2 large onions, chopped	½ teaspoon saffron
2 tablespoons butter	3 carrots, peeled and
6 cups water	grated
6 packages instant dry	salt and pepper to taste
chicken broth	2 egg yolks
chicken parts (such as	3 tablespoons lemon juice
backs, necks, wing	2 tablespoons flour
tips, giblets)	2 tablespoons cream

Sauté the onions in the butter until golden brown. Add the water, instant dry broth, chicken parts, saffron, carrots, salt, and pepper. Cover and simmer until the chicken is done (about 45 minutes). Beat the egg yolks and lemon juice together in a small bowl. Add them to the soup.

Remove the chicken parts from the soup and allow them to cool. Bone the pieces and return the meat to the soup. Ladle a cupful of hot soup into a small bowl and stir in the flour with a wire whisk to prevent lumping; then return the thickened soup to the pot and stir. Simmer briefly. Just before serving, float the cream on top of the soup.

Lettuce Soup

(Soup-e Kahoo)

(Serves 6–8)

2 tablespoons butter	1½ cups milk
6 tablespoons rice flour	2 egg yolks
6 cups water	2 tablespoons lemon juice
1 can chicken or beef broth	1 teaspoon salt
1 head lettuce, finely chopped	¼ teaspoon white pepper

Melt the butter in a saucepan over a low heat. Using a wire whisk, stir in the rice flour. While stirring, gradually add the water and broth. Add the lettuce. Cover and simmer until the lettuce is tender (about 10 minutes).

Add the milk, simmer for 5 minutes, and remove from the heat. Beat the egg yolks and lemon juice together, and add them to the soup gradually, stirring constantly. Add salt and pepper.

Chicken Soup

(Soup-e Morgh)

(Serves 8–10)

1 chicken, or 3 pounds of chicken parts (such as backs, necks, wing tips, giblets)	2 potatoes, sliced or chopped
2 large onions, sliced a few sprigs fresh parsley	3–4 carrots, sliced or chopped
1 teaspoon salt	2–3 chicken livers
¼ teaspoon pepper	1 tablespoon butter
4 packages instant dry broth	2 egg yolks
	2 tablespoons lemon juice

Place the chicken, onions, parsley, salt, and pepper in a large kettle. Add enough water to cover. Add the instant dry broth. Cover and simmer gently for 1 hour. Add the potatoes and carrots and simmer for another 30 minutes. Remove the chicken, potatoes, and carrots. Mash the potatoes and carrots well and return them to the soup.

Sauté the chicken livers in the butter, mash well or chop fine, and add to the soup. In a small bowl beat the egg yolks and lemon juice together and add them to the soup. The chicken may be boned and the meat returned to the soup; or the chicken may be used in other dishes.

Vermicelli may be substituted for the potatoes. It should be added for the last 15 minutes of cooking; it should not be mashed.

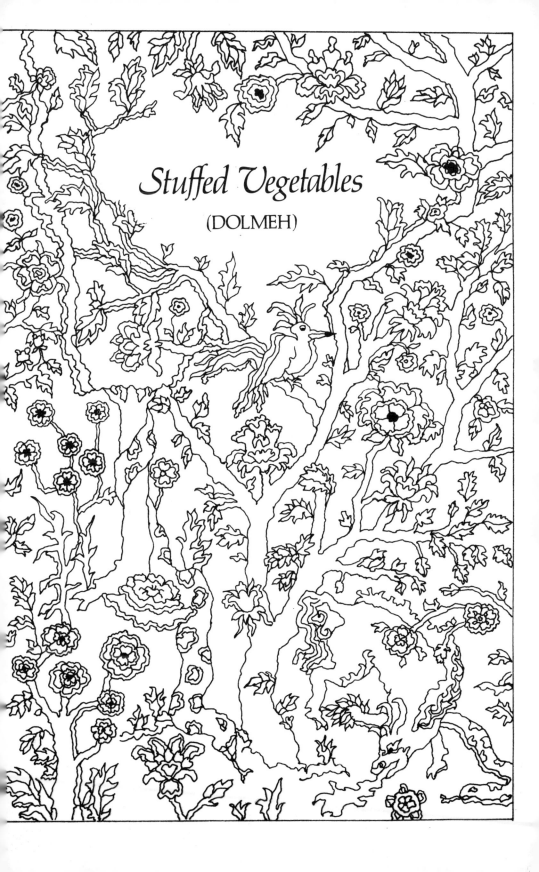

Stuffed Vegetables

(DOLMEH)

One author described *dolmeh* as small gourds crammed with force-meat and done in butter. They include stuffed vine leaves, cabbage leaves, tomatoes, squash—an infinite variety of exotic, delectable, and inexpensive dishes that can add zest and color to your menu. They may be served as a side dish or as a main course; they can be large and substantial, or small, light, and delicate. And wonder of wonders—they can all be prepared ahead of time and then re-heated! They are also delicious cold, served with yogurt on the side.

Stuffed Cabbage Leaves
(Dolmeh Kalam)

(SERVES 6–8)

2 large onions,
    chopped or grated
5 tablespoons butter
    or shortening
1 pound lean ground
    beef
2 teaspoons salt
¼ teaspoon pepper
1 tablespoon sugar
2–3 tablespoons lemon
    juice
1 tablespoon tomato
    paste
½ cup warm water
1 can bouillon or beef
    broth
1 bunch parsley, finely
    chopped

1 bunch scallions or
    leeks, chopped
½ cup fresh dill weed,
    chopped, or 4 table-
    spoons dried dill
    weed
¼ cup fresh tarragon,
    or 2 teaspoons dried
    tarragon (optional)
2–3 sprigs fresh mint
1 cup cooked rice
¼ cup yellow split peas
1 head cabbage
¼ cup tomato sauce
¼ cup cream or sour
    cream (optional)

To prepare filling:

Sauté the onions in 2 tablespoons of the butter or shortening until golden brown. Add the ground beef and sauté, stirring constantly until brown. Reduce the heat; add the salt, pepper, sugar, and lemon juice. Mix the tomato paste with the warm water and add to the meat mixture. Add ½ can of bouillon or broth, cover, and simmer for 20 minutes.

Sauté the parsley, scallions or leeks, dill weed, tarragon and mint in 2 tablespoons of the remaining butter, and add to the meat. Stir and simmer for 10 minutes. Add the cooked rice and stir well. Boil the yellow split peas in 1 cup of salted water for about 15 minutes, drain, and add to other ingredients.

To prepare cabbage leaves:

Separate the cabbage leaves from the main stem, drop them into boiling salted water, and boil gently for about 3 minutes. Drain in a colander, being careful not to break them. Spread the leaves out flat one at a time, and fill the center of each leaf with 2 or 3 tablespoons of filling.

Fold over the edges of the cabbage leaves and roll up from the stem end outward to the top of the leaf. (If necessary, the tough stems may be removed with a sharp knife.) In using the smaller leaves, 2 or 3 may be overlapped, filled, and rolled up.

Arrange the stuffed cabbage leaves in a baking dish. Warm the remaining tablespoon of butter and the remaining ½ can of bouillon or broth, stir in the tomato sauce, and pour over the stuffed cabbage. Bake in a medium oven (350° F.) for about 30 minutes. Warm the cream or sour cream, and spoon it over the stuffed cabbage just before serving.

Stuffed Grape Leaves

(Dolmeh-ye Barg-e Mo)

(SERVES 8 AS A MAIN COURSE, BUT MORE AS AN HORS D'OEUVRE)

½ cup rice
1 large onion, chopped or sliced
¼ cup butter or shortening
1 pound lean ground beef
1 bunch fresh parsley, chopped
1 bunch scallions, chopped
a few sprigs fresh mint, or 1 teaspoon dried mint
a few sprigs fresh tarragon, or 1 teaspoon dried tarragon
3 tablespoons dried dill weed

2 packages instant dry broth (chicken)
½ teaspoon salt
¼ teaspoon pepper
¼ cup lemon juice
4 tablespoons sugar
1 can grape leaves
½ cup water
yogurt or sour cream (optional)
6 prunes (optional)
¼ cup dried currants
¼ cup yellow split peas (optional)
3 tablespoons pine nuts (optional)

To prepare filling:

Put the rice into a pot of boiling salted water, and boil for 5 minutes. Drain and set aside. Sauté the onion in 2 tablespoons of the butter or shortening until golden brown. Add the ground beef and sauté well until brown, stirring frequently. Add the parsley, scallions, mint, tarragon, and dill weed. Add the instant dry broth, salt, pepper, boiled rice, 2 tablespoons of the lemon juice, and 2 table- spoons of the sugar. Mix well.

To prepare grape leaves:

Drain the grape leaves and spread out flat. Place a small amount of filling in the center of each grape leaf, fold the edges over, and roll up. (If larger *dolmeh* are desired, several leaves may be used, overlapping their edges.)

Arrange the stuffed grape leaves in a pan. In a small saucepan melt the remaining 2 tablespoons of butter, add the remaining 2 tablespoons of lemon juice, 2 tablespoons of sugar, and water. Pour this over the *dolmeh,* cover, and simmer over a very low heat until they are tender (about 30 minutes). Or bake in a 350° F. oven for 30 minutes.

Serve plain, or with yogurt or sour cream spooned over the top.

If desired, seeded prunes, currants, boiled yellow split peas, or pine nuts may be added to the filling.

Stuffed Tomatoes

(Dolmeh-ye Gojeh Farangi)

(Serves 6)

1 large onion, chopped or grated	1 bunch scallions, finely chopped
3 tablespoons butter or shortening	½ cup fresh dill weed, chopped, or 4 table- spoons dried dill weed
½ pound lean ground beef	
1 tablespoon tomato paste	¼ cup fresh tarragon, chopped, or 1 table- spoon dried tarragon
½ cup lukewarm water	2–3 sprigs fresh mint, chopped, or 1 tea- spoon dried mint
1 teaspoon salt	
⅛ teaspoon pepper	
1 tablespoon sugar	1 cup cooked rice
2 tablespoons lemon juice	12 tomatoes (medium)
½ can bouillon or beef broth	½ cup heavy cream or sour cream
1 bunch fresh parsley, finely chopped	

To prepare filling:

Sauté the onion in 2 tablespoons of the butter or shortening until golden brown. Add the ground beef and sauté, stirring constantly until brown. Dissolve the tomato paste in the water and add. Add the salt, pepper, sugar, lemon juice, and bouillon; reduce the heat and simmer until the meat is almost dry. Sauté the parsley, scallions, dill weed, tarragon, and mint briefly in the remaining 1 tablespoon of butter or shortening, and add to the meat. Stir in the cooked rice. Simmer, uncovered, over a low heat for 15 minutes.

To prepare tomatoes:

With a sharp knife, slice off the top fourth of each tomato and remove the crown. Do not discard. With a spoon, gently scoop out the inside of each tomato, being careful not to pierce the shell. Fill with the meat-rice mixture and then replace the tomato tops.

Arrange the stuffed tomatoes on a greased baking sheet, and bake in a medium oven (350°) for about 20 minutes. They should be done but not so soft that they fall apart. Spoon heavy cream or sour cream on top of each tomato, or serve the cream separately with the tomatoes.

Stuffed Potatoes I

(Dolmeh-ye Sib Zamini)

Using large, firm, raw potatoes, prepare the cases by peeling the potatoes, removing the tops, hollowing out the insides, and slicing off the bottoms so that they can stand up straight.

Fill with any *dolmeh* filling and arrange in a heavy kettle. Melt 3 tablespoons butter in 1 cup of hot broth and add salt and pepper to taste. Pour this around the potatoes in the bottom of kettle. Cover and simmer very gently until the potato cases are done but still firm enough to hold their shape (about 30 minutes).

Stuffed Potatoes II

(Dolmeh-ye Sib Zamini)

(SERVES 4–6)

2 large onions, chopped or sliced	3 tablespoons parsley, chopped
6 tablespoons butter or shortening	½ teaspoon salt
½ pound lean ground beef	¼ teaspoon pepper
1 tablespoon tomato paste	2 hard-boiled eggs, grated or chopped
¾ cup water or broth	6 large potatoes of uniform size

To prepare filling:

Sauté the onions in 2 tablespoons of the butter or shortening until golden brown; add the ground beef and sauté until brown, stirring constantly. Dissolve the tomato paste in ¼ cup of the water or broth, and add it to the meat. Add the parsley, salt, and pepper, and simmer gently for 15 to 20 minutes. Add the hard-boiled eggs.

To prepare potatoes:

Peel the potatoes and cut the tops and bottoms off flat. Scoop out the insides, being careful not to break through the shell. The cases should be about ⅜ inch thick on the sides and bottom. Melt 3 tablespoons of the butter and lightly brown the potato cases on all sides. Fill the potato cases with the meat mixture.

Arrange the stuffed potatoes in a baking dish. Heat the remaining 1 tablespoon of butter and the remaining ½ cup of water or broth; pour it over and around the stuffed potatoes. Bake uncovered in a 350° F. oven until the potatoes are cooked but still firm enough to hold their shape (about 50 minutes). Or you may arrange the stuffed potatoes in a heavy kettle, cover, and simmer very gently on top of the stove until done (about 45 to 60 minutes).

Stuffed Green Peppers

(Dolmeh-ye Felfel Sabz)

Cut off the tops of green peppers, hollow out the insides, scrape with a sharp knife, and remove all seeds. Boil in salted water for 3 minutes and drain.

Fill the pepper cases with any *dolmeh* filling. Arrange the stuffed peppers in a heavy kettle and pour over and around them 1 can of beef broth or consommé and 1 tablespoon of tomato paste dissolved in ¼ cup of warm water. Cover and simmer gently until the peppers are tender (45 to 60 minutes). They may also be baked, uncovered, in a 350° F. oven for 1 hour.

Stuffed Yellow Summer Squash

(Dolmeh-ye Kadoo)

(SERVES 4–6)

1 large onion, grated	1 tablespoon tomato
½ pound lean ground	paste
beef	½ teaspoon salt
¼ cup shortening or	⅛ teaspoon pepper
butter	4 tablespoons fresh or
½ can beef bouillon	dried dill weed
½ cup rice	1 teaspoon marjoram
1 bunch scallions,	6 yellow summer squash
chopped	¼ cup sour grape (or
½ bunch fresh parsley,	lemon) juice
chopped	

To prepare filling:

Mix the onion with the meat and sauté in 2 tablespoons of the shortening or butter until brown. Add the bouillon, cover, and simmer gently for 15 to 20 minutes. Parboil the rice in boiling, salted water for 8 to 10 minutes. Drain. Add the scallions and parsley to the rice. Stir in the tomato paste, salt, pepper, dill weed, and marjoram. Combine the rice mixture with the meat.

To prepare acorn squash:

Peel the squash with a sharp knife. (If they are young and tender, do not peel.) Cut each squash in half. With a narrow spoon or long, narrow, serrated-edged knife, scoop out the insides, being careful not to break through the shell. Stuff the shells with the meat filling.

Place the stuffed squash in a heavy kettle. Melt the 2 remaining tablespoons of shortening or butter and add the sour grape or lemon juice. Pour this mixture over and around the squash. Invert a china plate over the squash to press it down lightly. Cover the kettle with a lid and simmer gently until done (about 45 minutes or longer).

Stuffed Eggplants

(Dolmeh-ye Bademjan)

(SERVES 4–6)

1 large onion, chopped
  or grated
½ cup butter or
  shortening
½ pound lean ground
  beef
2 tablespoons tomato
  paste (or 2 cups
  tomato juice)
½ cup bouillon or beef
  broth
3–4 tablespoons lemon
  juice
½ teaspoon salt
⅛ teaspoon pepper
1 bunch leeks or
  scallions, chopped
½ bunch fresh parsley,
  chopped

a few sprigs fresh
  mint, chopped
a few sprigs fresh
  tarragon, chopped, or
  1 teaspoon dried
  tarragon
¼ cup rice
1 tablespoon sugar
2–3 hard-boiled eggs,
  grated (optional)
8 small Italian egg-
  plants
1–2 tablespoons lemon
  juice (optional)
1 tablespoon sugar
  (optional)
3–4 tablespoons cream
  or sour cream
  (optional)

To prepare filling:

Sauté the onion in 2 tablespoons of the butter or shortening until golden brown. Add the ground beef and sauté, stirring constantly, until brown. Lower the heat and add 1 tablespoon of the tomato paste diluted in ¼ cup of the bouillon or beef broth (or add 1 cup of the tomato juice), lemon juice, salt, and pepper, and simmer for 15 minutes. Sauté the leeks, parsley, mint, and tarragon briefly in 2 tablespoons of the butter or shortening, and add them to the meat. Stir briefly and remove from the heat. Parboil the rice for 10 minutes in boiling, salted water; drain and add to the meat. Add the sugar and stir until well mixed. If desired, 2 or 3 grated, hard-boiled eggs may be added. Set the filling aside while you prepare the eggplant cases.

To prepare eggplants:

Peel the eggplants thinly. Remove the tops by cutting a circle around them and slicing through just below the stem. Scoop out the insides, being careful not to perforate the bottoms or sides. Leave a shell approximately ¼ inch thick. Sprinkle the inside and outside of each eggplant shell with salt, and set them aside to "perspire" for about 20 minutes. Blot dry with paper towels. Stuff loosely with the meat mixture. Replace the eggplant tops, pressing them into place. Melt the remaining 4 tablespoons butter or shortening and brown the stuffed eggplant shells on all sides, turning gently to prevent breaking them.

Arrange the eggplants upright or sideways in a heavy kettle. Pour over and around them the remaining 1 tablespoon of tomato paste dissolved in the remaining ¼ cup of bouillon (or the remaining 1 cup of tomato juice). If desired, 1 or 2 tablespoons of lemon juice and 1 tablespoon of sugar may be added. Cover the kettle and place over a low heat, simmering gently until the eggplant shells are tender (about 45 minutes or longer). If necessary, more broth or tomato juice may be added in small amounts.

To serve, arrange the eggplants upright or sideways on a platter, and serve plain or with the following sauce: Stir 3 to 4 tablespoons of cream or sour cream into the pan drippings. Pour this over the eggplants, or serve it separately in a gravy boat.

Persian Souffles

(KOOKOO)

They have a Dish they call *Cookoo Challow* which is dry Rice and a Fritter of Eggs, Herbs, and Fishes.
(John Fryer, *A New Account of East India and Persia. Being Nine Years' Travel, 1672–1681.*)

A large omelette about two inches thick.
(James J. Morier, *The Adventures of Haji Baba of Isphahan.*)

The delectable *Kookoo* was called a "fritter" or "omelette" by early travelers to Persia. Neither word is quite adequate. The *kookoo* looks somewhat like a soufflé, and both are made with eggs and other ingredients. But there they part ways, for the *kookoo* is browned in butter, cannot collapse, and can be prepared ahead of time and reheated. There seems to be an almost endless variety of *kookoos;* many of them can be served as main dishes, with bread, yogurt, and a salad. Or they can be served as side dishes to supplement a skimpy meal or elaborate an already abundant table.

Green Herb Kookoo

(Kookoo-ye Sabzi)

(SERVES 6)

This is the finest and most delectable of all the *kookoos;* it tastes best when prepared with fresh herbs.

1 cup leeks or scallions
  (including half of the
  green stems), chopped
a few lettuce leaves,
  chopped
½ cup dill weed, chopped
1 cup parsley, chopped
¼ cup coriander (Chinese
  parsley), chopped
2 tablespoons butter
8 eggs

½ teaspoon baking soda
½ teaspoon turmeric (or
  saffron)
⅛ teaspoon cinnamon
½ teaspoon salt
¼ teaspoon pepper
3 tablespoons walnuts,
  chopped (optional)
3 tablespoons dried
  currants (optional)

Sauté the leeks or scallions, lettuce, dill weed, parsley, and coriander for 5 minutes in 1 tablespoon of the butter, stirring frequently.

Beat the eggs well. Add the baking soda, turmeric, cinnamon, salt, and pepper. Add the chopped greens. Melt the remaining 1 tablespoon of butter in a skillet, and pour in the egg-herb mixture. Do not stir. Cook over a medium heat until well browned; lift edge of the kookoo with a flat utensil to see if brown; then turn it over (as you would turn a large pancake) and brown the other side.

An easier method is to melt the remaining butter in an oblong Pyrex dish, pour in the egg-herb mixture, and bake in a 350° F. oven for 45 to 60 minutes, or until crisp on the bottom and light brown on top.

Serve with yogurt, or with thickened yogurt. This kookoo may be eaten either hot or cold, and it keeps well for use as a leftover.

To make this a festive dish, you may add a few tablespoons of chopped walnuts and/or a few tablespoons of dried currants.

If coriander is not available, you may substitute 1 cup chopped spinach.

String Bean Kookoo

(Kookoo-ye Loobia Sabz)

(SERVES 6)

1 pound string beans
1 large onion, grated
¼ cup butter
½ teaspoon saffron

6–8 eggs
2 teaspoons salt
¼ teaspoon pepper
¼ teaspoon baking soda

Cut the string beans into pieces about ¼ inch long. Boil in salted water until tender. Sauté the onion in 1 tablespoon of the butter until golden brown. Stir in the saffron. Beat the eggs well. Add the salt, pepper, baking soda, sautéed onion, and cooked beans. Melt the remaining 3 tablespoons butter in a skillet, pour in the egg mixture without stirring and cook over a medium heat until brown on one side. Lift edge of *kookoo* with a flat utensil to see if it is brown. Turn over (as you would a pancake) and brown the other side.

This *kookoo* can also be cooked by melting the remaining butter in a Pyrex dish, pouring in the egg mixture, and baking it in a 350° F. oven for 50 minutes or longer. It should be crisp along the edges and on the bottom and light brown on top.

Some Iranian cooks sauté the beans before adding them to the eggs. It may be done either way.

String Bean Kookoo with Ground Beef

(Kookoo-ye Loobia Sabz ba Goosht)

(SERVES 6)

1 pound string beans	½ teaspoon saffron
1 large onion, chopped	6–8 eggs
or grated	1 teaspoon salt
¼ cup butter	¼ teaspoon pepper
¼ pound ground beef	1 teaspoon baking soda
¾ cup bouillon or	
beef broth	

Cut the string beans into small pieces. Boil in lightly salted water until tender. Drain, reserving the liquid. Sauté the onion in 2 tablespoons of the butter until golden brown. Add the ground beef and sauté, stirring constantly. When well browned, add the bouillon or beef broth. Stir in the saffron. Cover and simmer for 30 minutes.

Beat the eggs well. Add the salt, pepper, baking soda, and cooked beans. Melt the remaining butter in a skillet, pour in half the egg mixture, and cook over a medium heat until brown on the underside. Spread the cooked meat over this. Pour the rest of the egg mixture over the meat. Cover and cook over a low heat for 15 to 20 minutes. Turn the entire *kookoo* over and brown the other side.

This *kookoo* can also be cooked by melting the remaining butter in a Pyrex baking dish, pouring in half the egg mixture, spreading it with the meat, covering with the remaining egg mixture, and baking in a medium oven (350° F.) for 45 to 60 minutes. It should be crisp along the edges and on the bottom and light brown on top.

Fava or Lima Bean Kookoo

(Kookoo-ye Shebet Baghala)

(SERVES 6)

2 cups dried fava beans
   (or 1 package frozen
   lima beans)
1 teaspoon salt
1 large onion, sliced
½ cup fresh dill weed,
   chopped, or 4 table-
   spoons dried dill weed

¼ cup butter
6 eggs
1 teaspoon salt
¼ teaspoon pepper
½ teaspoon baking soda

Soak the fava beans in water for at least 3 hours. Then add a little salt, cover, and simmer gently until tender. Cool with cold water. (If using lima beans, cook these according to the directions on the package. Drain, cool with cold water, and peel.) Put the beans through a food mill or grinder, or mash with a potato-masher.

Sauté the onion in 2 tablespoons of the butter. Add the dill weed and stir briefly. Beat the eggs well. Add the salt, pepper, baking soda, onion, and mashed beans. Mix well. Melt the remaining butter in a baking dish. Pour in the egg mixture and bake at 350° F. for 45 to 60 minutes—until the bottom and edges are crisp and the top is golden brown. Invert to serve.

Green Pea Kookoo

(Kookoo-ye Nokhod Farangi)

(SERVES 6)

2 cups peas (fresh,
    frozen, or canned)
1 tablespoon sugar
¼ cup butter
1 cup dill weed,
    chopped or 5–6

    tablespoons dried
    dill weed
6–8 eggs
1 teaspoon salt
    pinch of pepper

If using fresh or frozen peas, boil them with sugar until tender. Drain, and put the peas through a food mill or grinder, or mash them with a potato masher. Melt 1 tablespoon of the butter in a skillet and sauté the dill weed. (If dried dill weed is used, omit this step.) Beat the eggs well. Add the mashed peas, dill weed, salt, and pepper. Stir briefly.

Divide the remaining butter in half and melt it separately in 2 frying pans of the same size. Pour the egg mixture into one of these and cook until it is brown on the bottom. Invert the *kookoo* into the other pan, and fry until it becomes brown on the other side.

If desired, this *kookoo* may be baked in the oven. Melt the remaining butter in a baking dish, pour in the egg mixture, and bake it at 350° F. for 45 minutes or longer. It should be crisp around the edges and on the bottom and golden brown on top. Serve it directly from the baking dish or invert it onto a plate.

Eggplant Kookoo I

(Kookoo-ye Bademjan)

(SERVES 6)

1 medium eggplant
6 eggs
2 large onions, grated
1 package instant dry
    broth

1 teaspoon saffron
1 teaspoon soy sauce
1 teaspoon salt
¼ teaspoon pepper
¼ cup butter

Peel the eggplant, cut it into cubes or chunks, and drop them into boiling, salted water. Cover and simmer gently for 15 minutes. Drain, cool, and mash. Beat the eggs and stir in. Add the onions. Stir in the instant dry broth, saffron, soy sauce, salt, and pepper.

Melt the butter in a baking dish, pour in the eggplant mixture, and bake it in a medium oven (350° F) for 45 minutes or longer. Or melt the butter in a skillet, pour in the eggplant mixture, and cook until it is brown on the bottom. Turn it over like a pancake and brown the other side.

Eggplant Kookoo II

(Kookoo-ye Bademjan)

(SERVES 6)

This is the eggplant *Kookoo* recipe I use. It has always been a favorite with my American guests.

1 medium eggplant	2 tablespoons walnuts
1 large onion, grated	or pecans, chopped
1 tablespoon soy sauce	4 tablespoons butter
2 packages instant dry	3–4 tablespoons flour
broth	½ cup milk
1 teaspoon salt	2 tablespoons cream or
¼ teaspoon pepper	sour cream
1 tablespoon parsley,	5–6 eggs
chopped	

Peel the eggplant, cut it into chunks, and drop them into boiling, salted water. Cover and simmer 15 to 20 minutes, or until very tender. Drain the pieces in a colander; then place them in a bowl and mash well. Add the onion. Add the soy sauce, instant dry broth, salt, pepper, parsley, and walnuts.

Over a low heat, melt 2 tablespoons of the butter. Stir in the flour, using a wire whisk to prevent lumping. Gradually stir in the milk, making a white sauce. Then stir in the cream. Stir the white sauce into the eggplant mixture. Beat the eggs and stir them into the eggplant mixture.

Melt the remaining 2 tablespoons of butter in a Pyrex baking dish, pour in the eggplant mixture, and bake, uncovered, in a 350° F. oven for 45 minutes, or until the top is golden brown.

Zucchini Squash Kookoo

(Kookoo-ye Kadoo)

(Serves 6)

Follow the directions for either Eggplant *Kookoo* (*Kookoo-ye Bademjan*), substituting 4 zucchini squash for the eggplant. You may add 1 tablespoon of sugar, if desired.

Cauliflower Kookoo

(Kookoo-ye Gol Kalam)

(Serves 6)

1 small or medium cauliflower	1 teaspoon baking soda
6 eggs	2 teaspoons salt
1 teaspoon saffron	¼ teaspoon pepper
1 tablespoon soy sauce	1 large onion, grated
	¼ cup butter

With a sharp knife, separate the cauliflower flowerets from the main stem. Drop them into a pot of boiling, salted water, cover, and simmer for 15 minutes, or until tender. Drain in a colander. Mash them with a fork or potato masher. Beat the eggs. Stir in the mashed cauliflower, saffron, soy sauce, baking soda, salt, and pepper. Add the onion.

Melt the butter in a skillet, pour in the egg-cauliflower mixture, and cook over a medium heat until brown on the bottom. Turn it over and brown the other side. Or melt the butter in a baking dish, pour in the egg-cauliflower mixture, and bake it in a 350° F. oven for 45 minutes. It should be crisp around the edges and on the bottom and golden brown on top.

Leek Kookoo

(Kookoo-ye Tareh)

(SERVES 6)

1 pound leeks	¼ teaspoon pepper
6 eggs	½ teaspoon saffron
2 tablespoons bread	¼ cup butter
crumbs	1 cup walnuts, chopped
1 teaspoon baking soda	(optional)
2 teaspoons salt	

Wash the leeks, drain, and blot dry on paper towels. Chop fine, including about ⅓ of the stems. Beat the eggs well. Add the bread crumbs, baking soda, salt, pepper, saffron, and chopped leeks. Melt the butter in a skillet, pour in the egg-leek mixture, cover, and cook over a medium heat for 10 minutes to brown the bottom. Reduce the heat and cook gently until done all the way through (about 20 minutes). Turn over and brown, uncovered, on the other side.

This *kookoo* can also be cooked by melting the butter in a baking dish, pouring in the egg-leek mixture, and baking at 350° F. for 45 minutes or longer, until the bottom and edges are crisp and the top is light brown. With this method, you will need only 2 tablespoons of butter.

If desired, chopped walnuts may be added to the batter.

Leek Kookoo *with Walnuts*

(Kookoo-ye Tareh ba Gerdoo)

(SERVES 6–8)

1 cup walnuts	1 tablespoon flour
¼ cup butter	½ teaspoon turmeric
1 pound leeks	1 teaspoon salt
8 eggs	¼ teaspoon pepper

Put the walnuts into a food grinder or nut chopper and chop very fine. Sauté them in 2 tablespoons of the butter for 3 minutes. Chop the leeks fine, being sure to include about ⅓ of the stems. Beat the eggs well. Add the leeks, sautéed walnuts, flour, turmeric, salt, and pepper.

Melt the remaining 2 tablespoons of butter in a skillet. Pour in the egg-leek mixture and brown it on one side. Turn it over like a large pancake and brown the other side. Lower the heat and cook until done all the way through. It should be very crisp on the outside.

This *kookoo* can also be cooked by melting the remaining butter in a baking pan, pouring in the egg-leek mixture, and baking at 350° F. for 45 minutes or longer, until it is brown and crisp on the bottom and light brown on top. Serve with yogurt.

Cardoon Kookoo

(Kookoo-ye Kangar)

(SERVES 8)

Cardoons are also called "prickly artichokes." They have a very short growing season in Iran, where they are considered a delicacy because of their unusual and exquisite flavor.

2 pounds cardoons	*¼ teaspoon pepper*
4 tablespoons butter	*½ cup ground walnuts*
1 large onion, grated	*8 eggs*
2 teaspoons salt	

Wash the cardoons and pat dry with paper towels. Remove the stems and thorns. Chop them into small pieces. Sauté them briefly in 2 tablespoons of the butter. Add the onion, salt, pepper, and walnuts. Beat the eggs and stir them into the cardoons.

Melt the remaining 2 tablespoons of butter in a skillet. Pour in the egg-cardoon mixture and cook over a medium heat until brown on the bottom. Turn it over (as you would a large pancake) and brown the other side. Cut into wedge-shaped pieces and serve hot with yogurt. As with other *kookoos*, it may also be baked in the oven.

Chicken Kookoo

(Kookoo-ye Morgh—Choghortmeh)

(SERVES 8)

This *kookoo* is extremely popular in Resht, a town on the Caspian seacoast. It is a main dish but can also be used as a side dish.

¼ cup butter	2 teaspoons salt
2 large onions	¼ teaspoon pepper
1 teaspoon saffron	1 medium fryer chicken,
1 tablespoon lemon juice	cut up
1 tablespoon soy sauce	1 teaspoon baking soda
1 can chicken bouillon	1 tablespoon cold water
2 packages instant dry broth	10 eggs

Melt 1 tablespoon of the butter in a skillet. Slice 1 onion and sauté it in the butter until golden brown. Stir in the saffron, lemon juice, and soy sauce. Add the bouillon, instant dry broth, salt, and pepper. Place the chicken in the broth mixture, cover, and simmer until tender (45 to 60 minutes). Cool and bone. Mash to a pulp by putting the meat through a food mill or meat grinder.

Slice the other onion and sauté it in 1 tablespoon of the butter until golden brown. Dissolve the baking soda in cold water. Beat the eggs well. Mix together the chicken pulp, beaten eggs, baking soda, and sautéed onion. Melt the remaining 2 tablespoons of butter in a baking dish and pour in the chicken-egg mixture, patting the surface smooth with the back of a spoon. Bake at 350° F. for 45 to 60 minutes, until it is crisp on the bottom and lightly browned on top. Serve this *kookoo* with yogurt and a salad.

Fish Kookoo

(*Kookoo-ye Mahi*)

(SERVES 6)

2 fillets of flounder, haddock, or perch (or 2 7-ounce cans of salmon)	8 eggs
	½ teaspoon saffron
	2 teaspoons salt
	¼ teaspoon pepper
¼ cup butter	1 teaspoon baking soda
1 tablespoon lemon juice	1 tablespoon cold water
1 tablespoon soy sauce	

Dot the fish fillets with 2 tablespoons of the butter, sprinkle with the lemon juice and soy sauce, and broil until just done. Or melt the butter in a skillet and sauté the fillets until light brown on both sides; sprinkle with lemon juice and soy sauce, and set aside to cool. Flake with a fork.

Beat the eggs well. Add the flaked fish, saffron, salt, and pepper. Dilute the baking soda in cold water and stir in. Melt the remaining 2 tablespoons of butter in a frying pan, pour in the egg-fish mixture, and brown well on one side. Cut into wedge-shaped pieces, turn each piece over, and brown well on the other side. (If using canned salmon, drain, flake with fork, and proceed as above.) This dish is usually served with yogurt.

Brain Kookoo

(Kookoo-ye Maghz)

(SERVES 6)

2 *brains (beef or lamb)*	1 *teaspoon saffron*
5–6 *eggs*	½ *cup parsley, chopped*
1 *teaspoon salt*	4 *tablespoons butter*
pinch of pepper	

Drop the brains into boiling water and simmer gently for 10 minutes. Drain, blot dry on paper towels, and remove the transparent outer membrane. Put through a food mill or meat grinder, or mash to a pulp.

Beat the eggs. Add the salt, pepper, saffron, parsley, and mashed brains. Melt the butter in a frying pan. Pour in the egg-brain mixture. Cook it over a medium heat until crisp and brown on the bottom. Turn over and brown on the other side. Serve with lemon wedges or lemon juice.

Yogurt Dishes
(BORANI)

Borani is the Persian word for cold dishes made of yogurt mixed with various vegetables. Poorandokht was the daughter of a Sassanian King, Khosrow Parviz—and the first woman to rule Persia, 1300 years ago. It is said that she had a special fondness for yogurt and yogurt dishes; hence these dishes came to be called *Poorani,* and eventually *Borani.*

Yogurt is a popular dish throughout the Middle East, where it is widely believed to contribute to good health and longevity, and to cure stomach ailments. Modern science has indeed found that yogurt contains healthful bacteria that promote good digestion. A number of nutritionists today recommend yogurt as a general health food and of particular value when one is taking antibiotics or sulfa drugs.

In Iran yogurt is frequently taken as a cure for stomach upsets. Justice William Douglas related how some years ago while traveling through the Lar Valley in Northern Iran, he became very sick:

I had not eaten wisely and I was spending a miserable night. Word of it somehow went through the darkness to the Hedavand camp. About midnight a ragged, barefooted man of the tribe came to my bed with a bowl of mast (yogurt). Mast harbors no bacteria hostile to man and has some that kill many unfriendly ones. This mast

had a benign influence. After I had eaten most of it, I went to sleep
at once; and I woke up well.

> (William O. Douglas, *Strange Lands and Friendly People*.)

The popularity of yogurt in the Middle East can probably also be
attributed to the fact that for centuries there were abundant herds
of goats and sheep in the area, providing plentiful supplies of milk,
yet there were only primitive forms of refrigeration, and the keeping qualities of yogurt greatly surpassed those of milk. Thus yogurt
developed as an ideal form in which to consume milk. In Iran
yogurt is also dried into small balls for winter use, when it is called
kashk.

In addition to these virtues, yogurt can be the base for a delicious
variety of foods—hors d'oeuvres, vegetable dishes, and cold soups.
It can also provide a unique tart flavor to many meat dishes and
hot soups.

Yogurt

(Mast)

2 *quarts milk*	*bought at a store or*
¼ *cup yogurt (either*	*homemade)*

Pour the milk into a pan and place over a medium heat. Scald
for about 30 minutes (or until the milk reaches a temperature of
200° F.). Meanwhile, set the yogurt out to come to room temperature. Remove the milk from the heat and cool to lukewarm (about
30 minutes to a temperature of 135–140° F.). (If the milk is too
cool, the culture will not grow. If it is too warm, the heat will kill
the bacteria in the culture.) Pour the milk into a bowl. Stir in the
yogurt, cover the bowl, and set the bowl in a warm place (about
120° F.) for 8 to 12 hours. If you don't have a warm spot, heat your
oven to "warm." Place the bowl in the oven and immediately turn
off the heat. Keep the bowl there overnight. The milk should have
turned from liquid to a thick, custard-like consistency. Refrigerate.
The yogurt will stay fresh for 1 to 2 weeks.

If your starter yogurt is stale or sour, the resulting yogurt will
also taste stale or sour. So always be sure to start with sweet, fresh
yogurt.

Save about ½ cup of yogurt from each batch as a starter for
your next batch.

Yogurt Salad

(Mast-o-Khiar)

(SERVES 5–6)

2 cups yogurt
2 cucumbers, finely
  chopped or grated
1 teaspoon fresh mint,
  chopped, or dried mint
1 large onion, grated
2 teaspoons salt
3–4 radishes, grated

½ cup walnuts,
  chopped (optional)
1 teaspoon fresh
  dill weed, chopped,
  or dried dill weed
¼ cup dried currants
  or raisins

Pour the yogurt into a cheesecloth, draw the edges together, tie with a string, and suspend over a sink or bowl overnight, to allow all the water to drip out. The result will be a very thick, creamy yogurt. Mix all the ingredients together. With an ice cream scoop, shape the yogurt mixture into large balls and arrange them on lettuce leaves. If desired, the grated radishes may be sprinkled over the top rather than mixed in the salad.

Yogurt and Cucumbers

(Mast-o-Khiar)

Mix together any amount of yogurt and finely chopped cucumbers. Add salt and pepper to taste, chill, and serve cool.

For variety, add 1 teaspoon of chopped fresh mint and/or fresh dill weed and/or fresh tarragon.

Yogurt with Spinach I

(Borani-ye Esfenaj)

(SERVES 10)

1 10-ounce package
  spinach (fresh or
  frozen)

4 cups yogurt
2 teaspoons salt
½ teaspoon pepper

Boil the spinach until tender; then drain and chop it. When cool, stir it into the yogurt; season with salt and pepper, and chill in the refrigerator. Serve cold.

For added flavor, chopped herbs may be added to the spinach while it is boiling—dill weed, scallions, parsley, or mint, in any combination.

Yogurt with Spinach II

(Borani-ye Esfenaj)

(SERVES 5–6)

1 10-ounce package fresh spinach	1 large onion, chopped
2 teaspoons salt	1–2 tablespoons butter
¼ teaspoon pepper	2 cups yogurt

Boil the spinach in a small amount of water, with salt and pepper, until tender. Drain, chop, and set it aside to cool. Sauté the onion in the butter until golden brown and tender. Cool, and stir it into the yogurt. Add the spinach, mix well, and chill in the refrigerator. Serve cold.

Yogurt with Eggplant and Meatballs

(Borani-ye Bademjan ba Goosht)

(SERVES 4–5)

This is either a tantalizing side dish or a main dish.

1 large eggplant	1 tablespoon Kitchen Bouquet
½ cup butter	1 tablespoon lemon juice
2 large onions	4 cups yogurt
½ pound lean ground beef	1 teaspoon saffron
½ teaspoon salt	2 teaspoons dried mint flakes
⅛ teaspoon pepper	
½ cup beef broth	

Peel the eggplant, cut it lengthwise into 4 sections, then cut it crosswise into slices about ¼ inch thick. Sprinkle these pieces with salt and let them stand for at least 30 minutes. The eggplant will "perspire." Blot the pieces dry with paper towels, and sauté them in 5 tablespoons of the butter on both sides until golden brown. Grate 1 onion and mix it well with the ground beef. Add the salt and pepper. Shape it into tiny meatballs.

Chop or slice the remaining onion and sauté it in 2 tablespoons of the butter until golden brown. Add the meatballs and sauté until brown on all sides. Add the beef broth, Kitchen Bouquet, and lemon juice. Simmer, uncovered, for 20 minutes, turning the meatballs occasionally.

Arrange the meatballs in the bottom of a baking dish and place sautéed eggplant pieces on top. Mix the yogurt with the saffron, and pour it over the eggplant. Bake in a moderate oven (350° F.) for 20 to 30 minutes. Just before serving, sauté the mint flakes in the remaining 1 tablespoon of butter, and sprinkle them over the top.

Yogurt with Cardoons

(Borani-ye Kangar)

(SERVES 6–8)

3 cups yogurt	½ teaspoon salt
1 pound cardoons	¼ teaspoon pepper
¼ cup butter or shortening	

Pour the yogurt into a cheesecloth, tie the ends of the cloth together, hang it over a bowl, and allow it to drip overnight. By morning you will have yogurt of a thick, creamy consistency. Clean the cardoons, removing the prickles and thorns. Boil them in salted water until tender (about 20 minutes). Drain and mash them with a fork. Melt the butter or shortening in a skillet and stir in the mashed cardoons. Sauté briefly. Add salt and pepper; then add the yogurt, mixing well. Serve hot or cold. May be served as a side-dish, or as a spread with bread or crackers.

Yogurt with Eggplants

(Borani-ye Bademjan)

(SERVES 6)

1 large or 2 small
  eggplants
½ cup butter or
  shortening
1 cup beef broth or
  bouillon

½ teaspoon saffron
1 teaspoon salt
¼ teaspoon pepper
2 cups yogurt

Peel the eggplants. Cut them into thin rings or long slices. Sprinkle with salt, and set aside for 30 minutes or longer to "perspire." Blot the slices dry with paper towels. Melt the butter or shortening in a skillet and brown the eggplant slices on both sides. Drain on paper towels. Discard the fat. Return the eggplant slices to the skillet. Add the beef broth to the eggplant slices and simmer, uncovered, for 15 to 20 minutes.

Stir the saffron, salt, and pepper into the yogurt; pour it over the eggplant slices. Heat briefly on top of the stove or in the oven and serve hot. Or cool the eggplant slices, pound or mash them into a pulp, add the yogurt and seasoning, and serve with bread or crackers as an hors d'oeuvre. If desired, 2 tablespoons dried mint flakes may be sautéed in 2 tablespoons butter, and sprinkled over the top.

Yogurt with Meat and Lentils

(Borani-ye Goosht)

(SERVES 6)

2 large onions,
  chopped or sliced
3 tablespoons butter
1 pound shoulder of
  lamb (or chuck steak)
3 cups beef broth
  or bouillon
1 teaspoon salt

¼ teaspoon pepper
½ cup lentils
1 large or 2 small
  eggplants
2 cups yogurt
1 clove garlic,
  grated (optional)

Sauté the onions in the butter until golden brown. Cut the meat into small pieces, add to the onions, and sauté until brown. Add the beef broth, salt, and pepper. Cover and simmer for 1 hour. Add the lentils, cover, and simmer until all the ingredients are tender (about 30 minutes). Add water if necessary.

Peel the eggplant, slice or chop it into small pieces, and add it to the meat and lentils. Cover and simmer for 30 minutes. Allow the meat and vegetables to cool; then pour them into a bowl and pound them to a pulp or paste. Stir in the yogurt. Sprinkle the garlic over the top. This dish may be served hot or cold, with bread or crackers. It makes a marvelous hors d'oeuvre or luncheon dish.

Yogurt with Mushrooms

(Borani-ye Gharch)

(SERVES 4–6)

1 pound mushrooms	½ teaspoon salt
3–4 tablespoons butter	¼ teaspoon pepper
¼ cup chicken broth	1 clove garlic,
or water	grated (optional)
2 cups yogurt	

Wash the mushrooms and blot them dry on paper towels. Chop or slice them into small pieces, and sauté them in the butter. Add the broth or water, cover, and simmer until tender (about 20 minutes). Cool slightly and then stir in the yogurt. Add the salt and pepper. If desired, sprinkle grated garlic over the top. Serve warm.

Yogurt with Dates and Walnuts

(Kaleh-Joosh)

(SERVES 8–10)

This dish is typically made with liquid whey, but yogurt may be substituted.

2 large onions, grated	3 cloves garlic, grated
4–5 tablespoons butter or shortening	1 teaspoon saffron
1 tablespoon flour	1 teaspoon hot water
4 cups liquid whey (kashk) or yogurt	1 pound pitted dates
1 teaspoon dried mint flakes	½ cup walnuts, chopped or ground

Sauté the onions in half the butter or shortening until golden brown. Sprinkle the flour over the onions, stirring with a wire whisk. Add the liquid whey or yogurt. Bring the mixture to a boil and remove from the flame immediately. Sauté the mint flakes in 1 tablespoon of the butter or shortening and sprinkle them over the top. Sauté the garlic in 1 tablespoon of the butter or shortening and sprinkle this over the top.

Dissolve the saffron in hot water and sprinkle this over the top. Slice each date lengthwise into 8 slivers, and sprinkle this over the top, followed by the walnuts. This dish may be used as a side dish or as an hors d'oeuvre. As an hors d'oeuvre, decrease or eliminate the dates.

Yogurt with Squash

(Kashk-e Kadoo)

(SERVES 6–8)

This dish is made traditionally with liquid whey, but yogurt may be substituted.

6 yellow summer squash	½ cup water
3 medium onions, finely chopped	2 teaspoons salt
4 tablespoons butter	3 cups liquid whey (kashk) or yogurt
2 cloves garlic, chopped or grated	1 teaspoon dried mint flakes
1 teaspoon turmeric	

Cut the squash into small pieces. Sauté the onions in 2 tablespoons of the butter until golden brown. Add the squash and sauté, stirring occasionally. Add the garlic, sautéeing it briefly. Stir in the turmeric; then add the water and salt. Lower the heat and simmer until tender and all the liquid has been absorbed.

Pour the liquid whey or yogurt over the squash and simmer very briefly. Melt the remaining 2 tablespoons of butter in a small saucepan, stir in the mint flakes, and sauté for a few minutes. Sprinkle the mint flakes over the yogurt and serve warm.

Cold Yogurt Soup

(Ab Doogh Khiar)

(SERVES 4)

Delightfully refreshing on a hot summer's day.

2 *large cucumbers*	2 *teaspoons salt*
2 *cups yogurt*	¼ *teaspoon pepper*
1 *tablespoon mint,*	2 *cups cold water*
finely chopped	¼ *cup dried currants*
1 *tablespoon scallions or*	*or raisins*
leeks, finely chopped	

Peel the cucumbers and grate or chop them very fine. Mix all the ingredients together. Chill in the refrigerator. Just before serving, stir in a few ice cubes. Serve in bowls, as you would soup.

Cold Yogurt Soup with Chicken

(Ab Doogh Khiar ba Goosht-e Morgh)

(SERVES 8)

4 *large cucumbers*	¼ *cup dried currants*
4 *cups yogurt*	1 *large onion, grated*
1 *tablespoon tarragon,*	2 *teaspoons salt*
finely chopped, or	¼ *teaspoon pepper*
1 *teaspoon dried*	¼ *cup walnuts, chopped*
tarragon	2 *hard-boiled eggs,*
1 *tablespoon thyme,*	*chopped*
finely chopped, or	1 *whole breast of chicken*
1 *teaspoon dried*	*(boiled, broiled, or*
thyme	*roasted)*
3 *leeks, chopped*	2 *tablespoons dried mint*
2 *sprigs fresh mint,*	*flakes*
chopped	2 *tablespoons butter*

Peel the cucumbers and grate them; stir them into the yogurt in a medium-sized bowl. Add the tarragon, thyme, leeks, fresh mint, and currants. Add the onion, salt, pepper, walnuts, and hard-boiled eggs. Bone the chicken breast, chop or cut it up fine, and add. Mix well together. Sauté the mint flakes in the butter and sprinkle them over the top. Serve cold.

Yogurt Refresher
(Doogh)

(SERVES 1)

This delightfully refreshing drink is very popular in Iran, especially on hot summer days. It can be prepared very quickly and easily.

⅔ cup water	½ teaspoon salt
4–5 tablespoons yogurt	a few ice cubes

Combine all ingredients together. If desired, a few mint leaves may be floated on top.

Carbonated Yogurt Refresher
(Doogh-e Ab-Ali)

Follow the directions for Yogurt Refresher (Doogh), but substitute ⅔ cup soda water for the plain water.

Vegetables

(SABZIJAT)

Are you, perhaps, looking for new ways to prepare vegetables, to add diversity and unusual interest to carrots, spinach, or squash? The Persian way of cooking vegetables might provide the answer to the problem of making ordinary vegetables interesting and enticing.

Carrots

(Shesh-Andaz-e Havij)

(SERVES 6)

This dish transforms the humble carrot into something exotic and unusual. Try it for compliments galore.

1 pound carrots	2 tablespoons vinegar
3 tablespoons butter	(or pomegranate syrup)
2 large onions,	5 eggs
chopped or grated	¼ teaspoon salt
1 cup dates	¼ cup slivered almonds
¼ cup dried currants	¼ cup slivered pistachios
¼ cup raisins	

Peel the carrots and either chop them fine or cut them into thin slivers. Sauté them briefly in butter. Add the onions and sauté until golden brown. Pit the dates and cut into slivers. Add them to the carrots. Add the currants and raisins. Add the vinegar (or pomegranate syrup), cover, and simmer for 30 minutes over a low heat.

Beat the eggs well, and pour them over the carrot mixture; cook over a low heat until the eggs are firm. Sprinkle with salt. Sprinkle the almonds and pistachios over the top and serve.

Spinach with Eggs

(Nargessi Esfenaj)

(SERVES 4–6)

2 pounds fresh spinach	3 eggs
1 large onion, grated	salt and pepper
3 tablespoons butter	

Wash the spinach, drain, and blot dry on paper towels. Break each leaf in half. Place the spinach in a pot, without water, and simmer gently, covered, over a low heat until done (about 10 minutes). Sauté the onion in butter; add the spinach and sauté. Beat the eggs well with a fork, add salt and pepper, and pour them over the spinach. Cook gently until the eggs are firm but not dry.

Another method of preparing this tasty dish is to break the whole eggs over the spinach, and cook them gently on top of the vegetable until done.

Fava Bean and Lettuce Casserole

(Baghala ba Kahoo)

(SERVES 4)

1 pound shelled fresh fava beans, or 1 pound dried fava beans soaked overnight	10 sprigs fresh parsley
	12 small pearl onions
	2 teaspoons salt
1 head lettuce	¼ teaspoon pepper
1 teaspoon fresh thyme or ½ teaspoon dried thyme	¼ cup water
	3 tablespoons butter (or cream)

Shell the fava beans; peel the transparent skins off. Wash the lettuce, fresh thyme, and parsley; shake off the excess moisture, and chop these ingredients. Peel the onions and place them in a pot, together with the fava beans, lettuce, thyme, parsley, salt, pepper, and water. Cover and simmer over a low heat until done (about 30 minutes). Add the butter (or cream) just before serving.

Large lima beans may be substituted for the fava beans.

Fava Beans in Tomato Sauce

(Khorak-e Baghala)

(SERVES 4)

1 pound fresh fava beans	1 teaspoon salt
1 tablespoon tomato paste	¼ teaspoon pepper
	1 tablespoon flour
½ cup warm water	2 tablespoons milk

Shell the fava beans. Boil them in salted water until almost tender (about 25 minutes). Cool in cold water and peel. Place in a pot. Dilute the tomato paste with the warm water and add. Add the salt and pepper. Cover and simmer gently for another 15 minutes. Using a wire whisk, stir in the flour and milk, simmer briefly, and serve.

Fava Beans in the Pod

(Baghali-e Sabz)

(SERVES 6–8)

2 pounds young, green fava beans (in the pod)	2–3 scallions, sliced
2–3 teaspoons salt	⅓ cup fresh dill weed, chopped
¼ cup lemon juice	½ teaspoon sugar
½ tablespoon flour	3 cups water
¼ cup water	½ cup salad or olive oil
2 medium onions, sliced	

Wash the beans in the pod and make a slit down the side of each pod. Sprinkle with salt and lemon juice (to eliminate any trace of bitterness). Set aside for 15 minutes. Rinse the pods and drain.

Using a wire whisk, stir the flour into ¼ cup water. Pour this into a large pot. Add the onions, scallions, and dill weed. Add the sugar, water, and fava beans. Pour the oil over these. Cover and cook over a low heat until the beans are tender and the water has been absorbed.

Squash with Parsley

(Khorak-e Kadoo va Ja'fari)

(SERVES 4–6)

2 large onions, grated or finely chopped	6 acorn squash
	½ cup salad oil
3 cloves garlic, grated or finely chopped	2 cups water
	3 teaspoons salt
½ cup parsley, chopped	¼ teaspoon pepper

Mix together the onions, garlic, and parsley. Slice each squash lengthwise into 4 slices. Arrange these in the bottom of a pan. Sprinkle the onions, garlic, and parsley on top. Pour the salad oil and water over the squash. Add the salt and pepper. Cover and simmer until tender (about 20 minutes).

Lentil Puree

(Pooreh-ye Adas)

(SERVES 4)

2 large onions	¼ teaspoon pepper
2 cups lentils	1 cup croutons
2 teaspoons salt	

Peel and quarter the onions. Put the onions and lentils into a pot and cover with cold water. Add the salt and pepper; bring to a boil and cook until tender (about 20 minutes). Drain and put through a food mill or meat grinder 3 times; then press through a sieve.

(Or the vegetables may be blended in an electric blender.) Serve warm, topped with croutons. This makes an appetizing hors d'oeuvre served as a dip or spread.

Eggplant Casserole

(Mirza Ghassemi)

(SERVES 4–6)

This recipe comes from the province of Gilan.

2 medium eggplants	1 teaspoon turmeric
2 medium onions, chopped	½ teaspoon salt
8 cloves garlic, grated	¼ teaspoon pepper
¼ cup butter or	1 tomato
shortening	4 eggs

Roast the eggplants over a charcoal grill until brown. Or roast them in a 400° F. oven until brown on the outside and soft on the inside (test with a fork). Cool and peel. Mash the pulp. Sauté the onions and garlic in the butter or shortening until golden brown. Stir in the turmeric. Add the eggplant pulp and sauté briefly, stirring well. Add the salt and pepper.

Drop the tomato briefly into hot water to loosen its skin, and then peel. Chop it into small pieces, and stir them into the eggplant. Cook over a low heat for 5 minutes. Beat the eggs and pour them over the eggplant. When the eggs start to solidify, stir briefly, and serve.

Shiraz Eggplants

(Bademjan-e Shirazi)

(SERVES 4–6)

2 large eggplants	2 bunches scallions
½ cup butter or	(about 12), chopped
shortening	a few sprigs fresh parsley,
1 pound fresh tomatoes,	chopped
or 1 can tomatoes	2 teaspoons salt
(16-ounce)	¼ teaspoon pepper

Peel the eggplants and slice into thin rings. Melt the butter or shortening in a skillet and sauté the eggplant rings on both sides until light brown. If you wish, you may drain these on paper towels.

Drop the tomatoes briefly into boiling water to loosen their skins. Peel, cut into small pieces, and then mash them. (If using canned tomatoes, mash these.) Discard the fat and return the eggplant rings to the skillet. Pour the mashed tomatoes and their juice over the eggplant rings. Sprinkle the scallions and parsley over the tomatoes. Sprinkle with salt and pepper. Cover and simmer over a low heat for 20 minutes.

Mixed Vegetable Casserole

(Torsh-e Tareh)

(SERVES 4–6)

1 large onion, sliced	1 cup parsley, chopped
4 tablespoons butter	10 sprigs fresh mint,
2 cups pinto (or	chopped
cranberry October)	¼ cup coriander (Chinese
beans (soaked in water	parsley), chopped
for 2 hours)	2 pounds spinach
2 cups lentils	½ cup rice flour
8 cups water	¼ cup cold water
2 tablespoons salt	3 tablespoons undiluted,
¼ teaspoon pepper	frozen orange juice
3 cloves garlic, grated	4 eggs
½ cup dill weed,	1 tablespoon lemon juice
chopped, or 4	
tablespoons dried	
dill weed	

Sauté the onion in 2 tablespoons of the butter. Add the beans and lentils and cover with the water. Add the salt and pepper. Cover and boil gently until tender (about 1 hour and thirty minutes). In a separate skillet, sauté the garlic in the remaining butter. Add the parsley, dill weed, mint, and coriander to the garlic; stir and sauté briefly. Add the herbs and garlic to the beans and lentils.

Wash the spinach, drain, and chop coarsely. Add it to the beans. Simmer until tender (about 15 minutes). Place the rice flour in a small bowl and, with a wire whisk, stir in the cold water. Stir this gradually into the beans. Continue simmering until the dish thickens. If necessary, add more flour.

Stir in the undiluted, frozen orange juice. In a small bowl, beat the eggs and add the lemon juice; pour this into the beans. Stir briefly and serve. This dish should be like a thick soup. As a main dish, it may be served with rice; as a soup, it should be served with plenty of hot bread.

Vegetable Casserole with Meatballs

(Ghalieh-ye Esfenaj)

(SERVES 6)

⅓ cup black-eyed peas	4 tablespoons butter
⅓ cup lentils	2 packages (12 ounces)
⅓ cup yellow split peas	frozen chopped spinach
2 tablespoons salt	2 cups yogurt
1 large onion, grated	3 tablespoons fresh mint,
1 teaspoon salt	chopped, or dried mint
¼ teaspoon pepper	flakes
1 pound lean ground beef	

Soak the black-eyed peas, lentils, and yellow split peas for 2 to 3 hours. Then cover with cold water, add 2 tablespoons of salt, cover, and bring to a boil. Boil gently until tender (about 40 minutes). Add the onion, salt, and pepper to the ground beef. Mix well with the hands and shape into tiny meatballs, about the size of cherries. Sauté the meatballs in 2 tablespoons of the butter until brown on all sides. Drop these into the simmering pot of peas and lentils. Add the spinach and simmer gently for 15 minutes. Spoon some of the hot liquid into the yogurt and stir well; then stir the yogurt into the hot vegetables. Sauté the chopped mint in the remaining butter, and sprinkle this over the vegetables. This casserole may be served with rice or with hot bread.

Lentil-Squash Casserole

(Ghalieh-ye Kadoo)

(SERVES 5)

2 large onions, sliced	2 teaspoons salt
2 tablespoons butter	¼ teaspoon pepper
2 cups lentils	1 small onion, chopped
2 large butternut	(optional)
squashes	1 tablespoon butter
1 tablespoon lemon juice	(optional)

Sauté the onions in the butter until golden brown. Add the lentils and just enough water to cover; simmer until tender (about 20 minutes). Peel and slice the squashes. Add them to the lentils, cover, and simmer gently until the squashes are tender (about 20 minutes). Add the lemon juice, salt, and pepper. Stir well and serve. Just before serving, sautéed onion may be sprinkled over the top.

Spinach in Pomegranate Syrup

(Ghalieh Esfenaj)

(SERVES 6)

1 cup lentils	1 large onion, chopped
2 teaspoons salt	or sliced
2 pounds fresh spinach,	2 tablespoons butter
or 2 packages	3–4 tablespoons
(10 ounces) frozen	pomegranate syrup
spinach	(or yogurt)

Place the lentils in a pot; add the salt and enough water to cover. Bring to a boil and boil gently until done (about 20 minutes). Chop the spinach coarsely. Sauté the onion in the butter until golden brown. Add the spinach, sauté, cover, and simmer for 10 minutes. Add the spinach and onion to the cooked lentils. Add the pomegranate syrup. Cover and simmer for 15 to 25 minutes longer.

If yogurt is substituted for the pomegranate syrup, it should be heated with a few tablespoons of hot liquid from the pot before it is stirred into the vegetables. The yogurt should be added just before serving.

Baked Squash Boats

(Khorak-e Kadoo)

(SERVES 6)

6 cups water	½ cup fresh dill weed,
2 teaspoons salt	chopped, or 4
6 acorn squash	tablespoons dried
1 tablespoon butter	dill weed
8 ounces feta cheese	pinch of white pepper
2 eggs, beaten	radishes and tomatoes

Bring the water to a boil. Add the salt. Drop the unpeeled squashes into the boiling water for 25 minutes. When they are tender (but not too soft), remove them from the water and cool. Slice each squash into half lengthwise. Scoop out the seeds from each half, and discard them. Grease a baking pan and arrange the squash shells in it.

Crumble the feta cheese and mix it with the eggs, dill weed, and white pepper. Fill the squash shells with this mixture. Bake at 375° F. for 30 minutes. To serve, arrange radishes and tomato slices around the squash for decoration.

Salads
(SALAD)

Many of these salads are of Western origin, but over the years Persians have modified them almost beyond recognition. By adding their own special touch to these salads, Persians have ultimately made them their own.

The traditional Persian "salad" consists of fresh green herbs served on the side—tarragon, sweet basil, scallions, mint, and parsley.

.... but for Sallads it yields all that are desirable, both Herbs and Roots; and some of the most Medicinal Plants are of the Natural Growth of this Country.

(John Fryer, *A New Account of East India and Persia. Being Nine Years' Travels, 1672–1681.*)

Green Pea Salad with Yogurt

(Salad-e Nokhod ba Mast)

(SERVES 6)

2 cups yogurt
1 pound new potatoes
1 cup green peas
  (frozen, fresh, or
  canned)
4 tablespoons fresh or
  dried chopped dill
  weed

½ cup salad or olive oil
½ cup dill pickles,
  chopped
2 tablespoons lemon juice
salt and pepper to taste

Pour the yogurt into a clean cheesecloth, pull the edges together, and tie securely. Hang over a sink or bowl overnight to allow all the liquid to drip out.

Boil the potatoes, peel, and chop. Cook the frozen or fresh peas. Mix all the ingredients together and chill well in the refrigerator. Serve on lettuce leaves. If desired, an ice cream scoop may be used to shape the mixture into balls. This salad is especially attractive if it is decorated with radishes or fresh mint leaves.

Carrot Salad I

(Salad-e Havij)

(SERVES 4–6)

6 carrots
1 orange
1 lemon
¼ cup seedless raisins

½ teaspoon salt
4 tablespoons salad oil
1 teaspoon parsley,
  chopped

Peel the carrots and grate coarsely. Squeeze the juice of the orange into a small bowl. Soak the grated carrots in the orange juice for 1 hour. Squeeze the juice of the lemon and add the raisins. Mix together the carrots, orange juice, salt, and oil. Put the raisins and lemon juice on top. Sprinkle with the chopped parsley.

Carrot Salad II

(Salad-e Havij)

(SERVES 4–6)

1 pound carrots	salt and pepper to taste
1 pound peas,	4–5 slices canned beets
or 1 can peas	1 hard-boiled egg,
(16-ounces)	sliced
2 tablespoons parsley,	
chopped	

Peel the carrots and grate coarsely. Shell and boil the peas until tender. (Pour the liquid off the canned peas.) Add to the grated carrots. Add the chopped parsley, salt, and pepper. Add dressing to taste and toss gently. Decorate with slices of beet and hard-boiled egg.

Carrot Salad III

(Salad-e Havij)

(SERVES 4)

1 pound carrots	4 teaspoons vinegar
¼ cup salad oil	1 tablespoon parsley,
¼ teaspoon prepared	chopped
mustard	

Peel the carrots and grate them. Mix together the salad oil, mustard and vinegar, for a dressing. Pour the dressing over the grated carrots. Sprinkle with chopped parsley.

Spinach Salad I

(Salad-e Esfenaj)

(SERVES 4)

½ pound fresh spinach	salt and pepper to taste
1 tablespoon salad oil	1 hard-boiled egg,
1 tablespoon heavy cream	sliced or grated
3 tablespoons vinegar	radishes, whole or sliced
3 tablespoons yogurt	

Wash the spinach well and shake dry. Mix together the salad oil, cream, vinegar, and yogurt. Chop the spinach coarsely or break the leaves with your fingers. Sprinkle with the salt and pepper. Stir the yogurt mixture into the spinach. Decorate with hard-boiled egg and radishes.

Spinach Salad II

(Salad-e Esfenaj)

(SERVES 6)

> 1 pound fresh spinach
> ½ cup heavy cream
> salt and pepper to taste
>
> juice of 2 lemons
> 2 hard-boiled eggs

Wash the spinach well and drain in a colander. Break the leaves into small pieces with your fingers or chop them coarsely with a sharp knife. Mix together the cream, salt, pepper, and lemon juice to make a thick sauce. Pour it over the spinach. Chop the egg yolks and sprinkle over the salad. Slice the egg whites into rings for decoration.

Endive-Beet Salad

(Salad-e Laboo)

(SERVES 4)

> 3 tablespoons vinegar
> ¼ cup salad oil
> salt and pepper to taste
> 5–6 celery stalks, chopped
> ¼ cup walnuts,
>   chopped
>
> 2 apples, peeled and
>   chopped
> 1 can sliced or whole
>   beets, chopped
>   (16-ounces)
> 2 endives, chopped

Prepare a dressing by mixing together the vinegar, salad oil, salt, and pepper. Place the celery in a salad bowl and add the walnuts, apples, beets, and endives. Pour the dressing over all and toss lightly.

Green Salad

(Salad-e Sabz)

(SERVES 4)

4 potatoes	¼ teaspoon dry mustard
4 carrots	½ teaspoon salt
2 large dill pickles, chopped	¼ teaspoon pepper
1 stalk celery, chopped	¼ cup salad oil
2–3 scallions, chopped	½ cup mayonnaise (or heavy cream)
½ can green peas, drained	4 tablespoons vinegar

Peel, boil, and chop the potatoes. Grate the carrots. Mix together all the ingredients and chill in the refrigerator.

Watercress Salad

(Salad-e Sahrai)

(SERVES 4)

1 pound potatoes	½ cup mayonnaise
2 large bunches watercress	1–2 tablespoons vinegar
	salt and pepper to taste

Boil the potatoes, peel, and slice thinly. Wash the watercress and shake dry. Remove the stems from the watercress and mix with the potato slices. Add the other ingredients. Chill well before serving.

Pinto Bean Salad

(Salad-e Loobia Chiti)

(SERVES 4–6)

1 cup pinto beans (or kidney beans), cooked	¼ cup vinegar
3 large potatoes	1 head lettuce
½ cup salad oil	salt and pepper to taste
	2 hard-boiled eggs

Drain the liquid from the cooked beans. Boil the potatoes until done, cool, peel, and either slice thinly or dice. Mix together the salad oil and vinegar and set aside. Break the lettuce into pieces and place a layer in the bottom of a salad bowl. Cover with a layer of beans and then a layer of potatoes. Alternate the layers. Pour the oil and vinegar over all. Add the salt and pepper. Decorate with hard-boiled eggs, sliced, quartered, or grated.

Dill Pickle Salad

(Salad-e Khiar Shoor)

(SERVES 8–10)

4 large potatoes	5 sprigs fresh mint, chopped
3–4 carrots	
2 cups green peas	5 sprigs fresh tarragon, chopped
1 cup cranberry October (or pinto or kidney) beans	salt and pepper to taste
	¾ cup salad oil
20 radishes	⅓ cup vinegar
1 bunch scallions	½ cup heavy cream (or mayonnaise)
6–10 dill pickles	
½ head cabbage, grated or chopped	½ teaspoon prepared mustard
10 sprigs fresh parsley, chopped	

Boil the potatoes, carrots, peas, and beans separately until tender. Drain off all the liquid. Dice or slice the potatoes, carrots, radishes, scallions, and pickles. Mix all of the vegetables and herbs together. Season with salt and pepper. Mix together the salad oil, vinegar, cream and mustard. Pour over the salad. Chill well before serving.

Green Pepper Salad

(Salad-e Felfel Sabz)

(SERVES 6–8)

2 pounds potatoes	3 tablespoons salad oil
1 onion, sliced	2 tablespoons vinegar
2 pounds tomatoes, sliced	4 tablespoons heavy cream
3 green peppers, sliced	(or mayonnaise)
salt and pepper to taste	1 hard-boiled egg, chopped
1 tablespoon parsley, chopped	

Boil the potatoes until tender, peel, and slice. In a salad bowl, place 1 layer of potato slices, 1 layer of onion slices, 1 layer of tomato slices, and 1 layer of green pepper slices. Continue alternating layers until all the vegetable slices are used up. Sprinkle salt, pepper, and chopped parsley over the top. Mix together the salad oil, vinegar, and cream (or mayonnaise), and pour it over all. Decorate with hard-boiled egg.

Royal Salad

(Salad-e Saltanati)

(SERVES 6–8)

1 cup red kidney beans (or 1 cup cranberry October beans)	½ cup mayonnaise
	1 head lettuce
1 pound potatoes	2 large onions, thinly sliced
6 tablespoons salad oil	salt and pepper to taste
3 tablespoons lemon juice or vinegar	2 hard-boiled eggs

If using dried beans, cover with water and boil until done, drain, and cool. If using canned beans, drain off the liquid. Boil the potatoes in their jackets, peel, and dice. Mix together the salad oil, lemon juice or vinegar, and mayonnaise; pour it over the potatoes. Break the lettuce into pieces with the fingers; add it to the potatoes. Add the onions and beans, and toss the salad gently. Add salt and pepper. Grate the hard-boiled eggs over the top of the salad, or slice thinly and arrange the slices decoratively on top.

Russian Salad

(Salad Russe)

(SERVES 6)

As the name implies, this salad is of Russian origin. However, with the long tradition of cultural interchange between Iran and Russia, this salad has become commonplace on Iranian tables. It makes a wonderful hot weather supper, or it may be served as an hors d'oeuvre or as stuffing for raw tomatoes.

1 cup mayonnaise
(or ½ cup mayonnaise
and ½ cup heavy
cream)
4 tablespoons salad or
olive oil
4 tablespoons vinegar
½ cup fresh parsley,
mint, and tarragon,
chopped, or 1 teaspoon
of each, dried
1 cup boiled potatoes,
diced
½ cup canned or cooked
green beans, chopped

½ cup green peas, cooked
½ cup canned beets,
sliced or chopped
2 cups cooked chicken,
diced
½ cup dill pickles,
chopped
5–6 olives, sliced
salt and pepper to taste
1 hard-boiled egg
(for garnish)
dill pickles (for garnish)
1 tomato (for garnish)

Mix together the mayonnaise, salad oil, vinegar, and herbs. Add the rest of the ingredients and mix well. Garnish with slices of hard-boiled egg and/or dill pickle, or slices of tomato. Chill well before serving.

Potato Salad with Yogurt

(Salad-e Sib Zamini ba Mast)

(SERVES 4–6)

3 large potatoes
1 cup heavy cream or
sour cream
2 cups yogurt
1 teaspoon salt
¼ teaspoon white pepper
1 tablespoon fresh or

dried dill weed,
chopped
3 hard-boiled eggs,
finely chopped
4 large dill pickles
(or fresh cucumbers),
chopped

Boil the potatoes until tender; cool, peel, and dice. Beat together the cream and yogurt. Add the salt, pepper, and half of the dill weed. Mix together all of the ingredients. Sprinkle the remaining dill weed on top. Chill well.

Cardoon Salad

(Salad-e Kangar)

(SERVES 4–6)

2 pounds cardoons
3–4 potatoes
4 tomatoes
1 cup green peas, cooked
½ cup dill pickles, chopped

½ cup mayonnaise (or ¼ mayonnaise and ¼ cup heavy or sour cream)
salt and pepper to taste

Rinse the cardoons and set in a colander to drain. Remove the prickly stems. Boil in salted water until tender; drain. Boil the potatoes; peel and dice. Dice or chop the cardoons. Cut the tomatoes into thin slices or wedges. Combine all of the vegetables in a salad bowl, pour the mayonnaise over them, and add salt and pepper. Mix well. Chill before serving.

Chef's Salad

(Salad-e Ashpaz)

(SERVES 4–6)

2 large dill pickles
2 fresh cucumbers
2 tomatoes
a few sprigs parsley, chopped
2 spears asparagus, cooked
2 hard-boiled eggs

1 jar marinated artichoke hearts
6 pitted black olives
1 small can whole or sliced beets, drained
oil and vinegar as desired
salt and pepper to taste

Chop or dice all ingredients and mix together. Serve with desired dressing. This salad may be served with or without lettuce.

Mint Sauce

(Sekanjebin)

This sauce is used in Iran primarily as a dressing for romaine lettuce. I remember, as a child, when my family was visiting relatives, seeing large trays of carefully washed and separated romaine lettuce being brought in at teatime with bowls or small pitchers of *sekanjebin*. Each person would carefully dip the lettuce leaves in the mint sauce before eating them.

5 cups sugar	10 sprigs fresh mint
2½ cups water	1 cup vinegar

Boil the sugar and water together until the sugar is completely dissolved. Tie the mint sprigs together with a string, and drop them into the boiling syrup. Simmer for 20 minutes. Add the vinegar and simmer 10 minutes longer. Cool. This sauce should be the consistency of a thin syrup.

Mint-Cucumber Sauce

(Sekanjebin-e Khiar)

Prepare the Mint Sauce as directed above. Peel 1 cucumber and chop it very fine. Add it, together with crushed ice, to the Mint Sauce.

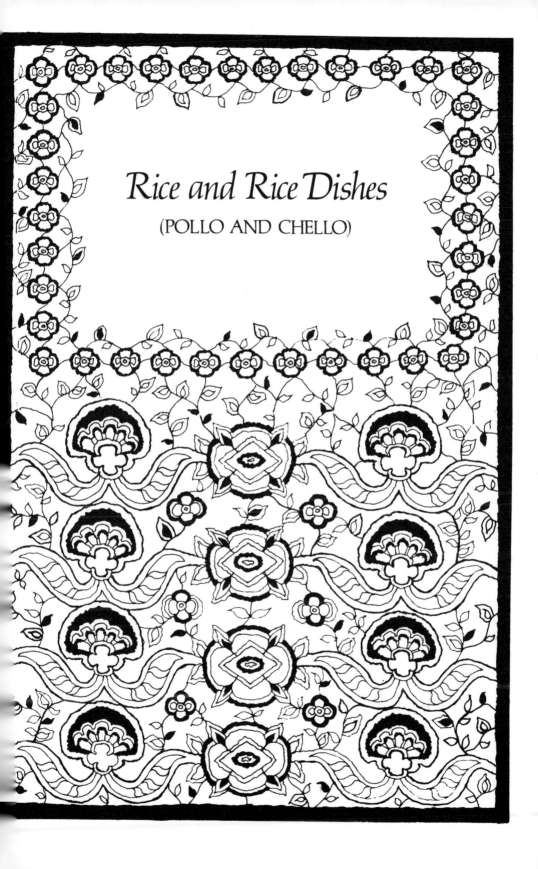

Rice and Rice Dishes

(POLLO AND CHELLO)

To make Pullow, *the Meat is first Boiled to Rags, and the Broth or Liquor being strained, it is left to drain, while they Boil the Rice in the same; which being tender, and the aqueous parts evaporating, the Juice and Gravy incorporates with the Rice, which is Boiled almost dry; then they put in the Meal again with Spice, and at last as much Butter as is necessary, so that it becomes not too Greesy or Offensive, either to the Sight or Taste; and it is then Boiled enough when it is fit to be made into Gobbets, not slabby, but each Corn of Rice is swelled and filled, not burst into Pulp.*

(John Fryer, A New Account
of East India and Persia.
Being Nine Years' Travels, 1672–1681.)

The Chilau, *which is a triumph of cookery, comes up in the form of a white pyramid of steamed rice, every grain of which is dry outside, but inside is full of juice, and is served with a large number of* entrees.

(Lord Curzon from same source)

The mainstay of Persian cuisine is rice, prepared in many different ways. It may be served in a fluffy white mound with *kabab* (when it is known as *chello*); or it may be served with stewed meat, or with meat or fowl folded into the rice, delicately seasoned, often with dried fruits and nuts added (when it is called *pollo*). John Fryer, who traveled in East India and Persia from 1672 to 1681, observed:

The most admired Dainty, wherewith they stuff themselves, is *Pullow,* whereof they will fill themselves up to the Throat and receive no hurt, it being so well prepared for the stomach.[1]

Another seventeenth-century traveler to Persia gave a charming account of a legend he heard during his sojourn there, which purported to explain the fondness of the Persians for rice:

And wot you forsooth why Rice is so generally eaten and so valuable? From a most reverent tradition delivered by their grand Annalist *Iacob-ben-Fiet-Ally,* a right Cabalist. And this it is. On a time, *Mahomet* being earnest in his prayers was accidentally conveighed into Paradize, where being very earnest in beholding its rare varieties, at length hee cast his eyes upon the glorious Throne of the Almighty; and (perceiving the Lord to turne about) fearing he should bee severely whipt for such presumption, blushes for shame, and sweats with terror; but loth to have it seene, wipes off his brow the pretious sweat with his first finger, and threw it out of Paradise: it was not lost, for, forthwith dividing it selfe into six drops, all of them became miraculous creatures: the first drop became a fragrant Rose (therefore is rose-water so much used there, and in honor of the Rose an Annuall feast solemnized:) the second, a grain of Ryce, (a holy graine:).[2]

Although this legend can be taken with a "grain of salt," it is indeed true that Iranians love rice and have used some of their national genius to develop innumerable imaginative rice dishes. Iranians take great pride in their ability to prepare rice that is extremely fluffy, with each grain separate. According to Sir John Chardin, in his *Voyages en Perse:*

Their rice ... is light, it refreshes, it is pleasant to the palate; it is quickly and easily digested.

Rare, indeed, would be the Iranian hostess who did not serve rice to her guests; in all likelihood there would be several varieties on the table, together with several kinds of meat or meat dishes. The exquisitely hand-tooled copper trays that tourists often bring

1. John Fryer, *A New Account of East India and Persia. Being Nine Years' Travels, 1672–1681,* The Hakluyt Society, Second Series No. XIX, Vol. II, London, 1909. (Edited by William Crooke.)
2. Sir Thomas Herbert, *Some Yeares Travels into Africa and Asia the Great.* Especially Describing the Famous Empires of Persia and Industant, London, 1638, Printed by R. Bip. for Jacob, Blome and Richard Bishop.

home as tabletops or wall hangings were once used as serving platters. Imagine a white tablecloth spread on the floor with guests sitting around it cross-legged; in the center of the tablecloth, amidst many delicacies, there would be a copper tray 4 feet long and filled with a mound of snow-white rice, on top of which would nestle a whole, roasted baby lamb.

The Persian method of cooking rice is unique and foolproof. Although this method does not attempt to conserve vitamins, it rinses out a lot of the starch, leaving the rice grains fluffy, separate, and extremely tasty. Once you have mastered this basic technique, you will find it easy to prepare the many interesting rice dishes that have been developed over the centuries.

Rice

(SERVES 4–6)

The Iranian housewife always soaks her rice in salted water at least overnight—Persian rice responds very well to this treatment. However, this step is not necessary with American long-grain rice and can be omitted. Some highly accomplished Iranian cooks will add a little vinegar or yogurt to the rice while it is cooking—to whiten the rice even more, they say. This, too, is not necessary. The method I use for cooking American long-grain rice is as follows:

3 cups rice   *4 tablespoons butter*
6 tablespoons salt

Bring a large pot of water to a rolling boil. Pour in the rice and salt. Stir once. Boil hard for exactly 10 minutes. Drain in a large colander; rinse well under cold water and drain. Melt the butter in a saucepan over a medium heat. Pour in the rice. Place a dish towel over the inside of the lid, bring the overlapping edges up over the top of the lid, and fasten them there. Cover the saucepan with the wrapped lid. (The cloth absorbs the moisture, preventing the drops of water that ordinarily form on the inside of the lid from dropping back into the rice and making it soggy.)

Steam over a medium heat for 20 to 25 minutes, or over a medium-low heat for 30 to 35 minutes. The rice will be ready when, upon lifting the lid, a cloud of steam emerges from the saucepan. The heat can then be turned very low, and the rice kept warm until ready to serve.

Always dish out the rice with a slotted spoon, fluffing it as you place it in a serving dish. A crust of *tah-dig* (literally, bottom-of-the-pan) will have formed on the bottom of the saucepan. To serve this in one unbroken piece, immerse the exterior of pan in cold water for a few minutes. Pry the *tah-dig* loose with a spatula.

A more exotic variety of *tah-dig* can be made by mixing 1 cup of the parboiled rice with 1 egg yolk and spreading it in the bottom of the saucepan before pouring in the rest of the rice. Or mix 1 cup of the parboiled rice with ¼ teaspoon of saffron and 3 tablespoons of yogurt and spread this over the melted butter in the bottom of the saucepan. Or, best of all, spread 2 or 3 thin layers of Lebanese mountain bread (also known as flatbread [*lavash*]) in the melted butter in the bottom of the saucepan before adding the rice. This makes a crisp delicacy fit for a king.

If you are using Persian long-grain rice (*domsiah*), rinse it very well until the water runs clear. Soak it in plain or salted water for several hours or overnight. When cooking, follow the directions given above, but reduce the boiling time to 5 minutes.

In any of the following recipes, turkey may be substituted for chicken.

Rice with Lentils

(Adas Pollo)

(SERVES 4–5)

The first time I served this dish to American friends, one of our guests commented, upon seeing the lentils, "Why, this is the first time I've ever seen rice cooked with chocolate chips!" Unfortunately, many Americans are not acquainted with this nutritious legume, which can be used in many intriguing dishes.

3 cups rice	¾ cup lentils
6 tablespoons salt	¼ cup butter

Bring a large kettle of water to a rolling boil. Add the rice and salt. Boil 10 minutes. Drain, rinse with cold water, and set aside to drain well. Boil the lentils in enough salted water to cover for about 10 minutes; they should be tender but not soft; drain. Melt the butter in a large pot. Pour in ⅓ of the rice. Sprinkle with ⅓ of the lentils. Continue alternating layers of rice and lentils. Cover with a lid that has been wrapped in cloth, and steam over a medium heat for 30 minutes.

For a more elegant dish, add ¼ cup toasted, slivered almonds, and ¼ cup dried currants (or raisins) just before steaming.

Rice with Lentils and Chicken

(Adas Pollo ba Morgh)

(SERVES 4–6)

Follow the recipe above for Rice with Lentils up until the butter is melted in a large pot. Set it aside and prepare the following:

¼ cup butter or shortening	3 tablespoons lemon juice
1 large fryer chicken, cut up, or 6 chicken breasts	1 tablespoon tomato paste
1 large onion, chopped	¼ cup warm water
1 teaspoon turmeric	2 tablespoons soy sauce
1 can chicken bouillon or consommé	½ teaspoon salt
	¼ teaspoon pepper
	1–2 tablespoons flour (optional)

Melt the butter or shortening in a skillet, and brown the chicken pieces on all sides. Remove from the pan. Brown the onion. Stir in the turmeric. Return the chicken pieces to the pan. Add the bouillon, lemon juice, tomato paste (dissolved in warm water), soy sauce, salt, and pepper. Cover and set in a slow oven (325° F.) for 2 hours. Turn the pieces occasionally. Remove from the oven and cool. Bone and skin the chicken. The drippings may be thickened with 1 or 2 tablespoons of flour.

After melting the butter in a large pot, pour in ¼ of the rice. Place ⅓ of the chicken on top, with several spoonfuls of drippings. Sprinkle over this ⅓ of the lentils and (if desired) toasted almonds and dried currants (or raisins). Continue alternating layers until the ingredients have all been used up, finishing with a layer of rice. Pour any remaining drippings over the top. Cover with a lid wrapped in a cloth, and steam over a medium heat for 30 minutes.

If desired, just before serving, dissolve ¼ teaspoon of powdered saffron in 2 teaspoons of hot water. Mix with several tablespoons of cooked rice. Sprinkle this over the top.

Serve the bottom crust *(tah-dig)* separately.

Rice with Chicken

(Morgh Pollo)

(SERVES 6–8)

1 teaspoon saffron	salt and pepper to taste
3 tablespoons hot water	4 cups rice
¼ cup butter	8 tablespoons salt
1 large fryer chicken, cut up, or 6 chicken breasts	¼ cup currants (preferably Persian currants, zereshk)

Dilute the saffron in the hot water. Melt 2 tablespoons of the butter and stir in the saffron. Baste the chicken pieces with this mixture, sprinkle with salt and pepper, and broil until well done (45–60 minutes).

Bring a large pan of water to a boil. Add the rice and 8 tablespoons of salt. Boil for 10 minutes; drain in colander, rinse with cold water, and set aside to drain well. Melt the remaining 2 tablespoons of butter in a large pan. Mix 2 tablespoons of the chicken drippings with 1 cup of the parboiled rice, and spread this over the bottom of the pan. Add half the rice. Arrange the chicken pieces, boned or unboned, over the rice, and sprinkle with the currants. Cover with the remaining rice. Pour the rest of the drippings over the rice. Cover with a lid wrapped in a cloth, and steam over a medium heat for 30 minutes or bake in the oven at 350° F. for one hour.

If desired, 2 or 3 tablespoons of caraway seeds may be sprinkled over the chicken before covering with rice.

Persian currants (zereshk) are quite tart in flavor and beautifully red, adding both zest and color to this tasty dish.

Jewel-Studded Rice

(Morasah Pollo)

(SERVES 6–8)

This rice is named for its highly decorative appearance, being "studded" with several varieties of colorful nuts.

Follow the recipe for Rice with Chicken (Morgh Pollo) and add ¼ cup slivered almonds, ¼ cup slivered pistachios, and ½ cup hazel nuts. These nuts should be sautéed lightly in several table-spoons of butter and then sprinkled decoratively over the rice before serving.

Sweet Rice

(Shirin Pollo)

(SERVES 4–6)

This is one of the most exotic and demanding of the Persian rice dishes, but it is also one of the most rewarding.

14 tablespoons butter	½ cup water
1 large fryer chicken, cut up	1 tablespoon sugar
2½ teaspoons saffron	3–4 ounces pistachios in the shell, or
1 can chicken bouillon or consommé	½ cup slivered or whole pistachios
3 tablespoons lemon juice	1 cup orange marmalade
1 tablespoon tomato paste	½ cup slivered almonds
¼ cup hot water	1 cup water
½ teaspoon salt	3 cups rice
¼ teaspoon pepper	6 tablespoons salt
2 cups carrots, cut into thin strips (1 inch long)	

Melt 6 tablespoons of the butter in a skillet, and brown the chicken pieces on all sides. Stir in ½ teaspoon of the saffron; add the bouillon, lemon juice, tomato paste (dissolved in the hot water), salt, and pepper. Cover and simmer gently over a low heat for about 1 hour. Or cover and place in a slow oven (325° F.) for 2 hours. Cool and bone.

Boil the carrots in ½ cup of water to which sugar has been added. When tender, drain and sauté in 2 tablespoons of the butter. Shell the pistachios and soak them for a few minutes in warm water; with a sharp knife, cut them into thin slivers. Add these to the carrots. Add the marmalade, slivered almonds, 2 teaspoons of the saffron, and 1 cup of water. Simmer these ingredients together, uncovered, for 15 minutes.

Bring a large kettle of water to a rolling boil. Add the rice and 6 tablespoons of salt. Boil for 10 minutes; drain, rinse with cold water, and set aside to drain well. Melt the remaining 6 tablespoons of butter in a large pan and pour in ⅓ of the rice. Arrange half of the chicken pieces over this, then add several spoonsful of the carrot marmalade mixture. Cover with ⅓ more of rice, then the rest of the chicken and carrot marmalade mixture. Cover with the remaining rice. Pour the chicken drippings over the top.

Cover with a lid wrapped in a cloth, and steam for about 30 minutes over a medium-low heat. This dish may be kept warm over a very low heat until ready to serve. Serve the *tah-dig* (bottom crust) separately. This dish may also be baked, covered, in the oven (350° F for 1 hour).

The pistachios may be left whole. Or they can be purchased already slivered from one of the stores listed in the Shopper's Guide.

To prepare the orange marmalade from scratch, boil 1 cup slivered orange peel in 4 cups water for a few minutes, then pour the water off. Repeat. Soak the orange slivers in 4 cups water for 24 hours. Boil 2 cups sugar with ¾ cup water for 5 minutes. Drain the orange slivers and add to the syrup. Boil until it thickens, stirring constantly to prevent burning.

Dill Weed Rice with Fava Beans and Lamb
(Baghali Pollo)

(SERVES 5–6)

2 large onions, sliced or chopped	6 tablespoons salt
½ cup butter	1 cup fresh dill weed, chopped, or 4–5 tablespoons dried dill weed
5 lamb shanks	
1 teaspoon turmeric	
1 can beef broth	1½ cups fresh fava beans, or ¾ cup dried fava beans (or 1 package frozen lima beans)
3 tablespoons lemon juice	
2 tablespoons tomato paste	
¼ cup hot water	½ teaspoon saffron
3 cups rice	2 teaspoons hot water

Sauté the onions in 4 tablespoons of the butter until golden brown. Add the lamb shanks and brown well on all sides. Place these in a heavy, ovenproof dish. Stir in the turmeric. Add the beef broth, lemon juice, and tomato paste (diluted in hot water). Cover and braise in the oven at 300° F. for 2½ hours. Cool and bone.

Bring a large pot of water to a rolling boil. Add the rice and salt. If dried dill weed is being used, add it to the water. Boil for 10 minutes; drain, rinse well with cold water, and drain again.

If using dried fava beans, soak them for 3 hours before boiling. They will require a much longer time to cook than fresh fava beans. Boil the fava beans in salted water until done but still firm (about 10 to 15 minutes for fresh beans and about 45 minutes for soaked, dried beans). Drain off the hot water; cool by covering the beans with cold water. Skin the fresh beans by pressing each bean on one edge so that it will slip out of its skin. (Dried fava beans do not have this skin.) If using lima beans, boil as directed on the package; remove from the heat while the beans are still firm. Cool and peel.

Melt the remaining 4 tablespoons of butter in a large pot. Add ⅓ of the rice. If fresh dill is used, sprinkle some of it over the rice. Cover with ⅓ of the beans, then ⅓ of the meat. Alternate layers until the ingredients are all used up. Cover the pot with a lid wrapped in a cloth, and steam over a medium heat for 30 minutes or longer.

Just before serving, dilute the saffron in 2 teaspoons of hot water. Mix this with 1 cup of cooked rice. Sprinkle this saffron-colored rice over the top.

This dish may also be prepared with stewed chicken. Although it is not in the Persian tradition to serve this dish with gravy, I find that my American friends like it that way. If you wish, therefore, thicken the meat drippings with a little flour, and serve it in a gravy boat. This dish is traditionally served with yogurt.

Tomato Rice with Lamb

(Eslamboli Pollo)

(SERVES 4–6)

3 cups rice
6 tablespoons salt
2–3 pounds shoulder
 of lamb
2 large onions,
 sliced or chopped
½ cup butter
1 teaspoon turmeric
1 can beef broth or
 bouillon
3 tablespoons tomato
 paste

¼ cup warm water
2 large cans
 (number 2½)
 tomatoes
1 teaspoon salt
¼ teaspoon pepper
1 tablespoon soy sauce
2 tablespoons lemon
 juice (or ½ cup
 white wine)

Bring a large pot of water to a rolling boil; add the rice and salt. Boil for 10 minutes and drain in a colander; rinse well with cold water and set aside to drain well.

Have your butcher bone the lamb. Cut off the excess fat and cut the meat into 1-inch pieces. Sauté the onions in 4 tablespoons of the butter until golden brown. Add the meat and sauté until brown. Stir in the turmeric. Add the beef broth, tomato paste (diluted in warm water), canned tomatoes, salt, pepper, soy sauce, and lemon juice. Cover and simmer until tender (about 1½ hours); or cook in a pressure cooker for 20 minutes, allowing the pressure to drop of its own accord.

Melt the remaining 4 tablespoons of butter in a large kettle, pour in ⅓ of the rice, then ⅓ of the meat mixture. Alternate layers of rice and meat until the ingredients have all been used up. Cover the kettle with a lid wrapped in a cloth, and steam over a medium heat for about 30 minutes.

This dish, when inverted onto a serving platter, will be quite red; it is very decorative as well as delicious.

Serve with a salad or green vegetable and yogurt.

Tomato Rice with Lamb and Green Beans

(Loobia Pollo)

(SERVES 4–6)

This is one of my favorites!

Follow the recipe above for Tomato Rice with Lamb (*Eslamboli Pollo*), except as follows:

Cut 1 pound fresh green beans into small pieces, about ¼ inch in length; add to the meat, together with ¼ teaspoon of cinnamon, for the last 20 minutes of simmering. Proceed as indicated.

Red Rice with Lamb and Peas

(Nokhod Pollo)

(SERVES 6–8)

Follow the recipe for Tomato Rice with Lamb (*Eslamboli Pollo*) except as follows:

Add 2 pounds of fresh green peas (shelled) or 1 9-ounce package of frozen green peas to the meat for last 10 to 15 minutes of simmering. Proceed as indicated.

Rice with Herbs and Lamb

(Ghormeh-Sabzi Pollo)

(SERVES 6–8)

3 pounds shoulder of lamb (or 1 pound lean ground beef)	½ cup water
1 large onion, sliced	3 tablespoons powdered Persian lime, or 1 whole dried Persian lime (or 3 tablespoons lemon juice)
9 tablespoons butter	
3 cups parsley, scallions, and leaf fenugreek, finely chopped	salt and pepper to taste
1 can beef broth or bouillon	4 cups rice
	8 tablespoons salt

Have your butcher bone the lamb. Cut it into 1-inch cubes and trim off the excess fat. Sauté the onion in 2 tablespoons of the butter (or, better still, in rendered fat trimmed from the meat). Add the meat and sauté it until brown. (If using ground beef: grate the onion and add it to the meat; add a little salt and pepper, mix well, and shape into small meatballs.)

Sauté the chopped green herbs in 2 tablespoons of the butter (or rendered fat). Add them to the meat. Add the beef broth, water, Persian lime (or lemon juice), salt, and pepper. Cover and simmer gently for 1½ to 2 hours. Or bake this dish in the oven, covered, at 325° F. for 2½ to 3 hours; or cook it in a pressure cooker for 20 minutes. Reduce the time if you are using meatballs.

Bring a large kettle of water to a boil. Add the rice and 8 tablespoons of salt. Boil 10 minutes, drain; rinse with cold water, and drain again. Melt 4 tablespoons of the butter in a large pan. Add half the rice. Cover the rice with the cooked meat and herbs, reserving a small amount of the liquid. Add the remaining rice. Melt the remaining 1 tablespoon of butter in the reserved liquid and pour it over the rice. Wrap a clean cloth around the lid, cover the pan tightly, and steam the rice over a medium heat for 30 minutes or longer.

Rice with Yellow Split Peas and Lamb

(Gheimeh Pollo)

(SERVES 6–8)

3 pounds shoulder of lamb	¼ teaspoon nutmeg
1 large onion, sliced	1 teaspoon salt
6 tablespoons butter	¼ teaspoon pepper
1 tablespoon turmeric	2–3 tablespoons powdered Persian lime, or 2–3 whole dried Persian limes (or 3 tablespoons lemon juice)
1 can beef broth or bouillon	
½ cup water	
2 tablespoons tomato paste	½ cup yellow split peas
¼ cup hot water	4 cups rice
¼ teaspoon cinnamon	8 tablespoons salt

Have your butcher bone the lamb. Cut it into 1-inch cubes and trim off the excess fat. This fat may be rendered by sautéeing it in a pan over medium heat for 15 minutes; it may be used instead of the butter, greatly enhancing the flavor of this dish. Sauté the onion in 2 tablespoons of the butter (or rendered fat). Stir in the turmeric. Add the meat and sauté it until brown. Add the beef broth and water. Add the tomato paste (diluted in hot water). Add the seasonings (including the Persian lime), cover, and simmer for 1½ to 2 hours. Add the yellow split peas for the last 30 minutes of cooking. This dish may also be covered and baked in the oven at 350° F. for 2 to 2½ hours.

Bring a large kettle of water to a boil. Add the rice and 8 tablespoons of salt. Boil for 10 minutes and drain in a colander; rinse well with cold water, and drain again.

Melt 2 tablespoons of the butter in a heavy kettle or pan. Mix 1 cup of the parboiled rice with a few tablespoons of the meat stock, and spread this over the bottom of the pan. Pour in ¼ of the rice, cover this with ⅓ of the meat. Continue alternating layers of rice and meat, ending with a layer of rice. Melt the remaining 2 tablespoons of butter in 4 tablespoons of meat stock, and pour this over the rice. Wrap a towel around the lid and cover the pan tightly. Steam for 30 minutes over a medium heat.

Rice with Cabbage and Meatballs

(Kalam Pollo)

(SERVES 6–8)

1 large onion, grated	1 can beef broth or
1 teaspoon salt	bouillon
¼ teaspoon pepper	1 teaspoon powdered
1 pound lean	saffron
ground beef	2 tablespoons soy sauce
6 tablespoons butter	2 tablespoons lemon juice
1 large head cabbage,	4 cups rice
finely shredded	8 tablespoons salt

Add the onion, salt, and pepper to the ground beef. Mix well with the hands and form into small meatballs. Melt 2 tablespoons of the butter in a heavy pan, and brown the meatballs on all sides. Add the shredded cabbage and sauté briefly. Add the beef broth, saffron, soy sauce, and lemon juice. If necessary, add a small amount of water. Simmer, uncovered, for 40 minutes, turning the meatballs occasionally.

Bring a large pan of water to a boil. Add the rice and 8 table-spoons of salt. Boil for 10 minutes; drain, rinse with cold water, and drain again. Melt the remaining 4 tablespoons of butter in a large pan. Mix ¼ cup of stock from the meatballs with 1 cup of parboiled rice. Spread this in the bottom of the pan. Pour in half of the rice; cover with the meat-cabbage sauce; top with the remaining rice. Wrap the lid in a cloth, cover the rice tightly, and steam over a medium heat for 30 minutes or longer.

The bottom crust (*tah-dig*) may be served separately.

Rice with Carrots and Lamb (or Chicken)

(Havij Pollo)

(SERVES 6–8)

2½–3 pounds shoulder of lamb (or 1 medium fryer or stewing chicken)	3–4 tablespoons lemon juice
2 large onions, sliced	3 pounds carrots
12 tablespoons butter	1 cup water
½ cup water	⅔ cup sugar
1 can beef broth	4 cups rice
	8 tablespoons salt
	1 teaspoon saffron

Have your butcher bone the lamb. Cut this into stewing-size pieces and trim off the excess fat. Sauté the onions in 2 tablespoons of the butter until golden brown. Add the meat and sauté it until brown. Add the water, beef broth, and lemon juice. Cover and simmer for 1½ hours (or 2½ hours in a 300° F. oven). (If using chicken: sauté the onions; add the chicken, water, broth, and lemon juice; cover and stew until tender; then cool and bone.)

Peel the carrots and boil them whole in enough water to cover until they are tender. Cut them into thin slivers. Sauté these in 5 tablespoons of the butter over a low heat for 5 to 10 minutes. Add 1 cup of water and the sugar, cover, and simmer for 10 minutes.

Bring a large pot of water to a boil. Add the rice and 8 table-spoons of salt. Boil hard for 10 minutes and drain in a colander; rinse well with cold water and drain again.

Melt the remaining 5 tablespoons of butter in a large pan, and pour in about ¼ of the rice. Cover this with a layer of cooked carrots, then a layer of meat (or chicken). Alternate layers of rice, carrots, and meat (or chicken), finishing with a layer of rice. Dissolve the saffron in 1 cup of warm stock, and pour this over the rice. Cover with a lid wrapped in a dish towel, and steam over a medium heat for about 30 minutes.

This dish may also be made with small meatballs, using lean ground beef, chopped onions, salt, pepper, paprika, and a dash of cinnamon. The meatballs should be well browned on all sides in hot butter.

Sour Cherry Rice with Chicken

(Albaloo Pollo)

(SERVES 6–8)

If you can get sour cherries, you might enjoy trying this colorful and exotic dish.

4 cups rice	¼ cup butter or
8 tablespoons salt	shortening
6 cups fresh sour	¼ cup slivered almonds
cherries	¼ cup slivered
6 cups sugar	pistachios
1 large fryer chicken	

Bring a large pot of water to a rolling boil. Add the rice and 8 tablespoons salt. Stir once. Boil for 10 minutes and drain in a colander. Rinse well with cold water and drain again.

Pit the cherries and place in a kettle; cover with sugar and cook over a low heat until thick (about 20 minutes).

You may cook the chicken according to your favorite method—baked, broiled, or stewed. Or you may roast it in the oven until tender (about 1½ hours at 350°), basting it frequently with the following sauce:

3 tablespoons salad oil	3 tablespoons lemon juice
½ can beef or chicken	(or ½ cup sherry
broth	or white wine)
1 tablespoon tomato	½ teaspoon saffron
paste	½ teaspoon salt
2 tablespoons soy sauce	¼ teaspoon black pepper
½ teaspoon turmeric	

If desired, the chicken may be cut into pieces and stewed in the above sauce on top of the stove over a low heat until tender.

Cook the chicken; skin and bone it. Thicken the drippings with 2 or 3 tablespoons of flour.

In a large pan, melt the butter or shortening, and pour in ¼ of the rice. Cover with about ⅓ of the cherry preserve; then add several chicken pieces and a couple of tablespoons of gravy. Alternate the layers of rice, cherry preserve, and chicken, finishing with a layer of rice. Cover with a lid wrapped in a dish towel, and steam over a medium heat for approximately 30 minutes.

To serve, sprinkle slivered almonds and pistachios on top. Serve the bottom crust *(tah-dig)* in a separate dish.

If fresh sour cherries are unavailable, a jar of sour cherry preserves (12 ounces) can be substituted. Do not add any sugar. Warm over low heat, stir in 2 tablespoons water, and proceed as above.

Molded Shirazi Rice with Chicken

(Shirazi Pollo-ye Ghalebi)

(SERVES ABOUT 8)

1 teaspoon saffron	3 tablespoons lemon juice
¾ cup butter	4 cups rice
1 3-pound fryer chicken, cut up	8 tablespoons salt
	1 medium eggplant
1 teaspoon salt	2 egg yolks, beaten
¼ teaspoon pepper	1 cup yogurt
½ can chicken broth or bouillon	½ cup currants (preferably Persian currants, zereshk)
½ cup water	

Dilute the saffron in 3 tablespoons of melted butter, and brush the chicken parts with this mixture. Sprinkle with salt and pepper. Add the chicken broth, water, and lemon juice. Cover and simmer for 1 hour, or until very tender. Cool and bone, reserving the stock.

Bring a large pot of water to a boil. Add the rice and 8 tablespoons of salt. Boil 10 minutes and drain; rinse with cold water and drain again.

Peel the eggplant and cut it into thin slices about 2 inches by 4 inches. Sprinkle it with salt and set it aside for about 20 minutes to "perspire." Blot dry on paper towels; sauté in 3 tablespoons of the butter until brown on both sides. Drain on paper towels.

Mix 2 cups of the parboiled rice with the egg yolks, yogurt, and 3 tablespoons of the chicken stock. Melt 4 tablespoons of the butter in a Pyrex baking dish or a shaped baking mold. Spread the rice-egg mixture over the bottom, pressing it down with the back of a spoon. Cover with half of the remaining rice. Arrange the sautéed eggplant slices over the rice; then add the boned chicken. Sprinkle with the currants, and cover with the rest of the rice.

Melt the remaining 2 tablespoons of butter in ½ cup of the chicken stock, and pour it over the rice. Bake in a 350° F. oven for 1½ hours, or until a golden crust has formed on the bottom of the mold. To serve, dip the mold in cold water up to the rim for a couple of minutes; then invert the mold onto a platter. You may sprinkle more currants over the top as a decoration.

Green Herb Rice

(Sabzi Pollo)

(SERVES 6–8)

This fragrant and devastatingly delicious dish is best when made with fresh herbs. The only ingredient that I have not been able to find in typical American grocery stores is fresh fenugreek (leaf); it can easily be omitted from this recipe. If you have a green thumb, you might try growing your own fenugreek at home.

The dried coriander and fenugreek available in most grocery stores are not from the leaves of these herbs, but from the seed; they *cannot* be used in this recipe.

4 cups rice	1 cup parsley, chopped,
8 tablespoons salt	or ½ cup dried
2 bunches scallions	parsley
¼ cup butter	1 cup coriander (Chinese
1 cup dill weed,	parsley), chopped
chopped, or 4–5	a few sprigs fenugreek,
tablespoons dried	chopped
dill weed	

Bring a large kettle of water to a rolling boil. Add the rice and salt, stirring just once. If using dried herbs, add them to the water.

Boil for 10 minutes and drain. Rinse well with cold water and drain again.

Discard the white bulbs of the scallions. Chop the green stems very fine.

Melt the butter in a large pan. Pour in ¼ of the rice; sprinkle over it ⅓ of the chopped herbs and scallion greens. Alternate layers, ending with a layer of rice. Cover tightly with a lid wrapped in a dish towel, and steam for 30 minutes over a medium-low heat.

In Iran this rice is traditionally served with pan-fried fish fillets, but it also goes very well with lamb (roasted, braised, or stewed) or with chicken or other fowl. It is especially good with roast turkey or duck.

Rice with Baked Lamb (or Chicken)

(Tah-Chin)

(SERVES 6–8)

The name for this dish means, literally, "arranged on the bottom of the pan." It can be prepared with either lamb or chicken. If you use lamb, try to obtain a young spring lamb or New Zealand lamb.

3–4 pounds leg of lamb (or 1 large fryer chicken)	1 teaspoon salt
	¼ teaspoon pepper
	4 cups rice
2 cups yogurt	8 tablespoons salt
2 large onions, sliced	2 egg yolks
2 teaspoons saffron	½ cup butter
2 tablespoons soy sauce	2 teaspoons hot water
2 tablespoons lemon juice	

Marinate the lamb (or chicken) overnight in a sauce made by combining the yogurt, onions, 1 teaspoon of the saffron, soy sauce, lemon juice, salt, and pepper. Remove the meat from the marinade, and reserve the marinade. Bake it in a moderate oven (325° F.) for 2 hours or longer. Cool and bone.

Bring a large pot of water to a rolling boil. Add the rice and 8 tablespoons of salt; stir just once. Boil 10 minutes; drain in a colander, rinse with cold water, and drain again.

Mix 2 cups of the parboiled rice with the marinade and egg yolks.

Melt 4 tablespoons of the butter in a pan, and spread the rice mixture in the melted butter over the bottom of the pan. Arrange the baked lamb (or chicken) over this, and cover with the rest of the rice. Cover with a lid that has been wrapped in a dish towel, and steam over a medium-low heat for 45 minutes.

Dissolve the remaining 1 teaspoon of saffron in hot water. Stir ½ cup of the cooked rice into the saffron water until golden. After arranging the rice and meat on a serving platter, garnish with the saffron rice. Melt the remaining 4 tablespoons of butter and pour it over the top.

There will be a thick crust of rice *(tah-dig)* at the bottom of the pan. To remove it in one piece, stand the pan in 2 inches of cold water for 2 or 3 minutes, then lift the crust out with a spatula.

Rice with Baked Lamb (or Chicken) and Spinach
(Tah-Chin Esfenaj)

(SERVES 6–8)

3–4 pounds leg of lamb (or 1 large fryer chicken)	4 cups rice
	8 tablespoons salt
2 cups yogurt	2 egg yolks
2 large onions, sliced	½ cup butter
2 teaspoons saffron	10 pitted prunes (or dried apricots)
2 tablespoons soy sauce	
2 tablespoons lemon juice	1 pound fresh spinach, or 1 package frozen spinach
1 teaspoon salt	
¼ teaspoon pepper	2 teaspoons hot water

Follow the recipe for Rice with Baked Lamb (or Chicken) *(Tah-Chin)* above. Boil the spinach until tender. After spreading the rice mixture over the bottom of the pan, spread the cooked spinach over the rice. Arrange the meat or chicken over the spinach, then place the prunes (or dried apricots) over the meat, and cover with the rest of the rice. Proceed as indicated.

Green Rice with Peas and Lamb
(Nokhod Pollo)

(SERVES 6–8)

3 pounds shoulder of
lamb, or New Zealand
leg of lamb, or
6 lamb shanks
3 medium onions, sliced
6 tablespoons butter
salt and pepper to taste
1 teaspoon saffron
1 cup consommé or
beef broth

2 cups fresh or frozen
green peas
2 cups dill weed,
chopped, or 6
tablespoons dried
dill weed
4 cups rice
8 tablespoons salt

If you are using shoulder of lamb, have the butcher bone it. Trim off the excess fat and cut the meat into 10 to 12 pieces. If you are using lamb shanks or leg of lamb, leave the meat whole. Sauté the onions in 2 tablespoons of the butter until golden brown. Add the meat and sauté until brown. Add the salt, pepper, and saffron. Add the consommé, cover, and bake in the oven at 350° F. for 2 hours or longer.

Meanwhile, cook the fresh or frozen peas until tender.

Bring a large kettle of water to a boil. Add the rice and 8 tablespoons of salt. If using dried dill weed, add it to the water. Boil 10 minutes. Drain in a colander, rinse well with cold water, and drain again.

If you are using leg of lamb or lamb shanks, bone. Melt the remaining 4 tablespoons of butter in a heavy pan, pour in ⅓ of the rice, then ⅓ of the braised meat, and ⅓ of the peas. Sprinkle with ⅓ of the chopped dill weed (if using fresh). Alternate layers of rice, meat, peas, and dill weed. Pour ½ cup or more of meat stock over the top. Cover with a lid that has been wrapped in a cloth, and steam over a medium-low heat for 40 minutes or longer.

Rice with Cardoons

(Kangar-Pollo)

(SERVES 4–6)

In the United States cardoons (prickly artichokes) are more available in the West than the East because they grow in arid regions. In Iran they are considered a delicacy and are often used in meat dishes and rice dishes.

3 pounds shoulder of lamb	¼ teaspoon pepper
2 large onions, sliced or chopped	1 tablespoon tomato paste
8 tablespoons butter	1 cup water
½ teaspoon turmeric	2 pounds cardoons
1 can beef broth or consommé	3 cups rice
	6 tablespoons salt

Have your butcher bone the lamb. Cut it into stewing-size pieces and trim off the excess fat. Sauté the onions in 2 tablespoons of the butter until golden brown; remove from the pan. Brown the meat; return the sautéed onions to the pan. Stir in the turmeric. Add the beef broth, pepper, and tomato paste (diluted in water).

Clean the cardoons, removing the prickly stems with a sharp knife. Chop the remaining stems into small pieces. Sauté them in 2 tablespoons of the butter and add them to the meat. Cover and simmer over a low heat for 2 hours until tender, or braise in a 350° F. oven for 2½ hours.

Bring a large pot of water to a boil. Add the rice and 6 tablespoons of salt. Boil for 10 minutes. Drain in a colander, rinse well with cold water, and drain again. Melt the remaining 4 tablespoons of butter in a large pan. Pour in ¼ of the rice; cover with ⅓ of the meat and cardoons. Alternate layers, finishing with a layer of rice. Pour any remaining stock over the top, or serve it separately as a gravy (it may be thickened with flour). Cover the pan with a lid wrapped in a cloth, and steam for 40 minutes over a low-medium heat.

Rice with Eggplant

(Bademjan Pollo)

(SERVES 6–8)

1 large eggplant	4 cups rice
5 tablespoons salt	1 large can (1 pound
1½ cups salad oil	12 ounces) tomatoes
2 large onions,	1 teaspoon dried
chopped or sliced	dill weed

Peel the eggplant, cut it into finger lengths, sprinkle it with 2 tablespoons of the salt, and set it aside to "perspire" for 20 minutes or longer.

Pour ¾ cup of the salad oil into a large pot, heat, and sauté the onions until golden brown. Add the rice and sauté for 5 to 10 minutes until golden brown. Add the tomatoes, the remaining 3 tablespoons of salt, pepper, and enough water to just cover the rice. Cover and simmer gently until all the liquid has been absorbed (20 to 30 minutes).

Blot the eggplant pieces with a paper towel. Heat the remaining ¾ cup salad oil and sauté the eggplant pieces until brown on both sides. Drain on paper towels. Fold the eggplant gently into the rice, sprinkle with the dill weed, cover with a lid wrapped in a dish towel, and steam for approximately 20 minutes over a low or medium-low heat.

Noodle-Rice with Meat and Dates

(Reshteh Pollo)

(SERVES 6–8)

Reshteh is a homemade Persian noodle. The closest approximation would be Chinese Udon noodles. If they are not available, use canned Chinese noodles.

2–3 pounds shoulder of
    lamb or lamb shanks
  1 large onion, sliced
 ½ cup butter
 ½ teaspoon turmeric
 ¼ teaspoon pepper
  2 tablespoons lemon
    juice
  1 can beef broth or
    bouillon
 ¼ cup water

6–8 quarts water
  4 cups rice
  8 tablespoons salt
6–8 ounces Chinese
    Udon noodles, or
  1 large can
    Chinese noodles
 ¾ cup pitted dates,
    sliced
 ½ teaspoon saffron

If you are using shoulder of lamb, have the butcher bone it for you. Save the bones for later use in a soup, such as *ab goosht*. (If you are using lamb shanks, bone them after the meat has been cooked.) Trim the excess fat off the shoulder of lamb and cut the meat into stewing-size pieces. Sauté the onion in ¼ cup of the butter (or rendered fat); remove from the pan when golden brown. Add the meat to the pan and sauté until brown. Return the onion to the pan; add the turmeric, pepper, lemon juice, beef broth, and water. Cover and simmer over a low heat for 1½ to 2 hours, or braise in a slow oven (325° F.) for 2½ hours, or pressure-cook for 20 minutes.

In a large kettle, bring 6 to 8 quarts of water to a rolling boil. Add the rice and 8 tablespoons of salt; boil rapidly for 10 minutes. Drain in a colander, rinse well with cold water, and drain again. Melt the remaining ¼ cup of butter in a kettle. Pour in a layer of rice.

Boil the Udon noodles in salted water according to the directions on the package. Drain well.

Cover the rice with a layer of cooked Udon noodles (or canned Chinese noodles), then a layer of dates, then a layer of cooked meat. Alternate layers of rice, noodles, dates, and meat. Dissolve the saffron in the remaining meat stock and pour it over the top. Cover with a lid that has been wrapped in a dish towel, and steam over a medium heat for 30 minutes.

Rice with Yellow Fava Beans

(Dampokht)

(SERVES 4–6)

2 large onions, sliced	5–6 cups water
4 tablespoons butter	3 cups rice
1½ tablespoons turmeric	1½ tablespoons salt
1 cup dried yellow	½ cup melted butter
fava beans	(optional)

Sauté the onions in the butter until golden brown. Stir in the turmeric. Add the fava beans and 1 cup of the water. Cover and simmer for 5 minutes. Add the rice, salt, and the rest of the water. Cover and cook over a low heat for about 20 minutes, or until all the water has been absorbed. Cover the inside of the lid with a cloth, replace it on the pot, and continue cooking over a low heat until the rice is fairly dry (another 20–30 minutes).

If desired, just before serving, pour ½ cup melted butter over the rice. This dish is traditionally served with yogurt. It goes well with broiled chicken or roast lamb.

Tomato Rice with Eggplant

(Dami Eslamboli)

(SERVES 6–8)

1 large or 2 small	1 teaspoon turmeric
eggplants	2 cans (16 ounces)
2 tablespoons salt	tomatoes
½ cup butter or	1 can bouillon (beef or
shortening	chicken)
2 large onions, sliced	2 teaspoons salt
or chopped	4 cups rice

Peel the eggplant and slice thinly. Sprinkle with salt and set aside for 20 minutes or longer to "perspire." Dry with paper towels, and sauté in 6 tablespoons of the butter until golden brown on both sides. Drain on paper towels and set aside. Sauté the onions in the remaining 2 tablespoons of butter until golden brown. Add the turmeric and stir. Add the tomatoes, bouillon, and salt. Bring to a gentle boil. Add the rice.

Cover and simmer gently until all the liquid has been absorbed (about 20 minutes) and the rice is fairly dry. Stir occasionally to prevent the rice from sticking to the bottom. Arrange the sautéed eggplant slices on top of the rice. Cover the inside of the lid with a cloth, replace on the pot, and steam over a low heat for another 20 minutes or longer.

Plain Rice

(Kateh)

(SERVES 4–6)

Unlike *chello* and *pollo*, *kateh* is not a fluffy rice, but is somewhat sticky. Thus, it is never served to guests, but is used for everyday family meals. It is easier and quicker to prepare than *chello* or *pollo* because there is no rinsing or draining.

3 cups rice	3 teaspoons salt
6 cups water	6 tablespoons butter

Pour the rice into a pot and add water and salt. Cover and cook over a low heat until all the water has been absorbed (about 20 minutes). Place the butter on top of the rice, cover, and cook over a very low heat for another 20 to 30 minutes.

If desired, *kateh* can be prepared in a mold. After the water has been absorbed, mix together 1 cup of cooked rice, 2 egg yolks, and 3 tablespoons of melted butter. Spread this mixture over the bottom of a greased mold. Add the remaining rice, and bake in a 350° F. oven for 1 hour. To unmold, dip the mold up to the rim in cold water for a couple of minutes, invert the mold on a platter. There should be a thick, golden crust over the rice.

Molded Rice

(Kateh Ghalebi)

(SERVES ABOUT 6)

Molded rice is popular in the Caspian provinces of Gilan, Mazenderan, and Gorgan. Unlike the fluffy mound of rice turned out by the Iranian urbanite, *kateh ghalebi* is baked in a mold and the rice is not rinsed or drained. Traditionally this dish is served with Stewed Lamb with Carrots. *(Khoresht-e Havij).*

3 cups rice	2 egg yolks, beaten
2 tablespoons salt	½ cup yogurt
6 cups water	¼ cup butter

Pour the rice into a pot and add the salt and water. Bring to a boil. Turn the heat to medium-low and cook, covered, until all the water has been absorbed (about 20 minutes). Mix 1 cup of cooked rice with the egg yolks, yogurt, and 2 tablespoons of melted butter. Press into the bottom of a ring mold. Spoon the rest of the rice into the mold. Melt the remaining 2 tablespoons of butter and pour this over the rice. Bake in a moderate oven (350° F.) for 45 to 60 minutes.

The rice will form a golden crust over the entire inner surface of the mold. To remove the rice, immerse the mold up to the rim in cold water for a few minutes. Run a knife around the edges, loosening the crust from the mold. Invert onto a platter and shake loose.

Molded Rice with Chicken and Dried Fruit
(Dami Ghalebi ba Morgh)

(SERVES 4–6)

3 cups rice	1 large onion, sliced
6 cups water	½ can chicken broth
4 teaspoons salt	¼ teaspoon pepper
⅛ cup pitted prunes	½ cup butter
(about 4–6 large)	1 teaspoon saffron
¼ cup pitted dates	½ cup yogurt
¼ cup dried apricots	¼ cup walnuts,
¼ cup dried peaches	chopped
4 large chicken breasts	¼ cup currants

Place the rice in a pot; add the water and 3 teaspoons of the salt. Bring to a boil, lower the heat, cover, and simmer gently for about 20 minutes, or until all the water has been absorbed. Cut the dried prunes, dates, apricots, and peaches into 3 or 4 pieces each. Soak these in a small amount of cold water while preparing the chicken.

Place the chicken breasts in a pot with the onion, chicken broth, the remaining salt, and pepper. Cover and simmer until tender (about 30 minutes). Cool and bone. Reserve the stock. Drain the dried fruits.

In a small saucepan, melt 4 tablespoons of the butter; stir in the saffron, 1 cup of cooked rice, and the yogurt. Coat the entire inner surface of a mold with this mixture. Over this rice mixture arrange first a layer of plain rice, then the soaked dried fruit, several chicken pieces, chopped walnuts, currants, and 1 or 2 teaspoons of the chicken stock. Continue alternating layers until the mold is full.

Melt the remaining 4 tablespoons of butter, add any remaining chicken stock, and pour this over the rice. Bake in a moderate oven (350° F.) for approximately 1 hour, or until a thick crust has formed over the entire inner surface of the mold. To unmold, dip the mold up to the rim in cold water for a couple of minutes, then invert onto a large platter.

This dish may be prepared without using a mold. Spread the butter, saffron, rice, and yogurt mixture in the bottom of a large pan. Alternate the ingredients as described above. Cover with a lid wrapped in a cloth. Steam for 30 minutes or longer, starting with a medium-high heat, and then gradually reducing the heat.

Stewed Meat and Rice
(KHORESHT)

Then in china basins and bowls of different sizes were the rag-outs, which consisted of hash made of a fowl boiled to rags, stewed up with rice, sweet herbs, and onions; a stew in which was a lamb's marrow-bone with some loose flesh about it, and boiled in its own juice . . . a fowl stewed to rags, with a brown sauce of prunes.

(James J. Morier,
The Adventures of Haji Baba of Isphahan.)

Khoresht (stewed meat or fowl) served with rice is the mainstay of Persian cooking. Every Iranian hostess will serve guests *khoresht* and rice as the entrée, no matter how many other elegant side dishes or main dishes there might be. Many hostesses will serve several different kinds of *khoresht*, which is part of the Persian tradition of hospitality.

For the American hostess, one such dish will be enough for several guests or a hungry family. In addition to being exotic and tasty, all these *khoresht* are economical because they stretch the meat. Since it is combined with various vegetables, fruits, and herbs, and served in a sauce, a cut of meat that would serve only 4 when roasted now serves 8 or 10! What's more, it tastes divine!

Once you have mastered the principle of making one *khoresht*, you will find that many of them are essentially just variations, using different vegetables, fruits, and seasonings, but the results are totally different. Lamb cooked with green herbs and black-eyed peas is quite different in appearance, flavor, and color to lamb cooked with green beans and tomatoes, yet the basic steps are similar. Even if you ordinarily don't care for lamb, you *will* like it prepared the Persian way! I have served lamb to numerous American guests who inquired what meat they were eating, and they were astonished to find out that it was lamb. "But it doesn't taste like lamb!" they invariably exclaim, which really means, "I don't generally like lamb, but I do like it cooked this way!"

Because of differences in the flavor of lamb (American lamb has a stronger taste than the Persian), it is necessary to season the *khoresht* more heavily in the United States. All of the recipes included here assume the use of American lamb, but they are also quite suitable for New Zealand lamb, which has less fat, or for short ribs of beef, or chuck steak.

In preparing these *khoresht*, use butter rather than vegetable shortening; better still, when cooking lamb, render the trimmed-off fat in a saucepan, and use this—it will greatly enhance the flavor of these dishes. Some readers may object to the amount of butter (or rendered fat) called for in these recipes. But let me warn you— don't skimp on the butter, for the dishes won't taste right if you do. No, they won't taste greasy. Yes, butter (or rendered fat) *is* fattening, but after all, you're not going to eat these dishes every day. Besides, it's truly worth it!

Stewed Lamb with String Beans
(Khoresht-e Loobia)

(SERVES 5–6)

This *khoresht* seems to be a favorite with my guests. Try it on yours and see how many compliments it brings.

2–3 pounds shoulder of lamb, or New Zealand leg of lamb	1 can beef bouillon or consommé
2 large onions, sliced	2 cans (16 ounces) tomatoes
4 tablespoons butter (or rendered lamb fat)	2 teaspoons salt
	1/4 teaspoon pepper
1 teaspoon turmeric	1/4 teaspoon cinnamon
2 tablespoons tomato paste	4 tablespoons lemon juice
2–3 tablespoons hot water	2 pounds string beans

Have your butcher bone the meat. Trim off the excess fat, and cut the meat into stewing-size pieces. Sauté the onions in the butter until golden brown. Or render the fat trimmed off the meat, and use this for browning the onions. Add the meat and sauté until brown. Stir in the turmeric. Dilute the tomato paste in hot water and add. Add the bouillon, tomatoes, salt, pepper, cinnamon, and lemon juice.

Cover and simmer gently for 1½ hours, or braise in a 350° oven for 2 hours or longer. Cut the string beans into ½-inch lengths. Add to the lamb for the last 20 to 30 minutes of cooking on top of the stove; the last 45 minutes in the oven. Serve with rice.

Stewed Lamb with Yellow Split Peas

(Khoresht-e Gheimeh)

(SERVES ABOUT 6)

2–3 pounds shoulder of lamb, or New Zealand leg of lamb	2 tablespoons tomato paste
2 onions, sliced	3–4 tablespoons warm water
3 tablespoons butter (or rendered fat)	4 tablespoons powdered Persian lime (or 4 tablespoons lemon juice)
1 can beef bouillon or consommé	
½ cup water	1 cup yellow split peas
1 teaspoon salt	1 can (1¾ ounce) potato sticks
¼ teaspoon pepper	

Have your butcher bone the lamb. Trim off the fat, and cut the meat into stewing-size pieces. Render the fat in a saucepan. Sauté the onions in the rendered fat (or butter) until golden brown. Add the meat and sauté until brown. Add the bouillon, water, salt, pepper, tomato paste (diluted in warm water), and powdered Persian lime (or lemon juice). Add half the yellow split peas (these will completely dissolve).

Cover and simmer over a low heat for 1½ hours. Add the remaining yellow split peas and continue simmering for another 15 to 20 minutes, or until the peas are just tender. Before serving, place the potato sticks in a serving dish. Pour the stewed lamb over these, and stir very briefly. Serve with rice.

This dish may also be prepared with unboned lamb shanks or short ribs of beef. Use 5 or 6 lamb shanks, allowing one shank per serving, or 5 or 6 beef short ribs.

Stewed Lamb with Yellow Split Peas and Prunes
(Khoresht-e Aloo)

(SERVES ABOUT 6)

Follow the recipe above for Stewed Lamb with Yellow Split Peas (*Khoresht-e Gheimeh*), adding ¾ to 1 cup of prunes for the last 30 minutes of cooking. If the prunes are sour, a little sugar may be added.

Stewed Lamb with Eggplant
(Khoresht-e Bademjan)

(SERVES ABOUT 6)

2–3 *pounds shoulder of lamb, or lamb shanks with bones*	¼ *cup hot water*
1 *large eggplant*	4 *tablespoons powdered Persian lime, or 4 whole Persian limes*
2 *tablespoons salt*	*(or 4 tablespoons lemon juice, although lemon juice is not as good)*
2 *large onions, sliced*	
½ *cup butter (or rendered fat)*	
1 *teaspoon turmeric*	¼ *teaspoon cinnamon*
1 *can beef broth or bouillon*	¼ *teaspoon nutmeg*
¼ *cup water*	1 *teaspoon salt*
2 *tablespoons tomato paste*	¼ *teaspoon pepper*

Have the butcher bone the shoulder of lamb. Trim off the excess fat and render this in a saucepan. Cut the meat into stewing-size pieces. If using lamb shanks, leave them whole. Peel the eggplant and cut it into slices about 2 inches by 4 inches. Sprinkle with 2 tablespoons salt and set it aside for 20 minutes or longer to "perspire."

Sauté the onions in 4 tablespoons of butter (or rendered fat) until golden brown. Add the meat and brown. Stir in the turmeric. Add the beef broth, water, tomato paste (diluted in hot water), powdered Persian lime, and other seasonings. Cover and simmer over a low heat for 1¾ hours.

Meanwhile, blot the eggplant pieces dry with paper towels. Sauté in the remaining 4 tablespoons of butter (or rendered fat) until golden brown on both sides. Drain on paper towels. Arrange carefully on top of the stewed lamb and simmer for 15 minutes, taking care not to break the slices. Serve with rice.

Stewed Lamb with Eggplant and Yellow Split Peas
(Khoresht-e Gheimeh Bademjan)

(SERVES ABOUT 6)

Follow the recipe above for Stewed Lamb with Eggplant (Khoresht-e Bademjan), with these changes:

When you add the beef broth and seasonings, add ½ cup yellow split peas (these will dissolve entirely). During the last 15 to 20 minutes of simmering, add another ½ cup yellow split peas, and continue simmering until these are just tender. Before serving, empty the contents of a 1¾-ounce can of potato sticks into a serving dish. Pour the stewed meat and eggplant over these. Serve with rice.

Chicken (or Lamb) in Pomegranate Sauce
(Khoresht-e Fesenjan)

(SERVES 6–8)

The ultimate test of a cook's ability in Persia is the quality of the *fesenjan* he or she can prepare. This delectable dish is the queen of the stewed meats and is usually considered a company dish. Once you have experienced its aroma and taste, you will know why.

In Resht, on the Caspian coast, this *khoresht* is always prepared with wild duck or pheasant. For my taste, it is exotic enough when made with chicken (or lamb).

Among the many culinary myths in Iran, one of the most prevalent is that certain foods are "hot" (meaning rich) while others are "cold" (meaning cooling)—*sard* and *garm*. This dish is one of those considered *garm*.

2 large onions, chopped or sliced	4–5 tablespoons pomegranate syrup
5 tablespoons butter	2–3 tablespoons sugar
1 large fryer chicken, or 5 whole chicken breasts	2–3 teaspoons salt
	½ teaspoon saffron (or turmeric)
1 can beef bouillon or consommé	¼ teaspoon cinnamon
1 cup water	¼ teaspoon nutmeg
2½ cups finely ground walnuts	¼ teaspoon pepper
	2 tablespoons lemon juice

Sauté the onions in 2 tablespoons of the butter until golden brown. Remove from the pan. Add 3 more tablespoons of butter and sauté the chicken pieces until light brown. Add the bouillon and sautéed onions. Cover and simmer gently for 30 minutes. Cool and bone.

Prepare the sauce by stirring the water into the ground walnuts. Stir in the pomegranate syrup and sugar, and simmer gently over a low heat for 10–15 minutes.

After the chicken has been boned, combine the cooked chicken with the walnut sauce; add the seasonings and the lemon juice; cover and simmer gently for another hour. Adjust the seasonings by adding a little sugar if too sour, or more pomegranate syrup if too sweet. The chicken pieces should be coated with a rich, dark, sweet-sour sauce; there should be plenty of thick sauce. Serve with rice.

This *khoresht* may also be made with meatballs (from ground beef) or lamb (cut into 1-inch cubes).

Chicken in Walnut-Lemon Sauce

(Khoresht-e Fesenjan)

(SERVES 6–8)

Follow the recipe above for Chicken in Pomegranate Sauce (*Khoresht-e Fesenjan*), except reduce the sugar to 1 tablespoon and increase the lemon juice to 4 tablespoons. Substitute 2 to 3 tablespoons of tomato paste for the pomegranate syrup.

Another variation of *fesenjan* is to substitute 5 tablespoons of undiluted frozen orange juice for the pomegranate syrup.

Stewed Lamb with Spinach and Prunes

(Khoresht-e Esfenaj va Aloo)

(SERVES 6)

2–3 pounds shoulder of lamb, or 6 lamb shanks or beef short ribs	½ cup water
	2 teaspoons salt
	¼ teaspoon pepper
3 large onions, sliced	1 tablespoon dried leaf fenugreek
2–3 tablespoons butter (or rendered fat)	2 pounds fresh spinach, or 2 12-ounce packages frozen chopped spinach
1 teaspoon turmeric	
1 can beef broth or bouillon	
¼ cup lemon juice (or sour grape juice)	4 bunches scallions, chopped
	10–12 pitted prunes (or Bokhara plums)

Have the butcher bone the shoulder of lamb. Trim off the fat, and cut the meat into stewing-size pieces. (If using lamb shanks or beef short ribs, do not bone; use whole.) Sauté the onions in the butter (or rendered fat) until brown. Add the meat and sauté until brown. Stir in the turmeric. Add the beef broth, lemon juice, water, salt, pepper, and leaf fenugreek. Cover and simmer over a low heat for 1½ hours. If using fresh spinach, wash, and drain; chop coarsely. (If using frozen spinach, do not defrost.) Add the spinach, scallions, and prunes for the last 30 minutes of cooking. Serve with rice.

Stewed Lamb with Carrots

(Khoresht-e Havij)

(SERVES 6)

2–3 pounds shoulder of
lamb, or New Zealand
leg of lamb
2 large onions,
chopped or sliced
¼ cup butter
1 pound carrots
1 can bouillon or
beef broth

½ cup water
½ teaspoon saffron
2 teaspoons salt
¼ teaspoon pepper
1 cup sour grape juice
(or lemon or
orange juice)

Have your butcher bone the lamb. Save the bones for making soup. Trim off the excess fat, and cut the meat into bite-size pieces. Sauté the onions in 2 tablespoons of the butter until golden brown. Or render the fat trimmed from the lamb, and substitute this for the butter.

Add the meat and sauté until well browned. Peel and slice the carrots thinly. Sauté the carrots in the remaining 2 tablespoons of butter for about 5 minutes and set aside. Add the bouillon, water, and seasonings to the meat. Cover and simmer gently for 1 hour. Add the carrots and the sour grape (or lemon or orange) juice. Simmer, covered, another 30 minutes. It is traditional to serve this dish with molded rice (Kateh Ghalebi).

Stewed Lamb with Green Plums

(Khoresht-e Gojeh)

(SERVES 6)

2–3 pounds shoulder of
lamb, lamb shanks, or
short ribs of beef
1 large onion, sliced
or chopped
¼ cup butter
1 can beef bouillon
1 tablespoon tomato
paste

4 tablespoons
warm water
1 teaspoon salt
¼ teaspoon pepper
1 teaspoon turmeric
1–2 tablespoons sugar
1½ pounds green plums

Have the butcher bone the lamb. Trim off the excess fat, and cut the meat into bite-size pieces. Render the fat and use this instead of the butter, if desired. (If using lamb shanks or short ribs, do not bone.) Sauté the onion in the butter or melted fat until golden brown. Add the meat and brown. Add the bouillon, tomato paste (diluted in warm water), and the seasonings.

Cover and simmer gently for 1½ hours. Wash and stem the green plums. Add to the stew, and simmer, covered, for another 30 minutes. Adjust the seasonings by adding more sugar if necessary. Serve with rice.

Stewed Lamb with Herbs and Plums

(Khoresht-e Na'na-Ja'fari va Gojeh)

(SERVES 6)

Follow the recipe above for Stewed Lamb with Green Plums (Khoresht-e Gojeh) but add 2 cups chopped fresh parsley and 6 sprigs fresh mint, chopped. Sauté the herbs briefly and add them to the onions after they have been browned. Proceed as indicated.

Stewed Lamb with Celery

(Khoresht-e Karafs)

(SERVES 6)

2–3 pounds shoulder of lamb	⅓ cup lemon juice
2 large onions, sliced	2 teaspoons salt
4 tablespoons butter	¼ teaspoon pepper
1 teaspoon saffron (or turmeric)	1 large bunch celery
	2 cups parsley, chopped
1 can beef bouillon or consommé	6 sprigs fresh mint, chopped, or 1 tablespoon dried mint flakes
½ cup water	

Have the butcher bone the meat. Trim off the excess fat, and cut the meat into bite-size pieces. Sauté the onions in 2 tablespoons of the butter until golden brown. Add the meat and sauté until brown. Stir in the saffron (or turmeric). Add the bouillon, water, lemon juice, salt, and pepper. Cover and simmer over a low heat for 1½ hours.

Wash the celery and cut it into 2-inch lengths. Sauté it, with the herbs, in the remaining 2 tablespoons of butter for about 5 minutes, stirring constantly. Add to the stew and continue to simmer, covered, for another 30 minutes. Serve with rice.

Stewed Lamb with Black-Eyed Peas

(Khoresht-e Ghormeh Sabzi)

(SERVES 6)

This dish is very time-consuming for the Iranian housewife to prepare because chopping the herbs takes so much time and patience. Lacking both, I have discovered a marvelous way to chop the parsley in seconds—in an electric blender! The scallions and leeks can be chopped by hand fairly simply. The main difficulty in preparing this dish in the United States lies in finding *leaf* fenugreek. I grow my own and dry it for winter use. If you cannot find fresh leaf fenugreek, you can order dried leaf fenugreek from one of the stores listed in the Shopper's Guide. Without fenugreek, this dish will *not* be absolutely authentic.

3 pounds shoulder of lamb, or New Zealand leg of lamb
⅓ cup dried black-eyed peas, or 1 package frozen black-eyed peas
2 large onions, sliced
4 tablespoons butter
1 can consommé or beef bouillon
¼ cup water
2 tablespoons salt
¼ teaspoon pepper
3–4 whole Persian dried limes (or 4

tablespoons lemon juice)
2 bunches parsley, finely chopped
8–10 sprigs leaf fenugreek, chopped, or 3 tablespoons dried leaf fenugreek
1 cup scallions, chopped (include half of the green stem)
1 cup leeks, chopped (include half of the green stem)

Have your butcher bone the meat. Trim off the excess fat, and cut the meat into stewing-size pieces. If using dried black-eyed peas, cover with salted water and cook until tender. Drain and set aside. Sauté the onions in 2 tablespoons of the butter (or rendered fat) until golden brown. Add the meat and sauté until brown. Add the consommé, water, salt, pepper, and Persian limes (or lemon juice). Cover and simmer gently for 1 hour.

Sauté the parsley, fenugreek, scallions, and leeks briefly in the remaining 2 tablespoons of butter and add them to the meat. Cover and simmer 30 minutes or longer. If using frozen black-eyed peas, cook according to the directions on the package. Just before serving, add the black-eyed peas to the stew. Serve with rice and yogurt.

Red kidney beans may be substituted for the black-eyed peas.

Stewed Lamb with Rhubarb

(Khoresht-e Rivas)

(SERVES 6)

2½–3 pounds shoulder of lamb, or lamb shanks	¼ cup lemon juice
	3 teaspoons salt
	¼ teaspoon pepper
2 large onions, sliced	½ cup water
4 tablespoons butter	2 bunches fresh parsley
1 teaspoon saffron	6 sprigs fresh mint
1 can consommé or beef bouillon	4–5 stalks rhubarb

Have your butcher bone the shoulder of lamb. If using lamb shanks, do not bone. Trim off the excess fat, and cut the meat into stewing-size pieces. If desired, render the fat and use it in place of the butter. Sauté the onions in 2 tablespoons of the butter or rendered fat until brown. Add the meat and sauté until brown. Stir in the saffron. Add the consommé, lemon juice, salt, pepper, and water. Cover and simmer gently for 1 hour.

Wash the parsley and mint, shake dry, and chop fine (this may be done in an electric blender). Sauté them briefly in the remaining 2 tablespoons of butter and add them to the stew. Cover and simmer 30 minutes or longer. Trim the ends off the rhubarb and cut into 1-inch or 2-inch lengths. Add them to the stew for the last 15 to 20 minutes of cooking. Serve with rice.

This dish may also be prepared without parsley or mint.

Lamb Stew with Sour Grapes

(Khoresht-e Ghooreh)

(SERVES 5–6)

2–3 pounds shoulder of lamb, or New Zealand leg of lamb	¼ teaspoon pepper
	1 tablespoon tomato paste
2 large onions, sliced	3–4 tablespoons warm water
3 tablespoons butter (or rendered fat)	1 pound sour grapes
1 can beef bouillon	2 tablespoons sugar (or more)
2 teaspoons salt	

Have your butcher bone the lamb. Trim off the excess fat, and cut the meat into stewing-size pieces. Render the fat, if desired, and substitute it for the butter. Sauté the onions in the butter (or rendered fat) until golden brown. Add the meat and sauté until brown. Add the bouillon, salt, pepper, and tomato paste (diluted in warm water).

Cover and simmer for 1½ to 2 hours (or 20 minutes in a pressure cooker). Remove the stems from the sour grapes, rinse, and add them to the stew. Cover and simmer for 15 to 20 minutes. Add the sugar, stirring until it is dissolved. Serve with rice.

Stewed Lamb with Quince

(Khoresht-e Beh)

(SERVES 6)

A delightful dish—tart and unusual.

2½–3 pounds shoulder of lamb, or lamb shanks, or short ribs of beef	¼ cup lemon juice
	2 teaspoons salt
	¼ teaspoon pepper
3 large onions, sliced	¼ cup water
4 tablespoons butter (or rendered fat)	1 large or 2 small quinces
1 teaspoon saffron	2 tablespoons sugar
1 can beef broth or bouillon	¼ cup yellow split peas (optional)

Have your butcher bone the shoulder of lamb. Trim off the excess fat, and cut the meat into stewing-size pieces. If desired, the fat may be rendered and substituted for the butter. If using lamb shanks or beef short ribs, do not bone. Sauté the onions in 2 tablespoons of the butter (or rendered fat) until golden brown. Stir in the saffron. Add the meat and sauté until brown. Add the beef broth, lemon juice, salt, pepper, and water. Cover and simmer gently for 1½ hours.

Peel the quinces, and quarter. Slice each quarter like an apple. Sauté them briefly in the remaining 2 tablespoons of butter. Add them to the stew; add the sugar; cover and simmer for 30 minutes.

If the stew is too tart, add more sugar.

If desired, ¼ cup yellow split peas may be added for the last 30 minutes of cooking.

Stewed Lamb with Cardoons

(Khoresht-e Kangar)

(SERVES 6)

2½–3 pounds shoulder of lamb, or New Zealand leg of lamb	1 teaspoon saffron
	2 pounds cardoons
1 large onion, sliced or chopped	1 can beef bouillon or consommé
	¼ cup water
¼ cup butter (or rendered fat)	⅓ cup lemon juice
	2 teaspoons salt
	¼ teaspoon pepper

Have your butcher bone the meat. Trim off the excess fat, and cut the meat into stewing-size pieces. If desired, render the fat and substitute it for the butter. Sauté the onion in 2 tablespoons of the butter (or rendered fat) until golden brown. Stir in the saffron. Add the meat and sauté until brown. Clean the cardoons, removing the prickly stems, slice them, and sauté them briefly in the remaining 2 tablespoons of butter. Add them to the meat, together with the bouillon, water, lemon juice, salt, and pepper. Cover and simmer for 2 hours, or until tender (or 20 minutes in a pressure cooker). Serve with rice.

Stewed Lamb with Cardoons and Herbs

(Khoresht-e Kangar ba Sabzi)

(SERVES 6)

Follow the recipe above for Stewed Lamb with Cardoons *(Khoresht-e Kangar)* and add the following:

> 1 bunch fresh parsley,
>   finely chopped
> 10–15 sprigs fresh
>   mint, finely
>   chopped

Sauté the herbs in 2 tablespoons of butter. Add them with the cardoons to the stew. Proceed as indicated.

Stewed Lamb with Apples

(Khoresht-e Sib-e Derakhti)

(SERVES 6)

2½ pounds shoulder of lamb, or New Zealand leg of lamb	¼ cup water
	2 teaspoons salt
1 large onion, grated	¼ teaspoon pepper
	¼ cup lemon juice
3 tablespoons butter	¼ cup yellow split peas
1 teaspoon saffron	3 pounds firm cooking apples
1 can beef bouillon or consommé	¼ cup sugar

Have your butcher bone the lamb. Trim off the excess fat, and cut the meat into bite-size pieces. If desired, render the fat and use it instead of the butter. Sauté the onion in the butter or rendered fat until golden brown. Add the meat and sauté until brown. Stir in the saffron. Add the bouillon, water, salt, pepper, and lemon juice. Cover and simmer for 30 minutes. Add the yellow split peas, cover again, and simmer for another hour.

Peel and halve the apples; core and cut each half into 3 or 4 pieces. Add the apple pieces and sugar to the stew, cover, and simmer gently for an additional 20 minutes. Serve with rice. If the apples are sweet, reduce the amount of sugar; if very tart, increase the sugar to taste.

Stewed Chicken with Yogurt

(Khoresht-e Mast)

(SERVES 6)

2 medium onions, sliced	¼ teaspoon pepper
2 tablespoons butter	1 large fryer or stewing
1 teaspoon saffron	chicken
1 can beef bouillon	½ cup candied
¼ cup water	orange peel
1 teaspoon salt	2 cups yogurt

Sauté the onions in the butter in a large kettle until golden brown. Stir in the saffron. Add the bouillon, water, salt, and pepper.

Add the chicken, whole or cut up. Cover and stew over a low heat about 1 hour, or until tender. Add the candied orange peel and simmer for 15 minutes over a low heat. Just before serving, stir 3 or 4 tablespoons of hot chicken broth into the yogurt. Then stir the yogurt into the chicken sauce. The chicken may be served whole or cut up, or boned and shredded. Serve with rice.

This dish may also be made with lamb. Use 2 to 3 pounds of shoulder of lamb, boned, trimmed of fat, and cut into bite-size pieces. Follow the directions above.

Stewed Lamb with Fava Beans

(Khoresht-e Gol dar Chaman—Baghala Ghatogh)

(SERVES 6)

This dish comes from Resht, the capital city of the province of Gilan.

2 cups fresh or dried
  fava beans
2½ pounds shoulder of
  lamb, or New Zealand
  leg of lamb
1 large onion, sliced
2–3 cloves garlic,
  grated
3 tablespoons butter

1 can beef bouillon
½ cup water
1–2 teaspoons salt
¼ teaspoon pepper
2 cups fresh dill weed,
  chopped, or 4–5
  tablespoons dried
  dill weed
3–4 eggs

If using dried fava beans, soak them for 3 or 4 hours in cold water. Have your butcher bone the lamb. Trim off the fat, and cut the meat into stewing-size pieces. Sauté the onion and garlic together in the butter or rendered fat. Add the meat and sauté until brown. Add the bouillon, water, salt, pepper, dill weed, and soaked dried fava beans. If using fresh fava beans, shell, peel, and add to the stew for the last 20 minutes of cooking.

Cover the stew and simmer gently for 2 hours. Beat the eggs and dribble them into the stew just before serving. Or hard-boil the eggs and grate them over the stew. Serve with rice.

This dish may also be prepared without meat.

Stewed Chicken Curry

(Khoresht-e Kari)

(SERVES 6)

2 medium onions, sliced
3 tablespoons butter
3–4 cloves garlic, grated
1 can beef broth or
  bouillon
¼ cup water
1–2 teaspoons salt
¼ teaspoon pepper
2–3 tablespoons
  lemon juice

1 stewing chicken
¼ cup slivered or
  whole almonds
2 teaspoons curry
  powder
3 tablespoons warm
  water

Sauté the onions in 1½ tablespoons of the butter until golden brown. Add the garlic. Add the beef broth, water, salt, pepper, and lemon juice. Add the chicken, cover, and stew until tender (1 hour or longer). Cool the chicken and bone.

Sauté the almonds in the remaining 1½ tablespoons of butter until light brown. Return the boned chicken to the drippings. Add the sautéed almonds and curry powder (dissolved in warm water). Simmer a few minutes longer. Serve with rice.

This dish can also be made with lamb or beef. For beef, allow about 2 hours for cooking.

Stewed Lamb with Squash

(Khoresht-e Kadoo)

(SERVES 6)

2½–3 pounds shoulder of lamb, or New Zealand leg of lamb	1–2 teaspoons salt
	¼ teaspoon pepper
	1 tablespoon tomato paste
2 medium onions, sliced	2–3 tablespoons warm water
6 tablespoons butter	3–4 tablespoons lemon juice
1 can beef bouillon or consommé	5 yellow summer squash
¼ cup water	

Have your butcher bone the lamb. Trim off the fat, and cut the meat into stewing-size pieces. Sauté the onions in 2 tablespoons of the butter until golden brown. Add the meat and sauté until brown. Add the bouillon, water, salt, pepper, tomato paste (diluted in warm water), and lemon juice. Cover and simmer over a low heat for 1½ hours.

Peel the squash; cut lengthwise into strips about 1 inch by 2 inches. Salt these strips lightly. Allow to stand for 20 to 30 minutes to "perspire." Blot dry with paper towels, and sauté in the remaining 4 tablespoons of butter until brown on both sides. Arrange them over the stew for the last 15 to 20 minutes of cooking. Serve with rice.

Stewed Lamb with Mushrooms

(Khoresht-e Gharch)

(SERVES 4–5)

This dish can be made with either chicken, beef, or lamb.

2 pounds shoulder of lamb, or lamb shanks	1 tablespoon soy sauce
2 medium onions, sliced	3 tablespoons lemon juice
4 tablespoons butter	1 pound fresh mushrooms, or
1 can beef bouillon or consommé	2 cans mushroom caps
¼ cup water	2 egg yolks
1–2 teaspoons salt	
¼ teaspoon pepper	

Have your butcher bone the meat. Trim off the excess fat, and cut the meat into cubes. Sauté the onions in 2 tablespoons of the butter until golden brown. Add the meat and sauté until brown. Add the bouillon, water, salt, pepper, soy sauce, and 2 tablespoons of the lemon juice. Cover and simmer over a low heat for 1½ hours.

Wash, dry, and slice the mushrooms. Sauté them in the remaining 2 tablespoons of butter for 3 or 4 minutes. Add them to the stewed meat for the last 30 minutes of cooking. If canned mushrooms are used, do not sauté; add them for the last 15 to 20 minutes of cooking. Just before serving, beat the remaining 1 tablespoon of lemon juice into the egg yolks, and pour this into the stew, stirring constantly. Serve with rice.

Stewed Lamb with Fresh Almonds

(Khoresht-e Chaghaleh-Badoom)

(SERVES 6)

Fresh almonds, with their fuzzy green outer shells and delectable, crunchy flavor, are a rare treat: they make this a truly exotic dish. They are available only for a very short period each spring, and should be picked while still young and tender.

2½–3 pounds shoulder
    of lamb, or
    lamb shanks
1 large onion,
    chopped or sliced
4 tablespoons butter
2 bunches fresh
    parsley, finely
    chopped
20 sprigs fresh mint,
    finely chopped

1 teaspoon turmeric
1 can beef bouillon
1–2 teaspoons salt
¼ teaspoon pepper
¼ cup sour grape juice
    (or lemon juice)
1 pound fresh
    almonds

Have your butcher bone the lamb. Trim off the excess fat, and render this for use instead of the butter, if desired. Cut the meat into bite-size pieces. Sauté the onion in 2 tablespoons of the butter or rendered fat until golden brown. Add the meat and sauté it until brown.

Sauté the chopped parsley and mint in the remaining 2 tablespoons of butter. Add to the meat. Stir in the turmeric. Add the bouillon, salt, pepper, sour grape (or lemon) juice, and cover. Simmer for 1½ hours. Add the fresh almonds. Cover and simmer for another 30 minutes. Serve with rice.

Stewed Lamb with Okra

(Khoresht-e Bamieh)

(SERVES 6)

2½–3 pounds shoulder
    of lamb, or New
    Zealand leg of
    lamb
1 large onion,
    sliced
3 tablespoons butter
    (or rendered fat)
1 tablespoon turmeric
2 cans tomatoes
    (16-ounce)

1 can beef bouillon
    or consommé
2 cloves garlic,
    sliced
2 teaspoons salt
¼ teaspoon pepper
1 red pepper, whole
    or chopped
2 pounds okra
1 cup pitted dates

Have your butcher bone the meat. Remove the excess fat, and cut the meat into stewing-size pieces. If desired, the fat may be rendered and substituted for the butter. Sauté the onion in the butter (or rendered fat) until golden brown. Add the meat and sauté it until brown. Stir in the turmeric. Add the tomatoes, bouillion, garlic, salt, pepper, and red pepper. Cover and simmer for 1½ hours.

Remove the tops and stems from the okra, sprinkle with salt, and set aside. Soak the dates in 1 cup of cold water. When quite soggy, put the dates through a meat grinder. Wash the okra well with cold water to remove the salt. Add the okra to the stew and simmer for 10 minutes. Add the ground dates, uncover the pot, and simmer for 10 to 15 minutes. Serve with rice.

Stewed Chicken with Tangerines

(Khoresht-e Narengi)

(SERVES 6)

2 large onions, sliced	½ cup candied orange
4 tablespoons butter	or tangerine peel
1 stewing chicken	1 tablespoon flour
1 teaspoon saffron	3 tangerines (or 2
1 can beef or chicken	small cans
bouillon	mandarin
¼ cup water	orange segments)
1–2 teaspoons salt	4 tablespoons
¼ teaspoon pepper	slivered almonds
4 tablespoons	and pistachios (or
lemon juice	just almonds)
½ pound carrots	

Sauté the onions in the butter until golden brown. Add the chicken, whole or cut up, and sauté until golden brown on all sides. Stir in the saffron. Add the bouillon, water, salt, pepper, and lemon juice. Cover and simmer over a low heat for 1 hour.

Peel the carrots and slice into thin, 1-inch slivers. Add, together with the candied orange or tangerine peel, to the chicken. Continue simmering until the peel is tender. Thicken the sauce with flour, using a wire whisk to prevent lumps. Peel the tangerines, separate into segments, and peel each segment. Add them to the stewed chicken. If using mandarin oranges, drain off the liquid and add. To serve, sprinkle with almonds and pistachios. Serve with rice.

Duckling in Pomegranate-Walnut Sauce
(Fesenjan-e Ordak)

(SERVES 8–10)

2 large onions,
   chopped or sliced
4 tablespoons butter
2 ducklings, cut up
1 can beef or chicken
   bouillon or
   consommé
2 tablespoons
   lemon juice

¼ cup water
1–2 teaspoons salt
¼ teaspoon pepper
6 tablespoons
   pomegranate syrup
3–4 tablespoons sugar
2½ cups finely ground
   walnuts

Sauté the onions in the butter until golden brown. Remove from the pan. Sauté the duckling pieces until brown on all sides. Return the sautéed onions. Add the bouillon, lemon juice, water, salt, and pepper. Cover and simmer gently for 45 minutes. Cool and bone the ducklings. Skim the excess fat off the surface of the cooking liquid.

Stir in the pomegranate syrup, sugar, and ground walnuts. Return the boned duckling to the pot, cover, and simmer gently for 1 hour or longer. If necessary, more bouillon or water may be added. If desired, the duckling may be cooked in a 350° F. oven for the last hour. Uncover the pan and continue cooking another 20 to 30 minutes. The sauce will become quite dark. Serve with rice.

Sour Chicken

(Khoresht-e Morgh-e Torsh)

(SERVES 6)

This is a famous recipe from the province of Gilan.

2–3 cloves garlic,
grated

4 tablespoons butter

1 large stewing
chicken, whole or
cut up

1 can beef or chicken
bouillon

¼ cup water

2 teaspoons salt

¼ teaspoon pepper

1 cup parsley,
chopped

1 cup scallions,
chopped

10 sprigs fresh mint,
chopped

¼ cup coriander
(Chinese parsley),
chopped

3 tablespoons yellow
split peas

½ cup frozen orange
juice, undiluted

3 tablespoons rice flour

6 tablespoons
cold water

3–4 eggs

Sauté the garlic in 2 tablespoons of the butter until golden brown. Brown the chicken on all sides in the garlic butter. Add the bouillon, water, salt, and pepper. Cover and simmer for 30 minutes. Sauté the chopped parsley, scallions, mint, and coriander in the remaining 2 tablespoons of butter, and add them to the chicken. Add the yellow split peas and frozen orange juice. Cover and simmer for 30 minutes.

Put the rice flour into a small bowl and make a thin paste by adding cold water and stirring. Stir this into the chicken sauce, using a wire whisk to prevent lumping. Beat the eggs briefly, and dribble them into the chicken sauce just before serving. The chicken may be served whole or cut up, or it may be boned and shredded. Serve with rice.

Fish in Herbs

(Ghormeh Sabzi ba Mahi)

(SERVES 4–6)

¼ cup dried red kidney beans (or dried black-eyed peas)	4 tablespoons butter or shortening
1 bunch fresh parsley, chopped	1 can beef or chicken broth or bouillon
1 bunch leeks, chopped	6 dried Persian limes
several tablespoons fenugreek, chopped	4–6 fillets of fish (perch, haddock, or halibut)
1 pound spinach, coarsely chopped	½–1 teaspoon salt
	¼ teaspoon pepper
	1 teaspoon turmeric (or saffron)

Rinse the kidney beans (or black-eyed peas), cover with salted water, and boil until tender (about 1 hour and 30 minutes). Sauté the herbs and spinach briefly in the butter or shortening. Add the beef broth, cover, and simmer gently for 10 minutes.

Break open one end of each dried Persian lime with a sharp knife, and drop them into the simmering spinach and herbs. Add the fish fillets, cover, and cook until they are flaky and tender (25–30 minutes). Add the salt, pepper, and turmeric (or saffron). Drain the kidney beans and add; simmer a few minutes and serve.

The dried Persian limes are added for flavor. Although they are not eaten, they are usually not removed from the dish before serving. For an uninitiated guest, however, it might save some embarrassment if the dried limes were removed before serving.

Stews, Casseroles, and Other Entrées
(KHORAK)

Any main dish that is not generally accompanied by rice is known as *khorak*.

Braised Lamb Shanks

(Khorak-e Mahicheh)

(SERVES 4)

3 tablespoons butter or shortening	1 tablespoon lemon juice
2 medium onions, sliced coarsely	1 teaspoon salt
4 lamb shanks	¼ teaspoon pepper
1 can beef broth or bouillon	¼ teaspoon paprika
¼ cup tomato sauce	½ cup water
	5–6 tiny carrots
½ teaspoon lemon peel, grated	1 bunch leeks
	2 tablespoons flour

Melt the butter or shortening in a deep kettle, and sauté the onions until golden brown. Add the lamb shanks and sauté until brown on all sides. Add the beef broth, tomato sauce, lemon peel, lemon juice, salt, pepper, paprika, and water. Cover and simmer over a low heat for 2 hours.

Peel the carrots and remove the stems. Remove the ends and stems of the leeks. Add the carrots and leeks to the pot. Cover and simmer another 15 minutes, or until these vegetables are tender.

Arrange the lamb shanks on a serving platter. Arrange the carrots and leeks decoratively around the meat. With a wire whisk, mix the flour with the drippings, and pour this sauce over the meat.

Plain Lamb Stew

(Khorak-e Bareh)

(SERVES 5–6)

3 pounds shoulder or leg of lamb, or lamb shanks	2 tablespoons lemon juice
3 small onions, chopped or sliced	1 teaspoon salt
3 tablespoons butter	10 peppercorns (wrapped in a small piece of cheesecloth and tied with a string)
1 teaspoon turmeric (or saffron)	several slices green pepper (optional)
1 medium-size can tomatoes (16 ounces)	2–3 tablespoons flour
1 can beef bouillon	
¼ cup tomato sauce	

Have your butcher bone the lamb for you. Cut it into 4 or 5 pieces, removing the excess fat. If using lamb shanks, do not bone. Sauté the onions in melted butter in a deep pot. Add the meat and brown on all sides. Stir in the turmeric (or saffron). Add the tomatoes, bouillon, tomato sauce, lemon juice, salt, peppercorns, and green pepper. Cover and simmer until tender (about 2 hours). Remove the peppercorns. With a wire whisk, add the flour to the drippings. Serve with rice, noodles, or potatoes.

Braised Lamb with Yogurt

(Khorak-e Goosht ba Mast)

(SERVES 4–6)

3 pounds shoulder of lamb, or lamb shanks	¼ cup water
2 large onions, sliced	½ teaspoon salt
3 tablespoons butter	¼ teaspoon pepper
1 teaspoon saffron	¼ teaspoon oregano
1 can beef broth or bouillon	½ cup yogurt
	1 can (1¾ ounce) potato sticks

Have your butcher bone the lamb. Cut it into 4 or 5 large pieces or bite-size cubes, removing the excess fat. Sauté the onions in the butter until golden brown. Add the meat and sauté until brown. Stir in the saffron. Add the beef broth, water, salt, pepper, and oregano. Cover and simmer for 2 hours.

Ladle a few tablespoons of hot broth from the meat into a small bowl and stir in the yogurt. Then stir the warm yogurt into the hot broth in the pot. Place the potato sticks in a serving dish, and arrange the pieces of meat in the center of the dish. Pour the sauce over the potato sticks. Serve immediately before the potato sticks become soggy.

Lamb Stew with Navy Beans

(Khorak-e Loobia)

(SERVES 4–6)

3 pounds shoulder of lamb, or New Zealand leg of lamb	½ teaspoon salt
1 cup dried navy beans	¼ teaspoon pepper
2 medium onions, sliced	1 cup parsley, chopped
3 tablespoons butter	1 bay leaf
1 teaspoon turmeric	2 tablespoons lemon juice
2 cans beef broth or bouillon	1 carrot, sliced

Have your butcher bone the meat. Cut into 5 or 6 pieces, trimming off the excess fat. Soak the beans in cold water for 2 to 3 hours. Place them in a pot of salted water and cover loosely; bring to a boil and simmer for 30 minutes. Sauté the onions in melted butter until golden brown. Add the meat and sauté until brown. Stir in the turmeric. Add the beef broth, salt, pepper, parsley, bay leaf, and lemon juice. Cover and simmer for 2 hours. Add the carrot to the stew for the last 30 minutes of cooking. Shortly before serving, stir in the cooked navy beans. Serve with rice, noodles, or potatoes.

Lamb Stew with Green Beans

(Khorak-e Loobia)

(SERVES 4–6)

3 pounds shoulder of lamb, or New Zealand leg of lamb, or lamb shanks	⅛ teaspoon cinnamon
	⅛ teaspoon nutmeg
	1–2 teaspoons salt
	¼ teaspoon pepper
1 large onion, sliced	1 tablespoon tomato paste
3 tablespoons butter	
1 tablespoon turmeric	¼ cup warm water
2 cans (16-ounce) tomatoes	1 pound green beans
	2 cans (1¾ ounce each) potato sticks
1 can bouillon	
2 tablespoons lemon juice	

Have your butcher bone the meat. Trim off the excess fat, and cut the meat into stewing-size pieces. If using lamb shanks, do not bone. Sauté the onion in the butter. Add the meat and brown, stirring occasionally. Stir in the turmeric. Add the tomatoes, ·bouillon, lemon juice, and seasonings.

Dissolve the tomato paste in warm water and add. Cover and simmer for 1½ hours. String the beans and cut into ¼-inch lengths. Add them to the stew and simmer for another 30 minutes. Just before serving, place the potato sticks in a serving dish and pour the stew over them; stir very briefly. Serve with hot bread or rolls.

Lamb Stew with Peas

(Khorak-e Nokhod Farangi)

(SERVES 4–6)

2½–3 pounds shoulder of lamb	1 teaspoon salt
2 large onions, chopped or sliced	¼ teaspoon pepper
3 tablespoons butter	2–3 pounds fresh peas
2 cans beef broth or bouillon	½ cup fresh dill weed, chopped, or 4 tablespoons dried dill weed

Have your butcher bone the lamb; trim off the excess fat, and cut the meat into stewing-size pieces. Sauté the onions in the butter until golden brown. Add the meat to the onions, and sauté until brown. Add the beef broth, salt, and pepper. Cover and simmer for 1½ hours. Shell the peas and add them to the stew. Add the dill weed, cover, and simmer another 30 minutes.

Breast of Lamb

(Boz Ghormeh)

(SERVES 4)

2 pounds breast of lamb	½ teaspoon saffron
2 large onions, grated or chopped	1 teaspoon dried mint flakes
4 tablespoons butter	½ cup ground walnuts
1 can beef broth	3 cloves garlic, grated (optional)
¼ cup water	1 tablespoon butter (optional)
½ teaspoon salt	
¼ teaspoon pepper	
1 cup liquid whey (or yogurt)	

Crack the breast bones with a sharp blow of a butcher's knife. Sauté the onions in 3 tablespoons of the butter until golden brown. Add the meat and sear on all sides. Add the broth, water, salt, and pepper. Cover and simmer over a low heat until the meat is tender (about 2 hours). Ladle a few tablespoons of the hot broth into the liquid whey (or yogurt) to warm it up before adding it to the meat. Stir in the saffron. Cover and simmer another 15 minutes.

Just before serving, sauté the mint flakes in the remaining 1 table-spoon of butter and sprinkle them over the meat. Sprinkle the ground walnuts over the top. If desired, sautéed, grated garlic may also be added to the top.

Chicken Croquettes

(Kotlet-e Morgh)

(SERVES 5–6)

2 *large onions, sliced*	1 *slice white bread*
¼ *cup butter*	1 *cup milk*
1 *teaspoon turmeric*	2 *eggs*
1 *3-pound fryer*	¼ *teaspoon pepper*
chicken	½ *cup flour*
2 *cans chicken or*	1 *cup bread crumbs*
beef broth	

Sauté the onions in 2 tablespoons of the butter until golden brown. Stir in the turmeric. Add the whole chicken and the broth. Cover and simmer gently for 1 hour, or until tender. Cool and bone. Put the chicken through a meat grinder. Soak the bread in the milk and add it to the ground chicken. Put the chicken mixture through the meat grinder again. Add 1 egg and the pepper, and mix well with the hands.

Wet the hands and shape the mixture into patties or croquettes. Dip each croquette into the flour until well coated, then into the remaining beaten egg, then into the breadcrumbs. Brown on all sides in the remaining 2 tablespoons of butter until golden brown. For a more piquant flavor, substitute packaged, seasoned fried bread mix for the bread crumbs.

Chicken-Potato Croquettes

(Kotlet-e Morgh-o Sib Zamini)

(SERVES 8–10)

1 2–3 pound fryer chicken	½ pound potatoes
1 can chicken bouillon	1 slice white bread
¼ teaspoon pepper	1 cup milk
2 tablespoons lemon juice	2 eggs, beaten
1 tablespoon soy sauce	1 cup flour (or breadcrumbs)
1 large onion, quartered or sliced	¼ cup butter or shortening

Place the chicken in a pot; add the bouillon, pepper, lemon juice, soy sauce, and onion. Cover and simmer until the chicken is tender (about 1¼ hours). Cool and bone. Put the boned chicken through a meat grinder or food mill. Boil the potatoes whole until done; then peel and grate. Soak the bread in the milk until soggy.

Mix together the chicken, potatoes, eggs, and soaked bread, working well with the hands. Shape into patties or croquettes. Dip into the flour (or bread crumbs), and brown on both sides in hot butter or shortening until golden brown. Drain on paper towels before serving.

Eggplant Casserole I

(Khorak-e Kashk-e Bademjan)

(SERVES 4)

2 medium onions,
    sliced
½ cup butter
1½ pounds boneless
    shoulder of lamb,
    or New Zealand
    leg of lamb
1 can beef bouillon
½ teaspoon salt
¼ teaspoon pepper
1 tablespoon tomato
    paste

3 tablespoons
    warm water
¼ cup yellow
    split peas
1 medium eggplant
1 cup yogurt (or
    liquid whey)
¼ cup chopped
    walnuts (optional)

Sauté the onions in 3 tablespoons of the butter until golden brown. Cut the meat into cubes, trimming off the excess fat. Add it to the onions and sauté until brown. Add the bouillon, salt, and pepper. Dilute the tomato paste in warm water and add. Cover and simmer for 45 minutes. Add the yellow split peas and simmer 15 minutes longer.

Peel the eggplant and cut it in half lengthwise. Slice crosswise into pieces about ⅛-inch thick. Sauté the pieces in the remaining 5 tablespoons of butter until brown on both sides. Drain on paper towels.

Pour the meat and yellow split peas into a baking dish. Arrange the eggplant slices on top and bake for 40 minutes at 325° F. Just before serving, gently warm the yogurt (or liquid whey) by stirring into it some of the hot meat sauce. Pour this over the top of the casserole. If desired, sprinkle some chopped walnuts over the top.

Eggplant Casserole II

(Khorak-e Bademjan)

(SERVES 4)

2 large onions,
chopped
½ cup butter (or
rendered lamb fat)
1½ pounds boneless
shoulder of lamb
1 teaspoon turmeric
1 pound fresh tomatoes,
or 1 medium-size
can tomatoes
(16 ounces)

1 can beef broth or
bouillon
¼ teaspoon pepper
½ teaspoon salt
1 large eggplant
1 green pepper,
thinly sliced

Sauté the onions in 3 tablespoons of the butter (or rendered lamb fat) until golden brown. Cut the meat into bite-size pieces, trimming off the excess fat. Add it to the onions and sauté until brown. Stir in the turmeric. Steep the fresh tomatoes briefly in boiling water; peel, slice and add them to the meat. (If using canned tomatoes, add the tomatoes and their liquid to the meat.) Add the beef broth. Cover and simmer for 1 hour over low heat. Stir in the pepper and salt.

Meanwhile, peel the eggplant and cut it into slices; sprinkle them with salt and set aside for 20 minutes to "perspire." Blot dry on paper towels and sauté in the remaining 5 tablespoons of butter (or rendered fat) until brown on both sides. Drain on paper towels.

Pour the meat and tomatoes into a baking dish. Arrange the green pepper slices over the meat and the eggplant slices over the green pepper. Bake in a 350° F. oven, uncovered, for 45 minutes. Add more broth or water if necessary.

Lamb Casserole

(Khorak-e Boz Ghormeh)

(SERVES 6)

This dish is a specialty of the province of Kerman.

3 pounds shoulder of lamb (or chuck steak)	¼ teaspoon salt
4 tablespoons butter	¼ teaspoon pepper
1 can beef broth or bouillon	3 medium onions, chopped or sliced
¼ cup water	3 cloves garlic, grated
1 teaspoon saffron	1 cup liquid whey (or yogurt)

Have your butcher bone the meat. Cut the meat into stewing-size pieces, trimming off the excess fat. Sauté it in 2 tablespoons of butter until brown. Add the beef broth, water, saffron, salt, and pepper. Cover and simmer gently for 1½ hours. Sauté the onions in the remaining 2 tablespoons of butter until golden brown. Sprinkle these over the meat. Sprinkle the garlic over the meat. Pour the liquid whey (or yogurt) over the meat; cover and simmer gently for 30 minutes.

Lamb Hearts

(Khorak-e Del)

(SERVES 4–6)

2 large onions, sliced	1 teaspoon salt
¼ cup butter	¼ teaspoon pepper
6 lamb hearts	¼ teaspoon cinnamon
3 tablespoons flour	
¼ cup beef broth or bouillon	

Sauté the onions in 2 tablespoons of the butter until golden brown. Rinse the lamb hearts under cold water and pat dry between paper towels. Cut into thin slices. Remove the onions from the skillet. Add the remaining 2 tablespoons of butter and sauté the heart slices until brown on both sides, pouring off any liquid that oozes out. Save this liquid.

Sprinkle the flour over the lamb heart liquid and stir well with a wire whisk to prevent lumping. Stir in the beef broth, salt, pepper, and cinnamon. Pour this over the sautéed hearts. Add the sautéed onions. Simmer over a low heat until done (20 to 30 minutes).

Okra and Lamb Casserole

(Khorak-e Bamieh ba Goosht)

(SERVES 4)

1½ pounds okra	shoulder of lamb
¼ cup vinegar	(or chuck steak)
1 tablespoon salt	1 can beef broth or
3 medium onions,	bouillon
grated	1 can tomatoes
4 tablespoons butter	(16-ounce)
or shortening	½ teaspoon salt
1 pound boneless	

Stem the okra. Add the vinegar and 1 tablespoon of salt to just enough water to cover the okra. Let it soak in this solution for 30 minutes. Meanwhile, sauté the onions in hot butter until golden brown. Cut the meat into stewing-size pieces; add it to the onions and sauté until brown. Add the beef broth, tomatoes, and ½ teaspoon of salt. Cover and simmer for 1½ hours until the meat is tender. Drain the okra and add it to the meat. Cover and simmer for 20 minutes, or until tender.

Beef Tongue with Lemon Sauce

(Zaban-e Gav ba Sauce-e Limoo)

(SERVES 8–10)

4 cloves	1 tablespoon tomato
2 large onions	paste
1 beef tongue	¼ cup warm water
1 carrot	3 tablespoons butter
1 bay leaf	2–3 tablespoons flour
2 teaspoons salt	1 tablespoon lemon
¼ teaspoon pepper	juice
4 packages instant dry	a few sprigs parsley,
chicken or beef broth	chopped

Stick the cloves into the onions. Place them in a large kettle, together with the beef tongue, carrot, bay leaf, salt, pepper, instant dry broth, and just enough water to cover the tongue. Dissolve the tomato paste in warm water and add. Cover and simmer very gently for 4 hours. Remove the tongue and allow it to cool. Slice thin.

Make a white sauce by melting the butter in a saucepan over a low heat; stir in the flour with a wire whisk and stir in about ½ cup of the warm broth. Add the lemon juice. Pour the sauce over the tongue slices and sprinkle with chopped parsley.

Kidney Casserole
(Khorak-e Gholveh)

(SERVES 4–6)

6 lamb kidneys	¼ teaspoon pepper
2 stalks celery	1 cup beef broth
1 carrot	2 tablespoons tomato
2 bay leaves	paste
4 small onions,	3–4 tablespoons warm
chopped	water
3 tablespoons butter	
or shortening	

Rinse the kidneys with cold water and pat dry with paper towels. Make a tiny slit in each kidney and peel off the transparent outer skin. Slice the kidneys thin. Tie the celery stalks, carrot, and bay leaves together in a bunch. Sauté the onions in the butter until golden brown. Add the kidney slices and sauté on both sides. Add the vegetables, salt, pepper, and beef broth. Dilute the tomato paste with warm water and add. Cover and simmer until tender (about 30 minutes). Discard the vegetables.

Liver and Kidney Casserole

(Khorak-e Jegar va Gholveh)

(SERVES 4–6)

1 large onion, finely chopped	or baby beef), chopped
3 tablespoons butter or shortening	1 pound fresh tomatoes, or 1 can tomatoes (16-ounce)
1 liver (lamb, calf, or baby beef), chopped	1 cup beef broth
2 hearts (lamb, calf or baby beef), chopped	¼ cup lemon juice
4 kidneys (lamb, calf,	¼ teaspoon salt
	¼ teaspoon pepper

Sauté the onion in the butter until golden brown. Add the liver, hearts, and kidneys to the onions and sauté. Steep the tomatoes briefly in boiling water to loosen the skins; peel, slice, and add. (If using canned tomatoes, drain off the liquid and add only the solids.) Add the beef broth, lemon juice, salt, and pepper. Simmer until done (about 30 minutes).

Calf's Tongue

(Khorak-e Zaban)

(SERVES ABOUT 8)

2 medium onions	3 bay leaves
2 calves' tongues	5 peppercorns
3–5 cups water	5–6 whole cloves
3 packages instant dry chicken or beef broth	

Sauce:

2 tablespoons butter	¼ teaspoon white pepper
⅓ cup flour	1 tablespoon lemon juice
1 cup tongue broth	a few sprigs parsley, finely chopped
1 cup milk	
1 teaspoon salt	

Slice, quarter, or halve the onions. Place the tongues in a large kettle, together with the water, instant dry broth, onions, bay leaves, peppercorns, and cloves. Cover and simmer for about 3 hours, or until tender. Remove the tongues from the kettle; cool and slice thin.

In a saucepan melt the butter over a low heat. With a wire whisk, stir in the flour, tongue broth, and milk. Add the salt, white pepper, and lemon juice. Pour this over the tongue slices. Sprinkle with chopped parsley.

Lamb Liver Casserole

(Khorak-e Jegar)

(SERVES ABOUT 6)

2 lamb livers	½ cup vinegar
5–6 tablespoons flour	2 tablespoons parsley,
3–4 tablespoons butter	chopped
or shortening	1 teaspoon salt
2 cloves garlic, grated	¼ teaspoon pepper

Remove the transparent skin from the livers. Slice thin. Sprinkle 3 tablespoons of the flour onto a board or plate; dip the liver slices into the flour, coating each side. Sauté the liver slices in the butter until brown on both sides; add the garlic. Add the vinegar, parsley, salt, and pepper; simmer for 10 minutes. Thicken the drippings with the remaining flour. Arrange the liver slices in a serving dish and pour the gravy over them. Serve with rice, potatoes, or noodles.

Lamb Brains I

(Khorak-e Maghz)

(SERVES 4)

In Iran brains and viscera are always purchased fresh (that is, from a newly slaughtered lamb) and cooked the very same day. This ensures their freshness, and thus a delicate flavor.

4 lamb brains	¼ teaspoon pepper
2 tablespoons lemon juice	¼ cup butter
¼ cup flour	or shortening
1 teaspoon salt	

Place the brains in salted water and put into the refrigerator for 30 minutes. Cut each brain in half down the middle. Drop the brains into boiling water to which lemon juice has been added, and simmer for a few minutes over a low heat. Remove the brains and blot dry. Dip each piece into the flour so that it will be well coated; season with salt and pepper; and sauté in the butter until golden brown on each side.

Lamb brains do not have to be boiled first. You may just dip the slices in flour; season with salt and pepper; and sauté until golden brown on both sides. Serve with lemon wedges.

Lamb Brains II

(Khorak-e Maghz)

(SERVES 3)

1 large onion, peeled	3 tablespoons vinegar
1 carrot, peeled	½ cup flour
3 teaspoons salt	¼ teaspoon pepper
10 peppercorns	4 tablespoons butter
1 bay leaf	or shortening
3 brains (lamb or beef)	2 eggs, well beaten

Place the onion and carrot in a pot, together with water, 2 teaspoons of the salt, peppercorns, and bay leaf; simmer gently for 10 minutes. Meanwhile, soak the brains in cold water for 10 minutes. Remove the thin outer membranes. Drop the brains into the pot of simmering vegetables; add the vinegar and simmer for 15 minutes. Drain and cool.

Cut each brain lengthwise down the middle, and then cut each piece in half. Mix the flour with the remaining 1 teaspoon of salt and the pepper. Dip the pieces of brain into the flour, then into the beaten eggs, then again into the flour, coating each piece well. Sauté on both sides in the butter until golden brown.

Persian Lamb Fries

(Khorak-e Donbalan)

(SERVES 4–5)

5 lamb fries*	1–2 teaspoons salt
4 tablespoons flour	¼ teaspoon pepper
2 eggs (diluted with 2 tablespoons water), well beaten	4–5 tablespoons butter or shortening
4 tablespoons bread crumbs	

Wash the lamb fries and cut each one in half. Remove the thin outer membranes. Slice each half in two. Dip the lamb fry pieces into flour, then into the beaten eggs, then into the bread crumbs. Sprinkle with salt and pepper. Brown on both sides in hot butter or shortening. Serve with green peas, sliced tomatoes, and buttered new potatoes.

Kidney, Liver, and Heart Casserole

(Khorak-e Del-o Gholveh-o Jegar)

(SERVES 6)

2 medium onions, grated	1 can tomatoes, drained (16 ounce)
¼ cup butter or shortening	2 tablespoons tomato sauce
2 lamb hearts	¼ teaspoon pepper
6 lamb kidneys	2 tablespoons lemon juice
1 lamb liver	2 tablespoons flour (optional)
1 can beef broth or bouillon	

Sauté the onions in the butter or shortening until golden brown. Remove the transparent outer membrane from the hearts, kidneys, and liver. Cut them into thin slices and sauté with the onions. Add the beef broth; the drained, canned tomatoes; the tomato sauce; and the pepper. Cover and simmer for 20 to 30 minutes. Add the lemon juice just before serving. If desired, the drippings may be thickened with flour.

* Also known as mountain oysters—these are the testes of the lamb.

Chicken in Orange Sauce

(Tala-Kooleh or Ghoorabeh)

(SERVES 4–6)

2 medium onions, sliced
4 tablespoons butter
1 stewing chicken
1 can consommé
¼ cup water
1 teaspoon salt
¼ teaspoon pepper
1 cup parsley, chopped
1 cup scallions, chopped
6 sprigs mint, chopped

¼ cup coriander (Chinese parsley), chopped
1 cup ground walnuts
½ cup orange juice
1 tablespoon frozen orange juice, undiluted
3 eggs, beaten (optional)

Sauté the onions in 2 tablespoons of the butter until golden brown. Place the chicken in a large kettle; add the onions, consommé, water, salt, and pepper. Cover and simmer until tender (about 1 hour). Sauté the chopped parsley, scallions, mint, and coriander in the remaining 2 tablespoons of butter; then add them to the stew. Add the ground walnuts, orange juice, and frozen orange juice. Continue to simmer gently for 30 minutes. If desired, stir in beaten eggs just before serving. Serve with rice or noodles.

Persian "Sloppy Joe"

(Beryooni)

(SERVES 6–8)

This and the following recipe come from Isfahan, the fabled city of blue-tiled mosques, splendid palaces, and exquisite carpets.

3 small onions, chopped or sliced
¼ cup butter or shortening
1 teaspoon turmeric
2 pounds lean beef, ground twice

1 can beef broth or bouillon
¼ cup water
⅛ teaspoon cinnamon
¼ teaspoon pepper

Sauté the onions in the butter or shortening until golden brown. Stir in the turmeric. Add the meat and sauté, stirring until brown. Add the beef broth, water, cinnamon, and pepper. Turn the heat low and simmer for 45 to 60 minutes, or until the meat is about the consistency of spaghetti sauce. Serve on bread. Or heat some Syrian bread in the oven and serve it with this dish. One can tear off a piece of this bread and use it as a scoop.

Mashed Lamb and Rice Casserole

(Shol-e Beryooni)

(SERVES 5–6)

1 large onion, sliced	2 cups rice
½ cup butter (or rendered lamb fat)	¼ teaspoon salt
	¼ teaspoon pepper
2 pounds boneless shoulder of lamb	4 cups water
	1 teaspoon cumin
2 cups beef broth	
peel from half an orange, grated or sliced	

Sauté the onion in 4 tablespoons of the butter until golden brown. Cut the lamb into 2 or 3 chunks, removing the excess fat; sauté until brown. Add the beef broth and orange peel. Cover and simmer until tender (about 1½ hours). Remove the meat and onions from the pan and put through a food mill or pound with a mortar and pestle.

Return the meat to the pan; add the rice, salt, pepper, and water. Bring to a boil and simmer gently until the rice is tender, stirring occasionally (about 20 minutes). If necessary, add more water. Sprinkle the cumin over the top. Melt the remaining 4 tablespoons of butter and pour over the top. Cover with a lid wrapped in a cloth and steam for 30 minutes over a low heat.

STEWS AND CASSEROLES

Leek Casserole

(Torsh-e Tareh)

(SERVES 4)

This recipe comes from the province of Gilan.

½ cup yellow split peas	1 teaspoon salt
3 tablespoons butter or margarine	¼ teaspoon pepper
	1 cup orange juice
2 pounds leeks, finely chopped	½ pound lean ground beef
½ bunch parsley, finely chopped	several cloves garlic, chopped or grated
1 cup water	6 eggs

Soak the yellow split peas in water for 20 minutes. Melt 2 table-spoons of the butter and sauté the chopped parsley and leeks briefly. Drain the split peas; add them to the herbs, together with the water, salt, and pepper. Cover and simmer gently until tender (about 30 minutes). Add the orange juice. In a separate skillet, sauté the ground beef until brown. Add it to the split peas and herbs. Sauté the garlic in the remaining 1 tablespoon of butter and sprinkle it over the dish. Just before serving, break the eggs on top, cover, and poach.

This dish may also be made without ground beef.

Persian "Ravioli"

(Kanali or Goosht-e Bareh)

(SERVES 4–6)

4 tablespoons butter	½ pound lean ground lamb (or beef)
4 eggs	
1 cup flour	¼ teaspoon nutmeg
2¼ teaspoons salt	¼ teaspoon pepper
2 tablespoons shortening	2 tablespoons tomato paste
2 large onions, grated	1 cup hot water

With an egg-beater or electric mixer, beat the butter until soft. Beat in the eggs, flour, and 1 teaspoon of the salt. A little water may be added if the dough is too stiff. Roll the dough out on a floured board with a rolling pin. Cut it into squares about 2 by 2 inches. Bring a pot of water to a boil, add 1 teaspoon of the salt and the shortening. Drop the squares into the boiling water one at a time; boil for 3 minutes, remove, drain, and set aside.

Sauté the onions with the meat in a frying pan until brown. Stir in the nutmeg, the remaining teaspoon of salt, and the pepper. Cool. Place 1 tablespoonful of the meat in the center of each piece of dough; roll up or fold over, pressing the edges closed with a fork. Place in a baking dish. Dissolve the tomato paste in hot water. Pour it over the meat-filled dough and bake at 350° F. for 30 minutes or longer.

Okra with Ground Beef
(Khorak-e Bamieh ba Gheimeh)

(SERVES 4)

1½ pounds okra	2 tablespoons
5 tablespoons vinegar	lemon juice
1½ teasoons salt	1 can beef broth or
3 large onions,	bouillon
grated or chopped	½ cup water
½ cup shortening	1 green pepper,
½ pound ground beef	finely chopped
3 fresh tomatoes, or	
1 can tomatoes	
(16-ounce)	

Remove the stems from the okra and soak them in vinegar, 1 teaspoon of the salt, and enough water to cover for 30 minutes. Sauté the onions in the shortening until golden brown. Add the ground beef and sauté until brown, stirring frequently.

Cover the fresh tomatoes with boiling water for 2 minutes to loosen the skins; peel and cut into small pieces. Add the fresh tomatoes (or drained, canned tomatoes) to the meat, together with the remaining salt, lemon juice, beef broth, and water. Add the green pepper to the meat. Cover and simmer over a low heat for 20 to 30 minutes. Drain the okra and add to the meat for the last 10 to 15 minutes of cooking time.

Okra with Chicken

(Khorak-e Bamieh ba Morgh)

(SERVES 4–6)

1½ pounds okra	1 can beef broth or
½ cup vinegar	bouillon
2 teaspoons salt	1 can (8-ounce)
3 large onions,	tomato sauce
chopped or grated	¼ teaspoon pepper
½ cup butter	1 tablespoon lemon juice
or shortening	2 green peppers,
1 teaspoon turmeric	sliced or diced
1 medium fryer	
chicken, cut up	

Remove the stems from the okra and soak them in the vinegar and the salt with enough water to cover. Sauté the onions in the butter or shortening until golden brown. Stir in the turmeric. Sauté the chicken pieces until brown on all sides. Add the beef broth, tomato sauce, pepper, lemon juice, and green peppers. Cover and simmer about 1 hour, or until tender. Drain the okra and add to the chicken. Continue simmering another 10 to 15 minutes.

Stuffed Whole Lamb

(Bareh-ye Shekam Por)

(SERVES 10–12)

In Iran this elegant dish is sometimes served at banquets, feasts, or weddings. The lamb is usually placed in the center of a huge mound of fluffy rice.

1 large onion, sliced	1 tablespoon slivered
3 tablespoons butter	pistachios
or shortening	½ cup raisins or
1 lamb liver	dried currants
1 cup rice	3–4 cloves garlic
½ teaspoon salt	1 8-pound baby lamb
¼ teaspoon pepper	2 teaspoons seasoned
1 teaspoon saffron	salt
½ cup slivered almonds	

To Prepare Stuffing:

Sauté the onion in the melted butter or shortening until golden brown. Cut the liver into thin slices and sauté it with the onions until brown. Boil the rice in salted water for 12 minutes, drain, and add. Add the salt, pepper, saffron, almonds, pistachios, and raisins or currants. Mix together lightly.

To Prepare Lamb:

Cut the garlic into slivers; pierce the skin of the lamb in several places with the tip of a sharp knife, and insert the garlic slivers under the skin. Fill the stomach cavity with the rice-liver stuffing. Close the cavity with small skewers and trussing string. Sprinkle the exterior of the lamb with seasoned salt. Roast in a 350° F. oven until well done and dark brown on the outside (approximately 4 hours).

Baked Lamb

(Tas Kabab)

(SERVES 4–6)

3 *pounds shoulder*	2 *tablespoons*
or leg of lamb	*hot water*
(or chuck steak)	1 *can beef broth or*
3 *tablespoons butter*	*bouillon*
2 *large onions, sliced*	2 *tablespoons*
12–14 *pitted prunes*	*lemon juice*
½ *teaspoon salt*	2–3 *large potatoes,*
¼ *teaspoon pepper*	*peeled and sliced*
¼ *teaspoon cinnamon*	1 *quince (optional)*
1 *tablespoon tomato*	
paste	

Have your butcher bone the meat. Trim off the fat, and cut the meat into thin slices about 1 inch by 2 inches. Melt the butter in a heavy baking pan. Arrange a layer of onion slices in the pan. Cover with a layer of meat, then a layer of prunes. Continue alternating layers of onions, meat, and prunes.

Sprinkle with the seasonings. Dilute the tomato paste in hot water. Pour over the meat, together with the beef broth and lemon juice. Bake, covered, in a 325° F. oven for 45 minutes. Arrange the potato slices over the meat. Bake, uncovered, 45 minutes longer, occasionally turning the potatoes.

This dish may also be made with 1 quince, peeled and thinly sliced. Arrange the slices in layers with the onions, meat, and prunes.

Pan-Fried White Fish Fillet
(Khorak-e Mahi Sefid)

Whitefish is a specialty of the Caspian Sea; it is highly regarded by most Iranians for its fine, delicate flavor. Those of you who do not have access to Caspian Whitefish can substitute sole, perch, halibut, or flounder.

Scrape the scales off the fish with a sharp knife; slit open the abdomen and clean out the insides. Cut it open down the back. Cut off the head (in northern Iran the head is considered a delicacy). Remove the backbone and cut the fish into fillets. Dip each piece in flour, and pan-fry in butter or shortening on both sides until golden brown. Sprinkle with salt and pepper to taste.

Another method of preparing these fillets is to dip each piece in a beaten egg, then in flour, and then pan-fry.

Traditionally, pan-fried fish fillets are served with Green Herb Rice (Sabzi Pollo). This combination is always eaten at the time of the New Year (No Ruz), which is the most important holiday of the year for Iranians, celebrating the arrival of spring at the time of the vernal equinox. The celebrations last for 13 days and involve much visiting among friends and relatives, and much feasting. Each family sets up a table with the traditional haft-sin, seven items whose names start with the Persian letter s—sepand, sib, sir, serkeh, sombol, sabzi, and somagh (wild rue, apples, garlic, vinegar, a hyacinth, green herbs, and sumac) are some of the articles traditionally used.

The festivities are concluded on the 13th day with a mass exodus to the countryside where families congregate along the banks of rivers, or on patches of grass, for a picnic accompanied sometimes by singing and dancing.

Ground Meat and Meatballs

(Shami and Koofteh)

If ground meat is prepared with some imagination, it need never be tiresome or boring. Iranians have some interesting ways of using ground meat in various dishes; you might enjoy trying some of them.

Shami is made by combining ground beef or ground cooked meat with various dried vegetables, such as yellow split peas or chickpeas.

Koofteh is a kind of meatball consisting of ground beef and various vegetables; sometimes the inside is stuffed with tantalizing surprises such as prunes or nuts.

Split Pea Patties

(Shami-e Pook)

(SERVES 6)

1 cup yellow split peas	1 teaspoon cold water
1 pound boneless shoulder of lamb (or chuck steak)	4 eggs, beaten
	½ teaspoon saffron
	1 teaspoon hot water
2 large onions, sliced	¼ teaspoon cinnamon
2 packages instant dry beef broth	¼ teaspoon nutmeg
	2 teaspoons salt
1 cup water	¼ teaspoon pepper
1 teaspoon baking soda	½ cup butter

Boil the yellow split peas in salted water until tender (about 25 minutes). Drain and set aside. Cut the meat into stewing-size pieces, and place in a kettle with the onions. Add the instant dry broth and water. Cover and simmer for 1 hour for lamb (2 hours for beef). Cool the meat; then put it through a meat grinder or food mill; run it through a second time together with the split peas. Dilute the baking soda in cold water and add it to the eggs. Dilute the saffron in hot water.

Combine all the ingredients (except the butter) and mix well, working with the hands. Shape into patties and press a hole through the middle of each one with the forefinger so that it resembles a doughnut. Heat the butter in a frying pan and sauté the patties over a medium heat until brown on both sides. They should be quite crisp on the outside. The patties may be served hot or cold.

Chick-Pea Patties I

(Shami-e Ard-e Nokhochi)

(SERVES 4–6)

1½ cups chick-pea flour	¼ teaspoon pepper
1 cup cold water	½ teaspoon saffron
1 pound lean ground beef	¼ teaspoon cinnamon
2 large onions, grated	¼ teaspoon nutmeg
1 teaspoon salt	½ teaspoon baking soda
	½ cup butter

Dissolve the chick-pea flour in the cold water; add it to the meat, together with the onions, salt, pepper, saffron, cinnamon, nutmeg, and baking soda. Knead well with your hands and shape into patties, pressing a hole through the center of each one with your thumb or forefinger. (This is not essential, but in Iran it is traditional and ensures that the meat will cook through in the middle.) Melt the butter in a frying pan and sauté the patties on both sides until brown. These may be served hot or cold.

If chick-pea flour is not available, you can make your own by putting dried chick-peas through a blender.

Chick-Pea Patties II

(Shami-e Nokhochi)

(SERVES 4–6)

1 pound boneless shoulder of lamb (or stewing beef), or 3 lamb shanks	¼ teaspoon pepper
	½ teaspoon saffron
	¼ teaspoon cinnamon
	¼ teaspoon nutmeg
2 large onions, sliced	¼ teaspoon oregano
1 cup water (or beef broth)	3 eggs, beaten
½ can chick-peas	½ teaspoon baking soda
1 teaspoon salt	½ cup butter

Simmer the meat and 1 of the onions in water (or beef broth), covered, until tender (1 hour for shoulder of lamb; 2 hours for beef or lamb shanks). If using lamb shanks, remove the bones. Grind the meat in a meat grinder or food mill. Drain the liquid from the canned chick-peas; add these and the remaining onion to the meat, and grind again. Add the seasonings, eggs, and baking soda. Mix well with the hands and shape into patties. Punch a hole through the middle of each patty and sauté in hot butter on both sides until brown and crisp.

Ground Beef Cutlets I

(Kotlet-e Goosht)

(SERVES 4)

1 large onion, grated	½ tablespoon butter
1 pound lean ground beef	½ can beef broth or bouillon
2 packages instant dry beef broth	2 tablespoons tomato sauce
¼ teaspoon salt	1 tablespoon lemon juice
¼ teaspoon pepper	2 tablespoons water

Mix the onion with the meat. Add the instant dry broth, salt, and pepper; mix well with your hands. Shape the meat into patties. Sauté them in butter on both sides until brown. Lower the heat; add the beef broth, tomato sauce, lemon juice, and water. Simmer, uncovered, for 20 minutes or longer, turning the patties occasionally.

Ground Beef Cutlets II

(Kotlet-e Goosht)

(SERVES 4)

1 small onion, grated	1 egg, beaten
3–4 tablespoons butter	2 packages instant dry beef broth
½ slice white bread	¼ teaspoon pepper
¼ cup milk	5 tablespoons flour
1 pound lean ground beef	

Sauté the onion in 1 tablespoon of the butter until golden brown. Soak the bread in the milk. Add the sautéed onion. Add the meat, egg, instant dry broth, and pepper. Mix well with your hands. Shape into patties. Dip the patties into the flour and brown in the remaining butter on both sides. Turn the heat low and cook, uncovered, until done all the way through (about 15 minutes).

Tart Ground Beef Patties

(Torshi Shami)

(SERVES 4)

This recipe comes from the northern city of Resht on the Caspian coast.

1 cup bread crumbs	1 pound lean ground
1 cup milk	beef
2 large onions, grated	2–3 tablespoons butter
1 tablespoon baking	2–3 tablespoons
soda	lemon juice
2 packages instant	3–4 tablespoons
dry beef broth	tomato paste
1 teaspoon salt	¼ cup warm water
¼ teaspoon pepper	

Place the breadcrumbs in a bowl; pour the milk over them. Add the onions, baking soda, instant dry broth, and seasonings; stir. Add the ground beef and mix well with your hands. Shape into patties, and punch a hole through the middle of each one with your forefinger or thumb so that the patties look like doughnuts.

Sauté them in the butter until brown on both sides. Lower the heat. Add the lemon juice. Dilute the tomato paste in the warm water and add. Simmer gently until all of the liquid has been absorbed, turning the patties over once or twice.

Parsley Meatballs
(Koofteh-ye Sabzi)

(SERVES 4–6)

¼ cup rice
4 tablespoons yellow
  split peas
2 large onions
1 bunch parsley, chopped
1 bunch scallions,
  chopped
1 pound ground beef
1 teaspoon salt
¼ teaspoon pepper
¼ teaspoon cinnamon

¼ teaspoon nutmeg
1 egg, beaten
2 tablespoons butter
2 tablespoons
  lemon juice
1 can chicken broth
2 tablespoons tomato
  paste
4 tablespoons
  warm water

Boil the rice and yellow split peas together in salted water for 15 minutes; drain and set aside. Grate 1 onion. Add the parsley, scallions, onion, rice, and yellow split peas to the meat; mix well. Add the seasonings and egg, and mix well. Shape into balls about the size of small apples.

Slice or chop the remaining onion; brown it in hot butter in a heavy skillet. Add the lemon juice, chicken broth, and tomato paste (diluted in warm water). Place the meatballs in this sauce, cover, and simmer for 45 minutes over a low heat; baste them occasionally. The meatballs can also be baked in a 350° F. oven for 1 hour.

Tabriz Meatballs

(Koofteh Tabrizi)

(SERVES 4-6)

The finest of all *koofteh* are supposed to be those made in Tabriz, the capital of Iranian Azerbaijan. Highly accomplished cooks in Tabriz are able to make one large meatball that contains a whole chicken! With more modest aims, our meatballs will be about the size of small apples, and will contain prunes, walnuts, currants, or eggs.

2 large onions	4 tablespoons dried
1 pound lean ground	currants or raisins
beef	¼ cup walnuts,
3 eggs, beaten lightly	halved
½ cup rice flour	3 hard-boiled eggs
(or ¼ cup yellow	2 tablespoons butter
split peas)	1 teaspoon turmeric
1 teaspoon salt	1 cup water
¼ teaspoon pepper	2 cups beef broth or
¼ teaspoon nutmeg	bouillon
¼ teaspoon cinnamon	1 tablespoon tomato
8 dried apricots or	paste
pitted prunes	

Grate 1 of the onions. Mix together the ground beef, grated onion, beaten eggs, rice flour, salt, pepper, nutmeg, and cinnamon. (If yellow split peas are used, boil these in salted water until very tender—about 15 minutes. Mash them well and add.) Shape the meat mixture into balls about the size of small apples, pressing into each one a prune or apricot; several currants or raisins; a walnut half; or a whole, half, or chopped hard-boiled egg. Seal and smooth the outsides of the meatballs.

In a large kettle, melt the butter. Chop or slice the remaining onion and sauté it in the butter until golden brown. Stir in the turmeric. Add the water, beef broth, and tomato paste. Arrange the meatballs in this sauce; turn the heat low and simmer, uncovered, for 45 minutes or longer. Turn the meatballs once or twice. Or bake them in the oven at 325° F. for 1¼ hours, turning them at least once.

Rice Meatballs
(Koofteh Berenji)

(SERVES 4–6)

1 cup rice
½ cup yellow split peas
2 large onions
1 pound ground beef
½ cup parsley, chopped
6 scallions, chopped
2 tablespoons dried dill weed
1 tablespoon mint flakes
1 teaspoon turmeric
2 eggs, beaten lightly
½ cup walnuts, chopped (optional)

2 tablespoons dried currants or raisins (optional)
1 teaspoon salt
¼ teaspoon pepper
2 tablespoons butter or shortening
1 can chicken broth
3 tablespoons lemon juice
1 tablespoon tomato paste
6 tablespoons warm water
yogurt or sour cream (optional)

Boil the rice and yellow split peas together in salted water for 20 minutes. Drain in a colander and set aside. Grate 1 of the onions. Mix together the ground beef, rice, yellow split peas, parsley, scallions, grated onion, dill weed, mint flakes, turmeric, eggs, walnuts, currants, salt, and pepper; work well with the hands.

Shape into balls about the size of small oranges. Chop or slice the remaining onion, and sauté it in the butter until golden brown. Add the chicken broth, lemon juice, and tomato paste (diluted in warm water). Arrange the meatballs in this sauce. Cover and simmer over a low heat for 45 minutes, or until all of the liquid has been absorbed. Or bake the meatballs in a 325° F. oven for 1¼ hours, turning them once or twice.

Yogurt or sour cream may be spooned over the meatballs before serving.

Curry Meatballs
(Koofteh-ye Kari)

(SERVES 4–6)

½ cup rice	1 teaspoon salt
2 onions	¼ teaspoon pepper
2 eggs, beaten lightly	2 tablespoons butter
1 pound lean ground beef	1 can chicken broth
2–3 tablespoons curry powder	½ cup water
¼ cup chick-pea flour	2–3 tablespoons lemon juice
1 cup parsley, dill weed, and scallions, chopped	

Boil the rice in salted water for 10 minutes; drain, and set aside. Grate 1 onion, and add it to the beaten eggs. Mix these with the ground beef, rice, curry powder, chick-pea flour, chopped herbs, salt, and pepper. Work well with the hands, and shape into small balls about the size of walnuts.

Slice the remaining onion, and sauté it in the butter until golden brown. Add the chicken broth, water, and lemon juice. Arrange the meatballs in this sauce. Cover and simmer over a low heat for 1 hour, or until all of the liquid has been absorbed. Turn at least once. Or bake the meatballs in the oven for 1 hour at 350° F., with the pan covered. Turn the meatballs over at least once.

You can make chick-pea flour by putting dried chick-peas through a blender.

Fava Bean and Dill Weed Meatballs

(Koofteh Shebet-Baghala)

(SERVES 4–6)

1 pound fresh fava beans (or lima beans), or 1 cup dried fava beans	tablespoons dried dill weed
½ cup rice	2 eggs, beaten lightly
2 large onions	1 teaspoon salt
1 pound lean ground beef	¼ teaspoon pepper
1 cup fresh dill weed, chopped, or 6–8	¼ teaspoon cinnamon
	2 tablespoons butter
	1 can chicken broth
	2 tablespoons water

If dried fava beans are used, they should be soaked in cold water for several hours. Then boil them in salted water until tender (about 1 hour or longer).

Boil the rice in salted water for 10 minutes. Drain in a colander and set aside. Shell the fresh fava beans, and boil them in salted water until tender (about 20 minutes); pour off the hot water, and cover with cold water. When cool, peel the beans by pressing on one side of each bean so that it slips out of its skin. Grate 1 onion. Mix it with the ground beef, peeled fava beans, rice, dill weed, beaten eggs, salt, pepper, and cinnamon. Shape this mixture into balls about the size of small peaches.

Slice the remaining onion, and sauté it in the butter until golden brown. Add the chicken broth and water. Arrange the meatballs in this broth. Bake, covered, in a 350° F. oven for 1 hour, turning occasionally. The meatballs may also be cooked in a covered pan on top of the stove over a low heat for 1 hour.

Chick-Pea Flour Meatballs

(Koofteh-ye Ard-e Nokhochi)

(SERVES 4–6)

2 large onions	2 tablespoons butter
1 pound lean ground beef	1 can chicken broth
1 teaspoon salt	¼ cup lemon juice
¼ teaspoon pepper	3 teaspoons sugar
2 cups chick-pea flour	½ teaspoon saffron

Grate 1 onion, and mix it well with the ground beef. Add the salt, pepper, and chick-pea flour. Work this mixture well with the hands, adding small amounts of water until it is smooth and elastic, and not sticky. Shape it into balls, about the size of a small apple.

Slice the remaining onion, and sauté it in the butter until golden brown. Sauté the meatballs until brown. Add the chicken broth, lemon juice, sugar, and saffron. Cover and simmer gently on top of the stove for 1 hour. Or bake the meatballs in a covered pan in a 350° F. oven for 1 hour or longer, turning them once or twice.

You can make chick-pea flour by putting dried chick-peas through an electric blender.

Kabab

Cabob *is roastmeat on skewers, cut in little round pieces no bigger than a sixpence, and ginger and garlick put between each.*

(John Fryer, *A New Account of East India and Persia. Being Nine Years' Travels, 1672–1681.*)

Kabab is the Persian word for meat or fowl cooked over a charcoal fire. It is often served with rice, but it may be wrapped in thin, flat, unleavened bread and served with fresh green herbs and yogurt.

... he set out before us on a sheet of bread a roast chicken, an onion, some salt, a round half of cheese, and some bunches of grapes; then, seeing that we hesitated as to the proper mode of attacking the chicken, he took it in his fingers, delicately pulled apart wings, legs, and breast, and motioned us again to eat ... Never did roast chicken taste so delicious!

(Gertrude Bell, *Persian Pictures.*)

Fillet of Lamb Kabab

(Kabab-e Barg)

(SERVES 4–6)

The finest of all *kababs* is *kabab-e barg*, prepared from lamb fillet. It is highly unlikely that you will find this cut of meat in an American supermarket. (American butchers usually cut the fillet (with the bone) into lamb chops.) However, by persuasion (and a willingness to pay the price) you may be able to get your butcher to cut the fillet from the bone for you. In Iran the fillet is laid out in a strip and sliced open lengthwise; then it is flattened out and cut crosswise to the grain into 2-inch pieces. The pieces are marinated overnight with grated or chopped onions, peppers, and a small amount of olive oil; or with yogurt and grated or chopped onions. The meat is then placed on skewers and cooked over a charcoal fire until well done but not dry. It is served with a mound of fluffy white rice, plenty of melted butter on the rice, and sometimes a raw egg yolk mixed into the rice while it is still hot. Over it all is sprinkled ground sumac.

Since I have a large family with enormous appetites, I usually substitute a more economical cut of meat for the fillet; I find that the results are quite satisfactory. This is what I do:

Have the butcher cut a 3-pound shoulder of lamb into slices approximately ¼-inch thick and 4 or 5 inches long, somewhat like pieces of Swiss steak. Pound each piece with a mallet, and place them in a shallow baking dish; pour either of the following two marinades over the meat:

*(1) 3 tablespoons
        vegetable oil
    1 large onion,
        chopped or grated
    1 tablespoon soy
        sauce
    1 teaspoon
        worcestershire
        sauce
    2 packages instant
        dry beef broth*

*½ cup pale dry
    cocktail sherry (or
    3 tablespoons
    lemon juice)*

*(2) 2 cups yogurt
    1 large onion,
        grated, chopped,
        or sliced*

Marinate the meat at least 24 hours. Cook on a grill over a charcoal fire until brown on one side. Turn and brown the other side. Season to taste with salt and pepper. Serve (as indicated above) with rice, egg yolk (if desired), plenty of butter, and ground sumac.

Shish Kabab

(SERVES 4)

Have the butcher bone a 3-pound shoulder of lamb. Cut the meat into 2-inch cubes, trimming off some (but not all) of the excess fat. Marinate overnight in one of the marinades listed for Fillet of Lamb Kabab. Place the meat on skewers, alternating it with cherry tomatoes.

Cook it over a charcoal fire until brown on one side; turn the skewers over and brown the other side. Serve with fluffy white rice, rice with lentils, or any other rice dish. Have little bowls of ground sumac on the table so that individuals may help themselves according to taste. Have fresh butter on the table to be served with the rice.

Chicken Kabab

(Kabab-e Joojeh)

(SERVES 6–8)

2 small fryer chickens	2 packages instant dry
6 tablespoons salad oil	beef broth
1 teaspoon saffron	1 teaspoon salt
1 tablespoon soy sauce	¼ teaspoon pepper
3 tablespoons lemon	¼ teaspoon nutmeg
juice	¼ teaspoon cinnamon

Cut the chickens into serving pieces. Mix all of the other ingredients together in a small bowl. Brush the chicken parts with this marinade and set aside for 2 hours at room temperature. Cook them over a charcoal fire for 1 hour. As the chicken is cooking, brush with any leftover marinade.

This chicken may also be broiled. Marinate as above, place on a baking-pan, place the pan on the lowest rack of the oven, and broil for 1 hour, turning 2 or 3 times.

The chicken may also be roasted whole. Marinate as above, then roast in a 350° F. oven for 2 hours, basting occasionally, and turning the chickens over once after 1 hour of roasting.

Ground Beef Kabab
(Kabab-e Koobideh)

(SERVES 4)

These delicious strips of charcoal-broiled ground meat are served with rice, egg yolk, ground sumac, and plenty of butter. They are easily prepared and equally well suited to a family picnic or a sumptuous outdoor barbecue.

1½ pounds ground beef	1 large onion, grated
2 packages granulated chicken or beef broth	½ teaspoon seasoning salt

   Mix all of the ingredients well with your hands. Shape into long, narrow strips (about 12 inches long by 2 inches wide); or into individual servings (about 3 inches long by 2 inches wide—somewhat like elongated hamburger patties). Cook on a grill over hot coals, turning once, until brown on both sides.

   If using skewers, they should be wide (1 inch in diameter). Also, ½ teaspoon baking soda and 1 egg should be added to the meat mixture to help hold it together around the skewers. The meat mixture should be refrigerated until cold. With wet hands, press the meat firmly around each skewer so that each one is coated with meat along its entire length except for the ends. Refrigerate until ready to cook. The charcoal should be very hot, and the meat should be cooked quickly so that it will not fall off the skewers.

Leg of Lamb Kabab
(Kabab-e Ran-e Bareh)

(SERVES 8)

This recipe is actually a substitute for stuffed whole lamb, which is traditionally served for the celebration of the holy day *Aid-e Ghorban*. The aroma and taste of roasted whole baby lamb as traditionally prepared are delectable, but this dish is not too practical for the typical American kitchen. Therefore, I have devised my own version of this delicacy; although it is not as exotic as the original, it is nevertheless quite tasty.

1 leg of lamb	4 tablespoons slivered
1 cup rice	almonds
10–15 chicken livers	4 tablespoons slivered
2 large onions,	pistachios
chopped	2 tablespoons
3 tablespoons butter	candied orange
2 tablespoons tomato	peel, cut in
paste	thin strips
½ cup hot water	2–3 cloves garlic,
2 teaspoons	slivered
lemon juice	

Have your butcher bone the leg of lamb. Boil the rice in salted water for 15 minutes; drain and set aside. Cut each chicken liver in half. Sauté the onions in the butter until golden brown. Add the chicken livers and sauté until brown. Dilute the tomato paste in the hot water, and pour it over the livers. Add the lemon juice, slivered almonds and pistachios, and candied orange peel; cover and simmer gently for 15 minutes. Stir in the drained rice.

Fill the leg of lamb with this stuffing, roll up, and truss well with string. Secure the ends well so that the stuffing will not spill out. Prick the outer skin in several fatty places, and insert slivers of garlic under the skin. They may be removed just before serving. Roast the lamb in the oven at 325° F. for 3 hours, or roast over a charcoal fire on a rotating spit until done. An elegant dish, I think you will agree.

Pheasant Kabab

(Kabab-e Gharghavol)

(ALLOW 1 POUND PER PERSON)

If you are lucky enough to know someone who enjoys hunting and who can occasionally present you with a pheasant, you might be able to prepare this unusual delicacy.

½ teaspoon saffron diluted	1 tablespoon soy sauce
in ¼ cup hot water	½ teaspoon turmeric
3 tablespoons salad oil	2 tablespoons lemon juice
2 packages instant dry	¼ teaspoon paprika
beef broth	

Combine all of the ingredients above, and marinate the pheasant (whole or cut up) in it for 2 hours or longer at room temperature.

Draw the bird (whole or cut up) onto a skewer or spit, and roast it in the oven or over a charcoal fire, turning it constantly so that it will brown evenly on all sides. Baste the pheasant as it is cooking with the remaining marinade. Set the oven at 300° F., allowing 15 to 20 minutes per pound. Allow longer if cooking it over a charcoal fire. The pheasant may also be broiled.

Saffron rice, chicken in pomegranate sauce (*pollo va khoresht-e fesenjan*) and feta cheese (*panir*).

Ground beef *kababa* before grilling.

Stuffed cabbage rolls (*dolmeh*), split pea hamburgers (*shami-ye pook*), small cocktail-size *shami* and pickled beets.

Various Persian spices and ingredients: *siyah-dooneh,* whole Parsian limes, dried *fenugreek,* pomegranate syrup, powdered Persian lime, pickled eggplant, Persian currants, yellow split peas, sumac.

Persian cookies (*nan-e shirini-ye khoshk*).

Rice and spinach soup (*ash*), thickened yogurt salad (*mast-e kiseh-i*), and flat bread (*lavash*).

Baklava.

Lamb shank soup (*ab-goosht*) and flat bread (*nan*).

Lamb stew with green beans (*khorak-e loobia*) and stuffed grape leaves (*dolmeh-ye barg-e mo*).

Game Birds

(KAPK AND GIHARGHAVOL)

These partridges—buff-colored and a bit larger than our Gambel's quail—have a low, fast, sweeping flight. They are difficult to hit. But when they are flushed from thistles there is a split second when they are vulnerable. They must first rise vertically three or four feet before they can take off. It is that instant when the Bakhtiari like to shoot them. We had several from each covey; and a Bakhtiari would carefully slit the throat of each. Otherwise the meat would be unclean by Moslem standards.

(William O. Douglas, *Strange Lands and Friendly People*.)

The origin of the ritual slaughter of animals was a sacrifice, made according to Muslim law and religion, in fulfillment of a vow, or to make atonement for certain transgressions.

Not all animals need to be slaughtered by the above ritual—for example, grasshoppers or fish. But for those animals which must be slaughtered strictly according to Muslim law and tradition the ritual consists of invoking the name of God, and slitting the throat, including the trachea and the esophagus. The head is not to be severed. The flesh of an animal not killed according to the prescribed ritual is considered unclean.

Many provisions of Muslim law emphasize the necessity to spare the animal any unnecessary suffering.

Roast Partridges with Cream

(Kabk)

(SERVES 3–5)

<table>
<tr><td>3 partridges</td><td>¼ cup heavy cream</td></tr>
<tr><td>¼ cup butter</td><td>1 teaspoon salt</td></tr>
<tr><td>1 pound cooking apples</td><td>¼ teaspoon pepper</td></tr>
<tr><td>½ cup water</td><td></td></tr>
</table>

Prepare the partridges for roasting by emptying the cavities and trussing. Sear them in hot butter. Remove them from the pan. Peel the apples and slice; sauté briefly; add the water and simmer, covered, for 15 minutes. Warm the cream somewhat and then add. Add the salt and pepper.

Meanwhile, roast the partridges in the oven (300° F.) until brown (about 45 minutes). Baste occasionally with some of the cream sauce. To serve, arrange the apple slices around the partridges; either pour the rest of the sauce over the birds or serve it separately.

Braised Partridges with Cream

(Kabk)

(SERVES 2–4)

<table>
<tr><td>2 partridges</td><td>1 cup beef broth</td></tr>
<tr><td>2 teaspoons salt</td><td>(or water)</td></tr>
<tr><td>¼ teaspoon pepper</td><td>¼ cup lemon juice</td></tr>
<tr><td>4 tablespoons butter</td><td>½ cup heavy cream</td></tr>
<tr><td>8 small white onions,</td><td>1 cup mushrooms,</td></tr>
<tr><td>peeled</td><td>chopped or sliced</td></tr>
</table>

Split the partridges in half lengthwise. Sprinkle with salt and pepper. Sauté them in 2 tablespoons of the butter. Add the onions and sauté them as well. Add the beef broth (or water) and lemon juice; cover and simmer until tender (about 1½ hours). Arrange the partridges on a serving platter and keep warm in a slow oven. Add the cream to the drippings. Brown the mushrooms in another skillet in the remaining 2 tablespoons of butter, and sprinkle them over the partridges. Just before serving, pour the cream drippings over the birds.

Partridges in Tomato Sauce

(Kabk ba Sos-e Gojeh-Farangi)

(SERVES 3–5)

3 partridges	1 can chicken broth
1 large onion, sliced	½ cup butter
2 bay leaves	1 tablespoon flour
1 carrot	1 tablespoon tomato
¼ teaspoon pepper	paste
1 teaspoon of salt	

Split each partridge lengthwise in two. Place them in a pot, together with the onion, bay leaves, whole carrot, pepper, salt, and chicken broth. Cover and simmer until tender (about 30 minutes). Remove the partridges and blot dry on paper towels. Melt the butter in a large pan and sear the partridges until brown on both sides. Remove them from the pan.

With a wire whisk, stir the flour into the melted butter. Stir in the liquid in which the partridges were cooked, discarding the bay leaves and carrot. Stir in the tomato paste. Simmer gently over a low heat until thickened. Just before serving, pour the sauce over the partridges.

Stuffed Pheasant

(Gharghavol-e Shekam Por)

(SERVES 2)

Stuffing:

2 medium onions, chopped	1 teaspoon salt
2 tablespoons butter	¼ teaspoon pepper
1 partridge liver, chopped	½ teaspoon saffron (or turmeric)
¼ pound ground beef	2 tablespoons beef broth

Pheasant:

½ cup butter
1 pheasant
½ pound mushrooms,
   chopped
3 cooking apples,
   peeled and chopped

½ pound chestnuts
1 cup beef broth
1 tablespoon flour

For the stuffing, sauté the onions in the butter; add the liver and ground beef and sauté. Season with salt, pepper, and saffron (or turmeric). Add the beef broth. Mix all of these ingredients well. Stuff the inside cavity of the pheasant and truss.

Melt 4 tablespoons of the butter and sear the pheasant on all sides. Sauté the mushrooms lightly in the remaining 4 tablespoons of butter. Add the apples to the mushrooms. Peel the chestnuts and add them to the mushrooms. Sauté briefly. Add the beef broth, and pour these ingredients over and around the pheasant. Cover and simmer over a low heat until tender (about 45 minutes). Or bake the pheasant in the oven at 350° F. for 1½ hours, turning the bird occasionally. Just before serving, thicken the drippings with flour.

Pheasant with Cream

(Gharghavol ba Khameh)

(SERVES 2)

1 pheasant
1 cup lemon juice
½ cup butter
   or shortening
1 tablespoon flour

1 teaspoon turmeric
2 cups chicken broth
1 teaspoon salt
¼ teaspoon pepper
½ cup heavy cream

Cut the pheasant into 6 pieces. Marinate it for 24 hours in the lemon juice. Remove and blot dry on paper towels or a clean cloth. Melt the butter or shortening in a heavy skillet and sauté the pheasant pieces on both sides until brown. Remove the pieces; reduce the heat and stir the flour into the drippings with a wire whisk. Add the turmeric. Add the chicken broth, salt, and pepper. Return the pheasant pieces to the skillet; cover and simmer until tender (about 1 hour). Just before serving, add the cream to the warm liquid, stirring until well blended. Arrange the pheasant pieces on a platter and pour the sauce over them.

Duck à la Perse

(Ordak)

(SERVES 6–8)

2 ducklings	¼ teaspoon nutmeg
4 cloves garlic	¼ teaspoon oregano
2 tablespoons butter	1 cinnamon stick
1 medium onion, chopped or sliced	2 bay leaves
2 cans chicken broth	4 tablespoons yellow split peas
2 tablespoons lemon juice	2 carrots
1 teaspoon salt	1 tablespoon flour
¼ teaspoon pepper	

Remove the liver, giblets, and neck from the inside cavity of each duckling. Peel the cloves of garlic and place inside each cavity. Melt the butter and sauté the onions in it until brown. Sear the ducklings on all sides. Chop the livers and giblets and sauté them until brown. Pour the chicken broth over and around the ducklings, onions, giblets, and livers. Add the lemon juice, salt, pepper, nutmeg, oregano, cinnamon stick, bay leaves, yellow split peas, and whole carrots.

Bake, uncovered, in the oven (325° F.) until tender (about 2 hours), turning the birds once or twice. Remove the cinnamon stick, bay leaves, and garlic cloves. Skim off the excess fat. Thicken the drippings with flour, and serve either in a gravy boat or poured over the ducklings.

Cut-up ducklings may be used instead of whole ones.

Bread
(NAN)

There are many different Persian flat breads, all of them either round or oval, ranging in thickness from paper-thin to ½ inch thickness, all of them a culinary treat. In Iran bread is usually purchased daily, and served fresh, often warm, from the bakery. It is fascinating to watch bread being prepared in a Persian bakery, the men kneading and slapping the dough with rhythmic, dance-like motions, a great furnace blazing behind them, casting the shadows of their movements onto the walls, the fragrance of freshly baked bread permeating the air. The dough is stretched into shape on a long-handled wooden paddle, tossed into the inferno-like oven, and a few minutes later retrieved with a long prong, some *(sangak)* with hot gravels still studding the surface, to be brushed off hastily by the baker. Some are sprinkled with sesame seeds *(barbari)*, some dark *(taftoon)*, some light *(barbari)*, some sweet *(ghandi)*, some thick *(shirmal)*, some tissue-thin *(lavash)*, but all of them inviting, enticing, and delicious.

In the larger cities in Iran bread is not usually baked in the home; but in the villages, and among the tribespeople, bread baking is a daily chore. And how do villagers and migrating tribeswomen bake bread? And in what ovens? Their ovens are usually deep holes dug into the ground, the walls of which are washed smooth. Their fuel is often thistles. Their rolling-pins are often thin, smooth, straight sticks. With these bare essentials, and with a little flour and water, they are able to turn out the necessary bread for their families. The dough is rolled thin, then slapped onto the walls of the hot "oven" where it adheres for a few minutes until lightly browned. A light touch with a home-made prong pries it loose.

For those of you who would like to try baking Persian bread at home, I am including two bread recipes, one paper-thin (lavash), and one about ½-inch thick (barbari).

Persian Bread

(Nan-e Barbari)

(MAKES 2 SHEETS)

1 package dry activated yeast	1–2 tablespoons melted butter
1 cup lukewarm water	a few tablespoons sesame seeds
1 tablespoon salad oil	
4 cups flour, or enough to make a soft dough	

Dissolve the yeast in the warm water. Stir in the salad oil. Place the flour in a large mixing bowl, and stir in the dissolved yeast and oil. Mix well, stirring with a wooden spoon. Turn the dough out onto a floured board and knead until smooth and elastic (about 5 minutes). Cover with a dry cloth and allow to rise in a warm place for 2 hours.

Spread the dough onto a greased cooking sheet, flattening it with the palms of the hands, and shaping it into an oval approximately ¼ inch thick. With the forefingers of both hands press 3 or 4 ridges lengthwise over the surface of the dough. Brush the surface with melted butter. Sprinkle with sesame seeds. Allow to rest for 30 minutes. Preheat oven to 350° F. Place on the lowest rack of the oven and bake for 20–25 minutes until golden brown in color. If desired, it may be put under the broiler for about 10 seconds. Serve hot.

This bread does not keep well. It should be served while still very fresh.

Flat Bread

(Nan-e Lavash)

(MAKES ABOUT 30 THIN SHEETS)

½ *package dry activated yeast*	2 *teaspoons oil*
3 *cups lukewarm water*	½ *cup yellow corn meal*
2½ *pounds flour*	½ *cup flour*
1 *tablespoon salt*	

Dissolve the yeast in ½ cup of the lukewarm water. Place the flour, salt, and oil in a large mixing bowl. With a wooden spoon stir in the dissolved yeast and the remaining lukewarm water. Mix well, turn out onto a floured board, and knead until smooth and elastic (about 5 minutes). Cover with a dry cloth, set in a warm place, and allow to rise for 2 hours. Pinch off a piece the size of a small apple, and roll it into a ball. Repeat until all the dough has been rolled into balls. Cover with a dry cloth, and allow to rise for 30 minutes.

Preheat oven to 450° F. Mix the corn meal with the ½ cup flour in a small bowl. Roll each ball of dough in this mixture until coated. Sprinkle a little of the corn meal-flour mixture onto a bread board, and dust a little of it onto a rolling-pin. Roll out each ball of dough until paper-thin. Cover each sheet of dough with a sheet of plastic-wrap. Stack them up until the dough has all been rolled out. Place one sheet of dough on a lightly floured wooden board with a handle. With a light flick, flip the dough off the board onto the floor of the oven. Bake each sheet for 15 seconds until lightly browned. If desired, place under the broiler for 3 or 4 seconds for further crisping and browning.

This bread keeps well wrapped in plastic bags. It also freezes well.

Cookies, Pastries, and Confections
(SHIRINI)

In Iran "dessert" is almost invariably fresh fruits in season—melons, pomegranates, peaches, or other fruit. Consequently, pastries and confections are seldom served after meals, although they are frequently eaten between meals, particularly for afternoon tea. However, I have found that a number of the traditional pastries make excellent desserts (in the Western sense) and that my American guests are absolutely delighted to be served a pastry such as *baklava* at the end of a meal.

As for cookies, I know of no others that match the Persian varieties for delicacy of taste and keeping qualities. Most of them are quite easy to make.

Among the many charming Persian customs relating to food, that of *ta'arof* comes to mind particularly where cookies and pastries are concerned. It is customary in Iran for a visitor or guest to be served tea and cookies before the visit—or business discussion—can start in earnest. It is also customary for the guest to first refuse the proffered dainties, whereupon the host will insist that he partake of them. The guest might refuse politely, and the host insist, 2 or 3 times before he or she finally accepts the offered food.

When my husband and I first came to the United States many years ago, and were graciously invited to American homes, we at first would politely (we thought) refuse the food offered to us. To our absolute astonishment the food was then whisked away never again to reappear. After going hungry a few times we quickly learned to drop the Persian custom of *ta'arof!*

Baklava (with Walnuts)

(Baghlava ba Gerdoo)

(MAKES ABOUT 13 PIECES)

An elderly neighbor of mine called this pastry the "food of the Gods." It deserves this praise.

4 ounces filo dough (strudel dough)	*2 teaspoons ground cardamom*
1 cup unsalted butter (no substitutes)	*1½ cups walnuts, chopped*
½ cup sugar	*½ cup honey*

Filo dough is usually purchased frozen. It takes only a few minutes to thaw out. When working with this dough, do not unwrap all of it at the same time because it dries out very quickly.

Melt the butter. Mix together the sugar, cardamom, and chopped walnuts. Using a pastry brush, butter the bottom and sides of a 10-inch by 13-inch baking pan. Cut the dough with scissors so that it will be the same size as the pan. Place 1 layer of dough on the bottom of the pan. Brush it with melted butter. Repeat for 3 or 4 layers. Sprinkle a few spoonfuls of the walnut mixture over this. Continue building up the layers of dough brushed with melted butter and sprinkled with the walnut mixture until the pan is full. End with 2 or 3 layers of dough. Pour any remaining butter over the top.

Bake in a 325° F. oven for 1 hour, or until the dough is crisp and flaky. Remove from the oven. Cool. With a sharp knife cut into squares or diagonals approximately 2 inches by 2 inches. Pour the honey slowly over the pastry—between the cracks, around the edges, and over the top. Sprinkle a few tablespoons of chopped walnuts or pistachios over the top. Using a spatula, lift the pieces out of the baking pan and arrange them on a serving platter.

In Iran a rose-water syrup is often used in place of honey. It is prepared by boiling 3 cups of sugar with 1½ cups of water until the syrup thickens, then adding 2 tablespoons of rose water.

Baklava (with Pistachios)

(Baghlava ba Pesteh)

Follow the directions for Baklava (with Walnuts), substituting chopped or ground pistachios for the walnuts.

Baklava (with Almonds and Pistachios)

Follow the directions for Baklava (with Walnuts), substituting ¾ cup of almonds and ¾ cup of pistachios for the walnuts.

The Iranian cook will prepare this baklava by immersing the almonds in narcissus petals in a tightly covered tin, replacing the narcissus petals with fresh ones each day. After a few days the almonds will have completely absorbed the fragrance of the petals.

Persian Cookies

(Nan-e Shirini)

(MAKES ABOUT 20)

6 egg whites	orange rind (or
1 cup sugar	½ teaspoon vanilla
2 tablespoons lemon juice	extract)
1 tablespoon grated	1 cup walnuts, chopped

Beat the egg whites in a bowl until stiff. Add the sugar gradually and beat a few minutes longer. Add the lemon juice and orange rind (or vanilla extract). Add the chopped walnuts. Drop by spoonfuls onto a greased cookie sheet. Bake at 350° for 15 minutes, or until done.

In remote villages, where sugar is scarce and expensive, 1 cup of grape syrup is substituted for the sugar.

Flour Cookies

(Nan-e Ardi)

(MAKES ABOUT 20)

1 cup butter
1 cup confectioners sugar
2 cups flour
1 teaspoon ground
   cardamom

1 egg white
several tablespoons sesame
   seeds (or chopped
   walnuts)

Beat the butter until creamy. Beat in the confectioners sugar gradually. Stir in the flour and cardamom, mixing until well blended. Shape into round cookies. Brush the tops with egg white. Sprinkle the tops with sesame seeds (or chopped walnuts). Bake on a greased cookie sheet at 325° F. for about 20 minutes.

Walnut Cookies

(Nan-e Ard-e Gerdooi)

(MAKES ABOUT 30)

1 cup butter
1 tablespoon
   confectioners sugar
1 egg yolk
1 cup walnuts,
   coarsely chopped

4 cups flour
½ teaspoon vanilla
   extract (or
   cinnamon)
1 cup confectioners sugar

Beat the butter and 1 tablespoon of confectioners sugar together until creamy. Add the egg yolk and continue beating. Stir in the walnuts, flour, and vanilla extract until well blended. Shape into small balls. Place on an ungreased baking sheet and bake in a medium oven (350° F) for 30 minutes. Roll in confectioners sugar.

Tea Cookies

(Nan-e Chai)

(MAKES ABOUT 30)

1½ cups butter	2 egg whites, beaten
1½ cups confectioners	several tablespoons
sugar	slivered almonds
2 egg yolks	(optional)
4 cups flour	
½ teaspoon vanilla	
extract	

Beat the butter until creamy. Add the confectioners sugar gradually, beating until it is well blended. Add the egg yolks and beat a few minutes longer. Work in the flour gradually. Add the vanilla extract. Refrigerate for a couple of hours.

Roll out the dough between waxed paper to a thickness of ¼ inch. With floured cookie cutters, cut out cookies from the dough. Place them on greased baking sheets. Brush the tops with beaten egg whites. If desired, sprinkle the tops with slivered almonds. Bake in a 350° F. oven for 10 minutes; then reduce the heat and bake 2 minutes longer, or until the cookies are golden brown.

Persian Cookies

(Nan-e Shirini-ye Khoshk)

This is a basic recipe which can be varied by using different flavorings.

1½ cups butter	4 cups flour
1½ cups confectioners	1 egg yolk (or egg
sugar	white) (optional)
1 teaspoon vanilla	slivered almonds,
extract (or 2	ground walnuts, or
tablespoons cocoa,	ground pistachios
or 1 teaspoon	(optional)
cinnamon, or	
grated lemon or	
orange rind)	

Beat the butter and confectioners sugar together until creamy. Add the vanilla extract or other flavoring. Add the flour and blend well. Refrigerate for a couple of hours. Roll out the dough between waxed paper to the desired thickness. With floured cookie cutters, cut the dough into the shapes desired. Place on greased cookie sheets and bake at 350° F. for 10 to 12 minutes, depending upon the thickness of the cookies. If desired, the tops may be brushed with beaten egg yolk or egg white before baking, and/or sprinkled with slivered almonds, ground walnuts, or ground pistachios.

Blossom Cookies

(Nan-e Shokoofeh)

(MAKES ABOUT 30)

1½ cups butter	2 egg whites, beaten
1½ cups confectioners	(optional)
sugar	several tablespoons
4 cups flour	poppy seeds (optional)
½ teaspoon almond	
extract	

Beat the butter and confectioners sugar together until creamy. Work the flour in gradually, blending until smooth. Stir in the almond extract. Place this dough in a plastic bag and refrigerate for 24 hours. Shape the dough into small balls. If desired, these may be flattened down somewhat with the back of a fork; the tops may be brushed with beaten egg whites and sprinkled with poppy seeds. Bake on a greased cookie sheet in a 350° F. oven for 15 minutes; then lower the heat to 300° F. and bake 15 minutes longer, or until the cookies are golden brown.

Flourless Walnut Cookies

(Nan-e Gerdooi)

(MAKES ABOUT 20)

5 egg yolks	1 cup ground walnuts
3 tablespoons sugar	several tablespoons
¼ teaspoon vanilla extract	slivered or chopped
½ cup walnuts,	pistachios (optional)
chopped	

Beat the egg yolks with the sugar and vanilla extract. Add the chopped and ground walnuts. Line a cookie sheet with waxed paper. Drop the dough by spoonfuls on the lined cookie sheet. If desired, the tops may be sprinkled with slivered or chopped pistachios. Bake in a 300° F. oven for 20 minutes, or until golden brown.

Coconut Cookies

(Nan-e Nargili)

(MAKES ABOUT 30)

1 cup butter	several tablespoons
1¼ cups confectioners	slivered almonds
sugar	(or pistachios)
4 cups flour	
2 cups shredded	
unsweetened coconut	

Beat the butter and confectioners sugar together until creamy. Add the flour and blend well; then add the coconut. Roll out the dough between waxed paper to a thicknesss of ½ inch. Cut it into desired shapes with floured cookie cutters. Decorate each cookie with slivered almonds (or pistachios). Place on greased cookie sheets and bake in a 300° F. oven for 15 to 20 minutes.

Almond Cookies

(Nan-e Badami)

(MAKES ABOUT 15)

3 egg whites	several tablespoons
¾ cup confectioners	slivered almonds
sugar	(or pistachios)
1 cup blanched almonds	
½ teaspoon ground	
cardamom	

Beat the egg whites until stiff, and add the confectioners sugar gradually. Grind the blanched almonds 3 times in a meat grinder, or once in a Mouli grater. Stir the cardamom and ground almonds into the egg whites. Line a cookie sheet with waxed paper. Place spoonfuls of dough (about the size of walnuts) on the cookie sheet. Sprinkle the tops with slivered almonds (or pistachios) if desired. Bake at 350° F. for 7 minutes.

Spicy Nut-Date Balls

(Kalampeh)

(MAKES ABOUT 30)

This recipe is a specialty of Kerman.

1 package dry-active yeast	¾ cup walnuts, chopped
1 cup lukewarm water	¼ teaspoon cinnamon
4 cups flour	¼ teaspoon ground
1 cup butter	cardamom
1½ cups dates, pitted	¼ teaspoon nutmeg
	¼ teaspoon cloves

Dissolve the yeast in lukewarm water. Combine the flour with ¾ cup of the butter, working it in with your hands. Sprinkle the dissolved yeast slowly over the dough, working it in with your hands. Knead for a few minutes. Place the dough in a greased bowl and cover it with a damp cloth; set it in a warm place and allow it to rise for 2 hours.

Meanwhile, slice each date into 2 or 3 pieces. Mix together the walnuts, dates, spices and the remaining ¼ cup of butter. Shape the dough into small balls. Press a hole into each one with your thumb or forefinger, and fill it with the walnut-date mixture. Close the hole by pinching the dough together and smoothing it over. Bake on a greased cookie sheet at 300° F. for 30 minutes.

Chick-Pea Flour Cookies

(Nan-e Nokhochi)

(MAKES ABOUT 40)

Another traditional, tasty, and distinctively Persian cookie.

1 cup butter	1 teaspoon ground cardamom
1 cup confectioners sugar	2 cups chick-pea flour
1 egg yolk	

Beat the butter and confectioners sugar together until creamy. Add the egg yolk and cardamom. With your hands knead in the chick-pea flour until it is smooth. The Iranian cook will roll out the dough to ¼-inch thickness and then cut out cookies with a special, tiny, cloverleaf cookie cutter. Without this, pinch off tiny pieces of dough about the size of hazelnuts, and roll them into balls between the palms of your hands. Decorate the tops of the cookies by pricking them with the tines of a fork or by pressing the back of the tines horizontally onto the cookies. Arrange them on a lightly greased cookie sheet and bake in a slow oven (300° F.) for 30 minutes.

This dough is very "short" and needs to be well kneaded. For an even "shorter" dough, omit the egg yolk.

You can prepare chick-pea flour by putting dried chick-peas through an electric blender.

Rice Flour Cookies

(Nan-e Berenji)

(MAKES ABOUT 35)

This cookie is a very fine, traditional Persian cookie. It quite literally "melts in the mouth." As a child, I remember looking forward to festive occasions especially because I knew this cookie would be served.

2 cups butter (or 1 cup butter and 1 cup margarine)	2 tablespoons rose water (or 2 teaspoons vanilla extract)
¾ cup confectioners sugar	several tablespoons poppy seeds
2 eggs, separated	
4 cups very fine rice flour	

Beat the butter well. Add the confectioners sugar gradually, beating it in thoroughly. Add the egg yolks one at a time, beating continuously. Stir in the flour until well blended. Add the rosewater. Beat the egg whites until stiff, and fold them into the dough. Cover and refrigerate the dough for 24 hours.

Roll the dough out between waxed paper to a thickness of ¼ inch. Use a round cookie cutter to cut out the cookies. Score the tops with the tines of a fork or imprint them with a pattern. Sprinkle with poppy seeds. Bake on a greased cookie sheet in a 325° F. oven for 15 to 20 minutes. These cookies crumble very easily. They should remain white in color.

Some Persian women will make their own rice flour at home by soaking fine quality rice in cold water for 1 or 2 days, changing the water several times, and then draining the rice, pounding it to a pulp, pressing it through a sieve, drying it, and then pressing it through a still finer sieve.

Sunshine Pills
(Ghors-e Khorshid)

(MAKES ABOUT 20)

1 cup butter or shortening	1 teaspoon vanilla extract (or 1 tablespoon rose water)
¾ cup confectioners sugar	¼ cup ground almonds
1 egg, separated	¼ teaspoon ground cardamom
2 cups rice flour	

Beat the butter or shortening and ½ cup of the confectioners sugar until creamy. Add the egg yolk to the batter, beating it in well. Stir in the flour until well blended. Add the vanilla extract. Beat the egg white until stiff, and fold this into the dough. Put the dough in a plastic bag and refrigerate for 24 hours.

Pinch off small amounts of the well-chilled dough and roll them in the palms of your hands into small balls. Make a depression in each one and fill with a mixture of the remaining ¼ cup confectioners sugar, almonds, and cardamom. Close the depression and smooth over. Place on a lightly greased cookie sheet and bake in a slow oven (300° F.) for 45 minutes.

Elephant's Ears

(Goosh-e Fil)

(MAKES ABOUT 30)

A delicate, decorative, and very delicious pastry. The Iranian cook spends hours making this dough, but Americans can buy prepared filo dough.

1 cup confectioners sugar	2 ounces filo
1 teaspoon ground	(strudel dough)
cardamom	2 cups cooking oil

Mix together the confectioners sugar and cardamom and set aside. Unroll the filo dough onto a board in single or double layers. With a sharp knife cut rectangles approximately 3 inches by 4 inches. Gently gather each rectangle across the middle and form it into a bow. Heat the oil to 370° F. Drop 2 or 3 bows at a time into the hot oil. Deep-fry for about 30 seconds, or until just golden brown. Lift them from the hot oil onto paper towels. Cool. Sprinkle with the confectioners sugar and cardamom mixture.

Elephant's Ears

(Goosh-e Fil)

(MAKES ABOUT 40)

For those who are more ambitious and want to make the truly authentic dish, this is how to do it from scratch.

¼ cup milk	oil for deep frying
2 tablespoons melted	1 cup confectioners
butter	sugar
2 egg yolks, beaten	½ teaspoon ground
2 cups flour (enough for	cardamom
a smooth, elastic	
dough)	

Mix together the milk, melted butter, and beaten egg yolks. Gradually stir in the flour. When it is quite thick, turn the dough onto a floured board and knead in the remaining flour. When smooth, elastic, and non-sticky, put into a plastic bag (or wrap with a plastic sheet) and allow it to rest for 2 hours.

Turn a third of the dough out onto a floured board and roll out paper thin with a rolling pin, sprinkling the board and the rolling pin with flour to prevent the dough from sticking. With a sharp knife, cut the dough into rectangles about 3 inches by 4 inches, or into circles 2 or 3 inches in diameter. Gather each circle or rectangle across the middle—like a bow—and pinch.

Heat the oil in a deep pan to 370° F. and drop each bow into the hot oil, turning as necessary. Cook only briefly (about 30 seconds) until the bows become a delicate golden color. Lift out and drain on paper towels. When cool, sprinkle with a confectioners sugar, or with confectioners sugar flavored with cardamom. Proceed with the remaining two-thirds of the dough as above.

Chick-Pea Flour Squares

(Bereshtook Nokhochi)

(MAKES ABOUT 30)

2 cups shortening or butter	1 tablespoon ground cardamom
4 cups chick-pea flour	several tablespoons ground or slivered pistachios
2 cups confectioners sugar	(or almonds) (optional)

Melt the shortening or butter in a frying pan. Turn the heat very low and sift the chick-pea flour in gradually, stirring constantly with a wire whisk. Remove the pan from the heat, and allow it to cool slightly. Stir in the confectioners sugar and cardamom. Spread the dough out on a greased cookie sheet about ¼-inch thick, smoothing the top with a spatula. Bake in a 300° F. oven for about 1 hour. Cool, and cut into tiny squares with a sharp knife. If desired, decorate the tops with ground pistachios before baking.

You can prepare chick-pea flour by putting dried chick-peas through an electric blender.

Coconut Candies

(Loz-e Nargil)

(MAKES ABOUT 30)

1 pound sugar	Several tablespoons
1 cup water	slivered or chopped
1 pound shredded	pistachios
unsweetened coconut	

Boil the sugar and water together until it forms a thick syrup. Remove it from the heat and beat until creamy. Stir in the shredded coconut. Spread this out in a shallow pan, sprinkle with slivered or chopped pistachios, cool, and slice into diamond shapes.

Sweetfingers

(Bamieh)

(MAKES ABOUT 25)

This is a sweet, sticky confection.

4–5 tablespoons butter	3 eggs
¾ cup water	2 cups vegetable oil
1 cup flour	

Syrup:

2 cups sugar	a few drops of food coloring
½ cup water	(yellow, orange, or rose)
½ cup rose water	

Melt the butter in a saucepan. Add the water and bring to a boil. Add the flour all at once, and stir with a wire whisk until it thickens. Cool. Add the eggs one at a time, beating well after each addition. Heat the oil in a saucepan. Force the dough through a pastry tube and drope a piece the length of a finger into the hot oil. Fry until it is just golden brown. Lift it out with a slotted spoon and drain on paper towels. Repeat until all the dough has been used up. When it is cool, dip each piece in syrup until it is well coated.

To prepare the syrup, mix together the sugar, water, and rose water in a saucepan and bring it to a boil. Boil until the syrup thickens. Add the food coloring and continue boiling for another minute. Cool.

Honey-Almond Sweets

(Sohan Asali)

(MAKES ABOUT 25 PIECES)

The most famous *sohan* is made in the holy city of Qum, which is also renowned for its exquisite carpets and its shrines. This confection is seldom made at home in Iran, because it can easily be purchased. It is one of my favorite candies.

1 cup sugar	2 tablespoons hot water
2 tablespoons honey	several teaspoons
3 tablespoons butter	slivered almonds
1½ cups slivered almonds	(or pistachios)
1 tablespoon saffron	

Place the sugar, honey, and butter in a saucepan over a medium heat, stirring occasionally, until the sugar melts. Add the almonds and stir occasionally until the almonds turn golden brown. (Do not stir too much, or the butter may separate). Dissolve the saffron in hot water and add. Cool to lukewarm. Drop by spoonfuls onto a well-greased cookie sheet, and sprinkle each candy with a few slivers of almonds (or pistachios). When it is completely cool and firm, lift each piece off the cookie sheet with a knife. Store in an air-tight container.

"Window" Cookies

(Nan-e Panjarei)

(MAKES ABOUT 30)

Delicate and light as a whisper, this cookie is traditionally prepared with special "window"- (gridiron) shaped molds. They may also be prepared with French waffle irons.

⅔ cup cornstarch
1 cup flour
1 cup cold milk
4 eggs, beaten
2 teaspoons vanilla
  extract

oil for deep frying
1 cup confectioners
  sugar

Stir the cornstarch and flour into the milk to make a paste. Add the beaten eggs and vanilla extract.

Heat the oil to about 380° F. Dip the end of a mold (or French waffle iron) into the hot oil until it becomes hot, then into the dough until well coated. Working quickly, dip the coated mold into the oil briefly until the dough becomes golden brown. Shake the cookie loose from the mold. Lift it with a fork and drain on paper towels. When it is cool, sprinkle with confectioners sugar.

Almond-Filled Cakes

(Ghotab)

(MAKES ABOUT 20)

2 egg yolks
½ cup butter
½ cup yogurt
1½ cups flour

2 cups vegetable oil
1 cup confectioners
  sugar

Filling:

½ cup ground almonds
¼ cup confectioners
  sugar

1 teaspoon ground
  cardamom

Beat the egg yolks, butter, and yogurt until creamy. Stir in the flour gradually, and knead well with the hands. If the dough is sticky, add more flour. Place the dough in a plastic bag and keep it at room temperature for 2 or 3 hours.

For the filling, mix together the almonds, confectioners sugar, and ground cardamom.

Roll out the dough on a floured board to a thickness of ¼ inch. Cut it into circles with a floured cookie cutter. Place a small amount of filling in the middle of each cookie. Fold the edges up, pinch

234 / PERSIAN COOKING

together, and roll it in the palm of your hands into the shape of an egg. Heat the cooking oil in a deep saucepan to 375° F. Drop the cookies in and deep-fry until golden brown (3 to 5 minutes). Drain them on paper towels. While still warm, roll them in confectioners sugar. When they are cool, roll them again in confectioners sugar.

Cornstarch Cookies

(Masghati-e Borideh Shodeh)

(MAKES ABOUT 25)

1 cup cornstarch	2 teaspoons ground
4 cups cold water	cardamom
2 cups sugar	½ cup melted butter

Dissolve the cornstarch in the water, using a wire whisk to prevent lumps. Pour it into a saucepan and cook over a low heat, stirring constantly, until very thick. Add the sugar and cardamom and continue stirring and cooking a few minutes longer. Stir in the melted butter and cook 3 minutes longer. Spread the dough out on a cookie sheet, and slice it into diamond shapes. Dry the cookies by baking in a 300° F. oven for 30 minutes. Cool.

Persian Marzipan

(Toot)

(MAKES ABOUT 25)

2 cups ground almonds	(or 2 teaspoons
½ cup confectioners	vanilla extract)
sugar	1 cup sugar
¼ cup rose water	slivered pistachios

Mix the ground almonds and confectioners sugar. Add the rose water (or vanilla extract) and stir or beat until the mixture holds together. Shape the dough into small balls; then roll them between the palms of the hand to lengthen them somewhat in the shape of a mulberry (toot), which this confection is supposed to resemble. Roll each piece in sugar, and stick a slivered pistachio in one end (the stem). Store in a tightly covered tin. These candies will not keep for very long because they tend to dry out quickly.

The Iranian cook will enhance the aroma of her almonds by immersing them in narcissus blossoms for several days. If desired, you may place your almonds in an air-tight container with one vanilla bean.

Glazed Cherries

(Noghl-e Albaloo)

(MAKES ABOUT 60)

2 pounds sugar	1 tablespoon lemon juice
1 cup water	2 pounds sour cherries,
1 egg white	pitted

Boil the sugar and water together until the syrup will drop from a spoon in slow, thick drops. Reduce the heat. Beat the egg white until stiff. Beat the syrup until it turns white and fluffy. Add the egg white, beating constantly. Add the lemon juice. Drop the cherries into the syrup. Lift them out immediately and spread them on a tray to cool; work quickly because the cherries harden rapidly.

Syrup-Dipped Cakes

(Narenjak)

(MAKES ABOUT 20)

5 tablespoons butter	5 eggs
¾ cup water	2 cups cooking oil
1 cup flour	

Melt the butter in a saucepan. Add the water and bring it to a boil. Add the flour all at once, and stir with a wire whisk until it thickens. Cool. Add the eggs one at a time, beating well after each addition. Heat the oil in a deep saucepan to 375° F. Force the dough through a pastry tube and drop a piece the length of a finger into the hot oil. Fry it until it is lightly golden (about 30 seconds). Lift it out and drain on paper towels. When it is cool, dip each piece in caramel syrup until it is well coated.

To prepare caramel syrup:

1 cup sugar	*1 cup boiling water*

Place the sugar in a heavy saucepan over a medium heat and stir until dissolved. Add the boiling water all at once. Be careful not to burn yourself, for there will be a sudden burst of steam. Simmer over a low heat for about 20 minutes. Cool.

Strawberry Delight

(Deser-e Toot Farangi)

(MAKES ABOUT 60)

2 quarts fresh	*2 tablespoons rose water*
strawberries	*(or 2 teaspoons*
2 cups sugar	*vanilla extract)*
½ cup water	

Wash the strawberries and leave the stems on; drain on paper towels. Boil the sugar and water together. Add the rose water (or vanilla extract). Skim any foam off the surface with a slotted spoon. When the syrup reaches the soft-ball (or thread) stage, spread the strawberries out on a tray lined with waxed paper, and pour 1 teaspoon of syrup over each berry. When cool, loosen each berry with the tip of a knife. Arrange on paper doilies. When strawberries are not in season, almonds may be used and flavored with a strawberry extract.

To test for the soft-ball (or thread) stage, drop a small amount of syrup into cold water. It should form a small, soft ball. Or drop the syrup from a spoon; when it spins a thread about 3 inches long, it is ready.

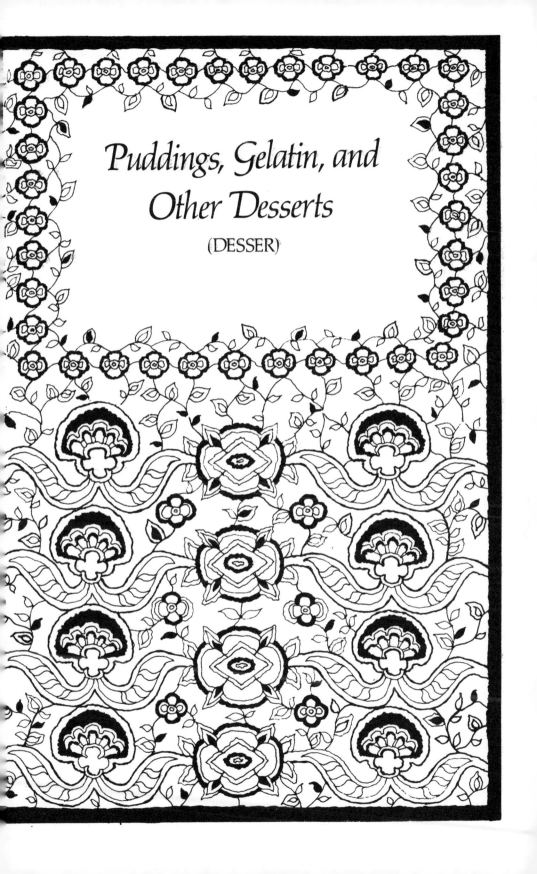

Puddings, Gelatin, and Other Desserts

(DESSER)

Layered Cherry Gelatin

(Desser-e Gele-ye Gilas)

(SERVES 10–12)

2 pounds fresh cherries,
  pitted
2 cups water
2 cups sugar
1 envelope unflavored
  gelatin
¼ cup cold water

½ cup heavy cream,
  whipped
several tablespoons
  pistachios (or other
  nuts), chopped or
  slivered

Boil the cherries in the water until tender. Put them through a food mill, catching and reserving the cherry juice in a bowl. Add the sugar to the cherry juice; pour it into a saucepan and bring it to a boil. Soften the gelatin in cold water; add it to the hot cherry juice and stir. Set the mixture in the refrigerator until it is partially firm. Pour a small amount into individual serving dishes, and cover with whipped cream. Then cover with another layer of gelatin, and top it with chopped or slivered pistachios (or other nuts). If desired, this gelatin may be molded into various attractive shapes.

This dessert can also be made with packaged, flavored gelatin.

However, for those of you who would like to make this dessert from scratch (as it is done in Iran), you will have the delicious taste of real cherries.

Strawberry Gelatin with Cream

(Gele-ye Toot Farangi)

(SERVES 8–10)

2 cups strawberries	juice of half a lemon
2 cups water	½ cup heavy cream
1 cup sugar	2–3 tablespoons
2 envelopes unflavored	confectioners sugar
gelatin	½ teaspoon vanilla
3 tablespoons	extract
cold water	

Hull, wash, and drain the strawberries. Slice or mash them. Boil the water and sugar together until it spins a thread. Sprinkle the gelatin over the cold water; then dissolve it by adding it gradually to the hot syrup. Stir the mixture over the heat for 1 minute; then set it aside to cool. Add the strawberry pulp and lemon juice. Beat the cream until it is stiff; then fold in the confectioners sugar and vanilla extract. Fold the cream into the gelatin-fruit mixture. Pour it into a wet mold. Chill in the refrigerator until firm (about 4 hours).

Marbled Cherry Gelatin

(Gele-ye Gilas)

(SERVES 10–12)

2 pounds fresh cherries, pitted	syrup dissolved in 2 cups water (or
3 envelopes unflavored gelatin	2 cups wild berry or other juice)
3–4 tablespoons cold water	1 cup heavy cream
¼ cup sweet cherry	1 teaspoon vanilla extract

Chop, grind, or crush the cherries. Sprinkle the gelatin over the cold water in a dish. Place the dish in hot water, and stir until all the gelatin crystals are dissolved. Cool slightly. Stir in the cherry juice and cherries. Refrigerate. Whip the cream until it is stiff and fold in the vanilla extract. Fold the cream into the gelatin mixture, creating a marbled effect. Pour it into a wet mold and refrigerate for at least 4 hours. To unmold, dip the mold up to the edge in hot water, place a plate over mold, invert, and shake loose.

Cantaloupe Gelatin

(Desser-e Talebi ba Gelatin)

(SERVES 4)

1–2 large apples	½ cup boiling water
10–15 cherries, pitted	1 cup heavy cream
10–15 strawberries, sliced	1 teaspoon vanilla extract
1 pound confectioners sugar	1 large cantaloupe
1 envelope unflavored gelatin	¼ cup slivered pistachios (or almonds)
2 tablespoons cold water	

Peel the apples and cut them into small pieces. Combine the apples, cherries, and strawberries. Sprinkle the fruit with confectioners sugar, reserving ¼ cup of sugar for later use. Sprinkle the gelatin over the cold water. Add the boiling water, stirring constantly until well dissolved. Cool. Pour over the fruit and refrigerate.

Meanwhile, whip the cream until stiff, and fold in the remaining sugar and the vanilla extract. Stir it into the gelatin-fruit mixture. Cut the cantaloupe in half and remove the seeds. Peel the cantaloupe, then cut a slice off the bottom of each half so that it will stand flat on a plate. Fill each half of the cantaloupe with the gelatin-fruit mixture. Chill well. Sprinkle slivered pistachios (or almonds) over the top.

This dish may also be made in a mold by pouring some of the gelatin mixture into the mold, then placing the peeled cantaloupe halves upside down in the mold. Or the cantaloupe may be cut into cubes or balls, and stirred into the fruit mixture.

Orange Delight

(Kisel-e Porteghal)

(SERVES 4)

4 tablespoons sugar	1 teaspoon vanilla
2 cups orange juice	extract
(fresh or frozen)	½ cup heavy cream
3 tablespoons	1–2 tablespoons
potato flour	confectioners sugar

In a small pan, combine the sugar and orange juice. Add the potato flour gradually, stirring constantly. Place the pan over the heat, and bring to a boil slowly. Cook until thick, stirring frequently. Cool slightly. Stir in the vanilla extract. Chill. Serve with heavy cream, whipped, and sweetened with confectioners sugar.

Fruit Medley

(Desser-e Miveh)

(SERVES 4–6)

1 cantaloupe	¼ cup seedless grapes
¼ cup strawberries,	5–6 tablespoons
sliced in half	confectioners sugar
¼ cup cherries,	1 cup heavy cream
pitted	1 teaspoon vanilla
¼ cup apricots or	extract
peaches, sliced	

Cut the cantaloupe in half and remove the seeds. With a small scoop, cut out melon balls. Mix all of the fruit together in a bowl. Sprinkle with 2 tablespoons of the confectioners sugar and refrigerate. Whip the cream until it is stiff and fold in the remaining sugar and the vanilla extract. Serve the cream separately or pile it on top of the fruit and serve.

Prune Compote

(Compot-e Aloo)

(SERVES 4)

½ pound prunes	1 teaspoon vanilla
1 cup sugar	extract
1 cinnamon stick	2 tablespoons
1 cup heavy cream	confectioners sugar

Soak the prunes in water to cover for 1 hour. Add the sugar, place on the stove, bring to a boil, then simmer gently until tender (about 20 minutes). Add the cinnamon stick. Allow to cool, pit the prunes, then chill in the refrigerator. Whip the cream; add the vanilla extract and confectioners sugar. Remove the cinnamon stick from the prunes, and fold in the whipped cream, making a marble effect. Or serve the prunes in individual bowls and top with the cream.

Apple Cobbler

(Boniyeh-ye Sib)

(SERVES 6)

6 apples	6 tablespoons shortening
5 eggs	or butter
6 tablespoons flour	1 tablespoon (or more)
1 cup sugar	confectioners sugar
1 teaspoon cinnamon	

Peel the apples and cut them into small pieces. Bring a pot of water to a boil, drop the apple pieces into the boiling water, and parboil for a few minutes. Put them through a food mill, or press them through a sieve or a potato-ricer. Beat the eggs well. Add the flour, beating constantly. Add the sugar, cinnamon, and apple pulp. Melt 3 tablespoons of the shortening or butter in a skillet; pour in the apple mixture and brown on one side. Have ready another hot skillet with the remaining 3 tablespoons of shortening or butter melted in it. Invert the apple cobbler into the second pan, and brown the other side. Just before serving, sprinkle with confectioners sugar.

Saffron Pudding
(Shol-e Zard)

(SERVES 8)

Shol-e Zard is a sweet pudding. It is traditionally prepared for the annual observance of the martyrdom of Imam Hassan and for the fortieth day of the observance of the martyrdom of Imam Hussein (Arba'ein). On these religious days *shol-e zard* is presented to one's family or friends, or to the poor and underprivileged.

In some families a newborn child is assigned a specific food as his religious offering *(nazr);* each year, on the above-mentioned holy days, the assigned food is prepared and distributed in his name to the poor and needy, thus calling down the blessings of God upon him. The specific food might be *halvah,* a sherbet, rose water, or very often *shol-e zard.*

2 cups rice	¼ cup rose water
6–8 cups water	1 tablespoon cinnamon
4 cups sugar	¼ cup slivered almonds
1 tablespoon saffron	2 tablespoons
3 tablespoons	pistachios, chopped
hot water	or slivered
¼ cup shortening	
or butter	

Rinse the rice well with cold water. Place it in a pot with water and bring it to a boil. Cook gently for 15 to 20 minutes, or until the rice is very tender. Skim the surface occasionally. Add the sugar, and continue boiling gently, stirring constantly, until the mixture thickens, like a custard. Dissolve the saffron in hot water and add. Melt the shortening or butter and stir in. Stir in the rose water. Continue stirring over a medium or low heat until quite thick.

Pour it into a baking dish, and bake for 30 minutes in a 300° F. oven. Sprinkle with cinnamon, almonds, and pistachios. Cool before serving.

Honeymoon Pudding

Kachi

(SERVES 8)

This is a sweet dessert, somewhat similar to *halvah*. It is traditionally served at wedding feasts, where symbolically it is supposed to restore the strength of the exhausted bride and groom.

2 cups shortening	2 cups water
or butter	2 tablespoons rose water
2 cups flour	1 tablespoon saffron
(or rice flour)	2 tablespoons hot water
2 cups sugar	

Melt the shortening or butter in a saucepan. Over a very low
heat, stir in the flour gradually, using a wire whisk to prevent
lumps. Boil the sugar and water together until the sugar is dissolved. Add this syrup gradually to the flour, stirring constantly.
Add the rose water. Dissolve the saffron in the hot water and add.
Cook until the mixture thickens to the consistency of a thin
pudding. It should be honey-colored. If it becomes too thick, add
a little more water. Serve warm.

Halvah

(SERVES 6–8)

During the month of Ramazan (Ramadan, in Arabic), the holy
month of fasting, many pious Muslims fast from dawn until dusk,
breaking their fast at sunset with a ritualistic meal that precedes
the main evening meal. This fast-breaking meal, known as *eftar*,
can vary, but is usually begun with ½ a cup of warm water, followed by a handful of dates. Then a soft-boiled egg is served, accompanied by hot tea, bread, jam or honey, butter, and *feta* cheese.
This is always followed by *halvah* and sometimes rice pudding. If
the family wishes to make this the main meal, rather than an in-
terim one, a thick soup (*ash*) will complete the meal.

Halvah is a sweet, honey-flavored dessert or spread.

1 cup shortening	½ cup water
or butter	¼ cup rose water
2 cups flour	1 teaspoon saffron
1 cup sugar	

Melt the shortening or butter in a saucepan, and stir in the flour gradually, using a wire whisk to prevent lumps. Stir it over a medium heat until golden in color. Remove from the heat. Boil the sugar and water together until the sugar is dissolved; then add the rose water and saffron. Stir this syrup into the browned flour, and keep on stirring until the mixture thickens. If too thin, cook it briefly over a medium heat, being careful not to let it burn. When thickened, press the halvah into a plate, smoothing the top with the back of a spoon. Cool before serving.

Halvah is traditionally served with a design imprinted on its surface. To do this, use the back of a spoon and imprint half-circles on the halvah at regular intervals—in straight lines, horizontally and vertically. To serve, slice into wedges.

May be eaten plain, or spread on bread.

Ice in Paradise
(Yakh dar Behesht)

(SERVES 5)

½ cup rice flour	1 cup cold water
¾ cup sugar	¼ cup pistachios,
1½ cups milk	chopped (or
½ cup cornstarch	slivered almonds)

Stir the rice flour and sugar into the milk and beat well until smooth. Dissolve the cornstarch in the cold water; strain it through a cheesecloth, and stir it into the rice flour mixture. Place over a low heat and cook, stirring constantly, until the mixture thickens. Pour it into individual serving dishes. Sprinkle with pistachios or almonds, and refrigerate until well chilled.

Cornstarch Pudding

(Masghati-e Kaseh-i)

(SERVES 6)

1 cup cornstarch	½ cup slivered almonds
5–6 cups cold water	½ cup butter, melted
2 cups sugar	3 tablespoons pistachios,
¼ cup rose water	grated or chopped
(or 2 tablespoons	(or slivered almonds)
ground cardamom)	

Dissolve the cornstarch in the cold water, using a wire whisk to smooth out any lumps. Pour it into a saucepan and cook over a low heat, stirring constantly until it thickens slightly. Add the sugar, rose water (or cardamom), and almonds; and continue stirring. Add the melted butter. Continue stirring a few minutes longer. Pour it into serving dishes. Sprinkle with pistachios or almonds. Chill.

Rice Pudding

(Shir Berenj)

(SERVES 6)

½ cup rice	cardamom (or
2 cups water	rose water)
3½ cups milk	½ cup cream
2 teaspoons ground	1 tablespoon cinnamon

Rinse the rice well with cold water. If possible, presoak it for 2 hours. Boil it in 2 cups of water until tender (about 25 minutes). Add the milk and simmer gently 25 minutes longer, or until the pudding thickens. Add the cardamom (or rose water), simmer another minute, and remove from the heat. Stir in the cream, and pour the pudding into a serving bowl or individual dessert dishes. Decorate by sprinkling cinnamon over the top. Chill. Serve with sugar, honey, or caramel syrup.

Rosewater Pudding
(Meshkoofi)

(SERVES 6)

1 cup cornstarch	1 teaspoon ground
8 cups water	cardamom
3 cups sugar	¼ cup rose water
½ teaspoon saffron	3 tablespoons slivered
1 cup slivered almonds	pistachios (or almonds)

Dissolve the cornstarch in the water. Strain it through a cheese-cloth, put it into a pan, and cook for 15 minutes, stirring frequently. Add the sugar, saffron, almonds, cardamom, and rose water. Cook briefly (about 5 minutes). Pour the pudding into individual dishes, sprinkle the tops with slivered pistachios (or almonds), and cool. Chill in the refrigerator before serving.

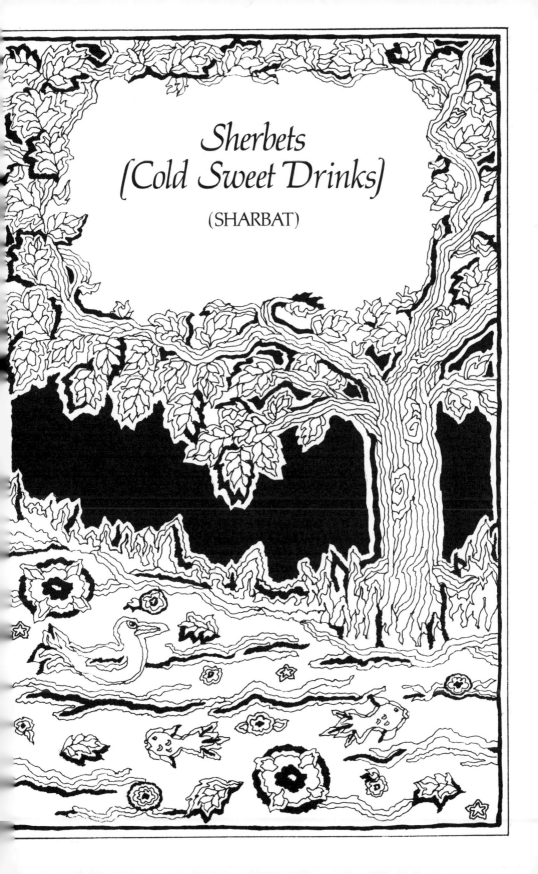

Sherbets
(Cold Sweet Drinks)

(SHARBAT)

But the sherbets were worthy of notice, from their peculiar delicacy: these were contained in immense bowls of the most costly china, and drunk by the help of spoons of the most exquisite workmanship, made of the pear-tree.

(James J. Morier, *The Adventures of Haji Baba of Isphahan.*)

The usual Drink is Sherbet, made of Water, Juice of Lemmons, and Ambergreece, which they drink out of long thin Wooden Spoons, wherewith they lade it out of their Bowls.

Sherbets are made of almost all Tart pleasing fruits as the Juice of Pomegranets, Lemmons, Citrons, Oranges, Prunella's, which are to be bought in the Markets. Thus by Diet, as well as Air, they procure not only a firmness of Constitution, but Properness and Tallness of Body, for none excell them either for Beauty or Stature.

(John Fryer, *A New Account of East India and Persia. Being Nine Years' Travels, 1672–1681.*)

On a hot day in an Iranian home, you would undoubtedly be served a cold, sweet, fruit-flavored drink called "sherbet," the very same refreshment described by travelers to Persia hundreds of years ago. The base for these drinks is a fruit syrup, usually prepared at home. When a guest arrives, a few tablespoons of the syrup are poured into a glass, water and ice are added, and a refreshing drink is ready. These syrups are made with such fruits as sour cherry, lemon, quince, or berries of various kinds. Here is a selection of sherbet syrups you will certainly enjoy.

In making syrups from acid fruits, such as sour cherries, quince, or lemon, it is best to use only an enamel or porcelain pan.

Any of these syrups can also be used as toppings or garnishes for ice cream, mousses, bavarian cream, or frozen desserts.

These syrups will keep at room temperature as long as the bottle
is sealed. Once it is opened it should be refrigerated.

    . . . while bowls of sweet and sour sherbets, with long-handled
spoons of pear-tree wood swimming in them, are placed within
their reach.

(James Baillie Fraser, Esq., Persia.)

Orange Syrup

(Sharbat-e Porteghal)

3 cups orange juice	*grated rind of 1 orange*
2 pounds sugar	

    Use only a porcelain or enamel pan. Boil the orange juice and
sugar together for 20 to 25 minutes, or until it thickens. Add
the orange rind and boil gently for a few minutes longer. Strain it
through a cheesecloth into a bowl. Cool and bottle. To serve, add
water and ice to taste.

Lemon Syrup

(Sharbat-e Ab-Limoo)

5 pounds sugar	*2 cups lemon juice*
6 cups water	*grated rind of 2 lemons*

    Use only a porcelain or enamel pan. Boil the sugar and water
together until it starts to thicken. Add the lemon juice and rind;
continue boiling until the syrup has a fairly thick consistency.
Cool and bottle. To serve, pour a few tablespoons into a glass, add
water and ice.

Quince-Lemon Syrup

(Sharbat-e- Beh-Limoo)

2 large quinces	*2 cups water*
2 pounds sugar	*¼ cup lemon juice*

Use only a porcelain or enamel pan. Peel, quarter, and core the quinces. Grate or chop them very fine. Boil the sugar and water together for 15 to 20 minutes, or until it starts to thicken. Add the quinces and boil 15 minutes longer. Add the lemon juice, simmer briefly, and strain the syrup through a cheesecloth into a bowl. Cool and bottle. To serve, pour a few tablespoons into a glass, add water and ice.

Sour Cherry Syrup

(Sharbat-e Albaloo)

This may be the queen of all the syrups—tart, yet sweet, a unique flavor.

> 2 pounds sugar
> 2–3 cups water
> 1 pound sour cherries
>
> ¼ teaspoon vanilla extract

Use only a porcelain or enamel pan. Boil the sugar and water together for 15 to 20 minutes. Add the sour cherries and boil gently another 20 to 30 minutes, or until the syrup thickens. Strain the liquid into a bowl through a cheesecloth, squeezing the cherries to extract all of the liquid. Add the vanilla extract. Bottle. To serve, add water and ice.

Dried sour cherries may be used instead of fresh ones. They should be soaked in cold water 6 hours or longer. Please consult the Shopper's Guide for addresses of stores where dried sour cherries may be purchased.

Crab Apple Syrup

(Sharbat-e Zoghal-Akhteh)

> 3 pounds sugar
> 3 cups water
> 1½ pounds crab apples
>
> ½ teaspoon vanilla extract

Boil the sugar and water together for 15 or 20 minutes, or until it starts to thicken. Add the crab apples and simmer gently until the syrup thickens. Add the vanilla extract, simmer briefly, and set aside to cool. Strain it through a cheesecloth into a bowl. Cool and bottle. To serve, add water and ice.

Strawberry Syrup

(Sharbat-e Toot-Farangi)

3 pounds sugar	½ teaspoon vanilla
3 cups water	extract
1½ pounds strawberries	

Boil the sugar and water together for 15 to 20 minutes, until it starts to thicken. Add the strawberries and boil gently until the syrup thickens. Add the vanilla extract. Strain it through a cheesecloth into a bowl. Cool and pour it into a bottle. To serve, add water and ice.

This syrup may be prepared from frozen, sliced strawberries. Use 2 packages of frozen strawberries, 2 cups of water, and 4 cups of sugar. Proceed as indicated above.

Raspberry Syrup

(Sharbat-e Tameshk)

Follow the directions for Strawberry Syrup.

A delicious syrup may also be made by combining strawberries and raspberries, either fresh or frozen.

Pickles
(TORSHI)

The Iranian housewife takes pride in the quality and variety of pickles she keeps in her pantry. Many of the following recipes are uniquely Persian and extremely palatable. In all my years of searching for the ingredients required for Persian cooking, there are only two that I have not been able to identify correctly in English. Both of them are used in making certain pickles; one of them is *golpar*, incorrectly identified in various Persian-English dictionaries as marjoram or oregano. It is neither. I have sniffed my way through countless spice jars in the United States, but without finding it. The second one is *siyah-daneh*, a tiny, pungent black seed, incorrectly identified in many dictionaries as fennel seed, which it is not. I am, therefore, using the Persian name for these two ingredients. They can be purchased by mail from an import store in New York whose address is listed in the Shopper's Guide.

In all the following recipes, if the jars are sterilized and sealed they can be kept at room temperature until opened. From then on they should be refrigerated. The contents will keep almost indefinitely.

Mixed Pickles

(Torshi-ye Makhloot)

1 small head cauliflower	2 quarts vinegar
2 pounds carrots	1 cup water
1 pound green peppers	1 pound small white
1 pound turnips	onions
1 cup green beans	1 pound cherry tomatoes
2 stalks celery	(preferably on the green
2 tablespoons coarse salt	side)

Trim the cauliflower and separate it into flowerets. Peel and slice the carrots. Seed the green peppers; and chop, slice, or shred them. Peel the turnips, trim, and dice. String the beans and cut them into ¼-inch pieces. Chop the celery. Sprinkle all the vegetables except the cauliflower and beans with coarse salt.

Boil the cauliflower and the beans in salted water for 5 minutes. Drain well. Pour the vinegar and water into a pot and and bring to a boil. Combine all the vegetables and put them into sterilized jars. Cover them with the vinegar. Seal the jars. Allow to stand for 15 days before using.

Pickled Italian Eggplant

(Torshi-ye Bademjan-e Riz)

2 green peppers	8 cloves garlic
2 stalks celery	10 small Italian
2 cups vinegar	eggplants
2 tablespoons coarse salt	1 teaspoon pepper

Two days ahead of time, seed the green peppers and shred or chop them. Chop the celery. Boil the vinegar. Add the coarse salt, garlic, celery, and green peppers; set aside.

Stem the eggplants. Boil them whole in salted water until just tender (10–12 minutes). Drain well; spread them out on a clean cloth and allow to dry overnight. Place the eggplants in sterilized jars. Add all the other ingredients and seal.

Pickled Eggplant I

(Torshi-ye Bademjan)

Iranians pickle eggplants by three methods, and each one is delicious. You will have to let your personal taste be your guide.

1 large eggplant	1 teaspoon siyah daneh
1 teaspoon golpar	¼ teaspoon pepper
6 cloves garlic, grated	2 teaspoons coarse salt
1 teaspoon mint flakes	2 cups vinegar

Top the eggplant, slit it down one side, and drop it into a pot of boiling salted water. Boil it until tender (12–15 minutes). Drain it well in a colander, placing a china plate and a heavy weight over the eggplant to ensure maximum drainage. Sprinkle the seasonings into the eggplant cavity, place it in a jar, pour over the vinegar, and cover the jar with a tight lid. In a few days pour out the vinegar and replace it with fresh vinegar. Refrigerate. It will keep almost indefinitely.

Pickled Eggplant II

(Liteh-ye Bademjan)

This is my favorite method of preparing pickled eggplant.

2 large eggplants	1 teaspoon fresh or
vinegar	dried coriander
¼ teaspoon pepper	(Chinese parsley),
2 teaspoon mint flakes	chopped
2 teaspoons fresh or	2 teaspoons siyah-daneh
dried parsley,	2 teaspoons golpar
chopped	1 teaspoon ground
8 cloves garlic, grated	coriander
1 teaspoon fresh or	1 teaspoon summer
dried dill weed,	savory
chopped	2 teaspoons salt
1 teaspoon fresh or	
dried tarragon,	
chopped	

Peel the eggplants and cut into large pieces. Place in a pot and add just enough vinegar to cover. Bring to a boil, and cook until tender (about 12 minutes). Drain into a colander, and mash the eggplant. Add all of the seasonings. Stir in enough vinegar so that the eggplant will have the consistency of mashed potatoes (about 1 to 1½ cups). Pour into jars. Refrigerate.

Pickled Eggplant III

(Torshi-ye Bademjan)

2 large eggplants	coriander, chopped
2 tablespoons coarse salt	garlic, grated
¼ teaspoon pepper	mint, chopped
1 teaspoon turmeric	celery leaves, chopped
2 teaspoons fresh:	parsley, chopped
spinach, chopped	fenugreek, chopped
leeks, chopped	basil, chopped
dill weed, chopped	beet leaves, chopped
tarragon, chopped	2 cups vinegar
summer savory, chopped	

Bake the eggplants in a hot oven, or roast them over a charcoal fire until well browned on the outside and tender on the inside. Cool slightly and peel. Mash well and add the seasonings. Place in jars, stir in the vinegar, and seal.

Pickled Cherry Tomatoes

(Torshi-ye Gojeh Farangi)

1 pound cherry tomatoes	vinegar
	dill seeds (optional)
½ ounce coarse salt	garlic cloves (optional)

The cherry tomatoes should be firm and fresh. Stem them and place them in jars. Sprinkle with salt. Cover with vinegar and seal. Traditionally no seasonings are used with pickled tomatoes, but dill seeds, garlic cloves, or other seasonings may be added if desired.

Pickled Cabbage I

(Torshi-ye Kalam)

1 head cabbage	2–3 tablespoons coarse salt
1 stalk celery	vinegar
10 sprigs fresh parsley	several peppercorns
a few sprigs mint, or	several cloves of garlic
2 teaspoons dried	
mint flakes	

Shred the cabbage, discarding the coarse stem. Chop the celery, parsley, and mint. Mix together all of these ingredients, place in jars, and sprinkle with coarse salt. Cover with vinegar. Add peppercorns and garlic cloves to each jar. Seal.

Pickled Cabbage II

(Torshi-ye Kalam)

1 large head cabbage	2 red peppers
3 tablespoons coarse salt	vinegar
2 pounds fresh peas	

Wash and chop the cabbage coarsely, discarding the stem. Sprinkle well with salt. Allow to stand for 24 hours. Pour the cabbage and its juice into sterilized jars. Shell the peas, boil in salted water for 5 minutes, drain, and add to the cabbage. Chop the red peppers and add. Cover with vinegar, and seal the jars.

Pickled Cauliflower

(Torshi-ye Kalam-Gol)

Follow the directions for Pickled Cabbage, using a cauliflower that has been separated into flowerets. Proceed as directed.

Seven-Tone Pickles I

(Torshi-ye Hafte-Bijar)

This is a marvelous pickle of fresh herbs. If you have an herb garden you will have no difficulty obtaining the fresh ingredients.

Equal amounts of fresh:	basil
spinach	beet leaves
leeks	
dill weed	½ ounce coarse salt
tarragon	fresh red peppers
summer savory	peppercorns
coriander	dried oregano
mint	dried marjoram
parsley	several cloves garlic
celery	black pepper
fenugreek	vinegar

Wash the herbs and spread them out on a towel to dry. Chop them very fine, mix, and pour them into jars. Sprinkle with coarse salt. To each jar, add half a red pepper, several peppercorns, some oregano and marjoram, 2 or 3 cloves of garlic, and black pepper. Cover with vinegar and seal.

Seven-Tone Pickles II

(Torshi-ye Haft-e Bijar)

a few sprigs of fresh coriander, or ½ teaspoon dried coriander	a few celery leaves, chopped
	10 small Italian eggplants
a few sprigs fresh mint, chopped, or 2 teaspoons dried mint flakes	1 pound tiny pickling cucumbers
	1 cup small, new potatoes
a few sprigs fresh tarragon, chopped, or 2 teaspoons dried tarragon	1 green pepper, chopped
	1 teaspoon turmeric
	1 teaspoon golpar
a few sprigs fresh basil, chopped, or 2 teaspoons dried basil	6–8 cloves garlic
	1 tablespoon coarse salt
	1 quart vinegar

Wash the herbs, drain, and spread them out on a towel to dry thoroughly. Remove the stems from the eggplants, and boil them in salted water until tender (12–15 minutes). Place them in a sieve or colander, cover with a china plate and heavy weight to drain off all the liquid. When thoroughly dry, cut the eggplants into bite-size pieces. Place them in a bowl. Chop the fresh herbs and sprinkle them over the eggplant pieces. Add all the other ingredients (except the vinegar) and mix well. Place in sterilized jars, cover with vinegar, and seal.

Pickled Turnips

(Torshi-ye Shalgham)

2 pounds turnips
4 cups vinegar
2 teaspoons dried
   mint flakes
4 cloves garlic

Boil the turnips until tender. Drain, and boil in vinegar for a few minutes. Add the remaining ingredients, pour into sterilized jars, and seal.

Pickled Beets

(Torshi-ye Laboo)

Follow the directions for Pickled Turnips, but substitute beets.

Dill Pickles

(Torshi-ye Khiar Shoor)

4 pounds small
   cucumbers
½ cup coarse salt
several cloves garlic
fresh red peppers
fresh or dried tarragon

fresh or dried mint
whole cloves
fresh dill
1 quart water
1 teaspoon salt
2 quarts vinegar

Wash and dry the cucumbers; place them in a large bowl, sprinkle them with coarse salt, and set them aside for several hours. Wash, drain, and dry them well. Place them in jars. To each jar add 1 clove garlic, half a red pepper, some tarragon, mint, several cloves, and 1 sprig of dill.

Bring the water, salt, and vinegar to a boil. Cover the cucumbers with this liquid, and seal the jars.

Pickled Cucumbers (Sour)

(Khiar Torshi)

2 pounds small cucumbers	a few sprigs of fresh parsley, or
¼ cup coarse salt	2 teaspoons dried parsley
8 cloves garlic	1 teaspoon fresh or dried coriander
a few sprigs fresh tarragon, or 2 teaspoons dried tarragon	several peppercorns 8 cups vinegar

Wash and dry the cucumbers. Pack tightly in jars. Sprinkle with coarse salt. Add garlic, herbs, and spices to each jar. Boil the vinegar for a few minutes, and pour it over the cucumbers. Cool and seal.

Pickled Shallots

(Torshi-ye Moosir)

fresh shallots	white vinegar
¼ cup coarse salt	

Peel the thin outer skin of the shallots, remove the stems, and slice thin. Soak in cold water for 48 hours, changing the water 2 or 3 times a day. Drain in a colander. Spread them out on a clean cloth and allow them to dry for 24 hours. Place them in jars, sprinkle with coarse salt, cover with vinegar, and seal.

Pickled Onions

(Torshi-ye Piaz)

2 *whole heads of garlic*	1 *pound small white*
3 *tablespoons dried*	*onions*
mint flakes, or a few	*coarse salt*
sprigs fresh mint	*vinegar*

Peel the garlic cloves and grate them or put them through a meat grinder together with the mint. Soak the onions in water for 2 hours. Drain them well, peel, and spread them out on a clean dish towel to dry thoroughly. Place a layer of onions in a sterilized jar, sprinkle them with coarse salt, mint, and garlic. Continue alternating layers. Cover with vinegar, and seal the jar.

Pickled Mixed Vegetables

(Torshi-ye Sabzi-ye Makhloot)

1 *small eggplant*	¼ *pound green peppers*
¼ *pound new potatoes*	3–4 *shallots*
¼ *pound green beans*	1 *stalk celery*
1 *small head*	¼ *teaspoon each,*
cauliflower	*fresh or dried:*
several tablespoons	*mint flakes*
coarse salt	*tarragon*
¼ *cup vinegar*	*parsley*
½ *pound carrots*	*coriander*
½ *pound small*	*basil*
cucumbers	*vinegar*

Bake the eggplant in a hot oven (400° F.) until it can be peeled easily and is tender inside. Cool it long enough so that it can be handled without burning your hands. Peel it and place the pulp in a colander; cover it with a plate and heavy weight, and allow it to drain for 12 hours. Peel the potatoes and boil them in salted water until tender. Drain, and dice or slice. Cut the beans into ¼-inch pieces and boil in salted water for 5 minutes. Separate the cauliflower into flowerets and boil them in salted water for 5 minutes.

Place the eggplant in a bowl. Sprinkle with coarse salt, add the vinegar, and mash to a pulp. Peel the carrots and cucumbers, seed the green peppers, and chop these vegetables very fine. Chop the shallots and celery. Combine all the vegetables, add the seasonings, stir in enough vinegar to make a thick, pulpy mixture. Spoon into jars and seal.

Pickled Mixed Fruits and Vegetables

(Torshi-ye Miveh-ye Makhloot)

½ pound fresh lemon and/or orange peel	1 teaspoon pepper
1 pound fresh apricots	1 teaspoon dry mustard
1 pound fresh peaches	1 teaspoon golpar
1 pound fresh pears	3 teaspoons powdered Persian lime
1 pound firm fresh apples	several coriander seeds, or 1 teaspoon powdered coriander
1 fresh quince	1 teaspoon pennyroyal
vinegar	1 teaspoon ginger
½ pound small new potatoes	1 teaspoon galangal
½ pound carrots	1 teaspoon tamarind
½ pound green beans	1 teaspoon anise
half head of cauliflower	1 teaspoon cinnamon
1 pound small cucumbers	1 teaspoon siyah-daneh
coarse salt	1 teaspoon cumin
⅓ pound confectioners sugar	1–2 fresh red peppers
1 teaspoon saffron	several cloves garlic, grated (optional)
1 teaspoon ground cardamom	

Boil the lemon and/or orange peel for a few minutes. Discard the water. Using fresh water, boil again, and then discard the water. Soak in fresh cold water for 24 hours, changing the water 2 or 3 times. Drain and spread the peel out on a clean towel to dry.

Peel the apricots, peaches, pears, apples, and quince; remove the stems, cores, and seeds; then cut the fruit into pieces. Sprinkle them with coarse salt, place them in a pot, cover with vinegar. Boil until the fruit is tender. Put the fruit and lemon and/or orange peel through a meat grinder or food mill. Stir in enough boiled vinegar to make a thin, pulpy mixture.

Peel the potatoes and carrots, and chop or dice. String the beans and cut into ¼-inch pieces. Separate the cauliflower into flowerlets. Chop or dice the cucumbers and red peppers. Place these vegetables in a bowl and sprinkle with coarse salt. Allow to stand for 24 hours. Drain off the liquid, and spread the carrots and cucumbers out on a clean towel to dry. Boil the potatoes, green beans, and cauliflower in salted water for 5 minutes. Drain, and spread out to dry.

Dried apricots and peaches may be used. These should be soaked in water for 2 hours.

Mix together the fruit pulp, the vegetables, and all the spices and seasonings. Stir in a little more boiled vinegar to achieve the consistency of mashed potatoes. Pour into sterilized jars and seal.

If desired, grated garlic may be added to this pickle.

Pickled Mixed Fruits

(Torshi-ye Miveh)

1 pound each of the following:	prunes
watermelon	vinegar
grapes	1 teaspoon nutmeg
pears	(or more)
apples	1 teaspoon cinnamon
figs	(or more)
apricots	coarse salt
peaches	

Use fresh fruit if possible; otherwise, dried fruit may be substituted. Stem and seed the fruit, cut into pieces, and boil until soft and mushy. Press through a sieve, or food mill. Boil the vinegar and stir in just enough to make a thin mixture. Stir in the seasonings, pour the fruit into sterilized jars, and seal.

Pickled Dates

(Torshi-ye Khorma)

1 cup sumac	¼ teaspoon each:
1 cup dried tamarind	cinnamon
3 cups cold water	nutmeg
½ cup lemon juice	salt
1 pound pitted dates	pepper
1 whole head garlic	

Soak the sumac and tamarind separately, each in 1½ cups cold water, for 24 hours. Strain through a cheesecloth, reserving the liquid. Mix the liquid with the lemon juice and boil for a few minutes. Put the dates through a meat grinder and add them to the boiling liquid. Peel the garlic cloves, grind or press them, and add. Boil for 2 minutes. Add the seasonings, pour the date mixture into sterilized jars, and seal.

Pickled Lemon Rind

(Torshi-ye Poost-e Limoo Torsh)

1 cup fresh lemon rind	½ teaspoon each:
coarse salt	leaf coriander
3 cups vinegar	golpar
1 teaspoon mint flakes	black pepper

Boil the lemon rind for a few minutes. Pour off the water. Repeat, using fresh water. Soak the rind for 24 hours in cold water. Drain, sprinkle with coarse salt, and spread the rind out on a clean cloth for 2 or 3 days to dry. Boil the vinegar for a few minutes. Place the lemon rind in jars, and cover with the boiled vinegar. Add the mint flakes, leaf coriander, *golpar*, and black pepper to each jar. Stir and seal.

Pickled Orange Rind

(Torshi-ye Poost-e Porteghal)

1 cup fresh orange rind	dash of salt
3 cups vinegar	dash of pepper

Boil the orange rind in enough water to cover. Pour off the water. Repeat. Soak the rind in cold water for 24 hours, changing the water 3 or 4 times until every trace of bitterness has been removed. Spread the orange rind out to dry for several days. When quite dry, put the rind through a meat grinder or food mill. Cover with vinegar, and boil until slightly thick and syrupy. Add salt and pepper, pour into sterilized jars, and seal.

Pickled Grapes

(Torshi-ye Angoor)

This is a specialty of Ghazvin.

3 pounds firm white grapes	4 cups white vinegar 1 tablespoon coarse salt

Stem the grapes and discard any soft ones. Wash the grapes and drain. Set them aside to dry. Boil the vinegar and salt together for a few minutes. Cool. Place the grapes in sterilized jars, pour the vinegar over them, and seal.

Pickled Quince

(Torshi-ye Beh)

2 large quinces	several coriander seeds,
2 cups water	or 1 teaspoon
½ cup sugar	powdered coriander
4 cups vinegar	several cloves garlic,
1 teaspoon powdered ginger	grated
	1 teaspoon tamarind
	½ teaspoon paprika

Cut the quinces into small pieces, removing the cores and seeds. Drop the pieces into boiling water, add the sugar, and boil until thick and syrupy. Add all the remaining ingredients, boil a few minutes longer, pour into sterilized jars, and seal.

Pickled Dried Peaches I

(Torshi-ye Barg-e Holoo)

2 pounds dried peaches	1 teaspoon turmeric
4 cups vinegar	1 teaspoon dry mustard
1 teaspoon cinnamon	½ teaspoon paprika
1 teaspoon golpar	1 teaspoon siyah-daneh

Soak the dried peaches overnight in water. Drain. Add the vinegar and cook for a few minutes. Stir in the spices. Pour the mixture into sterilized jars, and seal.

Pickled Dried Peaches II

(Torshi-ye Barg-e Holoo)

2 cups dried peaches	several cloves garlic, grated
4 cups vinegar	
1 cup sugar	1 teaspoon tamarind
1 teaspoon ginger	½ teaspoon paprika
1 teaspoon powdered coriander, or several coriander seeds	

Soak the dried peaches in the vinegar for 2 or 3 days. Add the sugar and seasonings, bring to a boil, and cook for 1 hour. Pour the mixture into sterilized jars, and seal.

Pickled Dried Mangoes

(Torshi-ye Anbeh)

2 pounds dried mangoes	cardamom
2½ cups lemon juice	cinnamon
1 cup tomato paste	confectioners sugar
½ teaspoon each:	coarse salt
saffron	2½ cups vinegar

Soak the dried mangoes in lemon juice overnight. Mix in the tomato paste and the seasonings. Stir in the vinegar, and cook for 30 minutes. Pour the mixture into sterilized jars, and seal. This pickle should be of a fairly thick consistency.

Pickled Cherries

(Torshi-ye Gilas)

1 pound firm, large cherries	coarse salt
vinegar	several tarragon leaves
	several peppercorns

Stem the cherries, and discard any that are overripe or soft. Boil the vinegar and coarse salt together for a few minutes. Cool. Place the cherries in sterilized jars. Pour the vinegar and salt over them. Add some tarragon and peppercorns to each jar. Three days later pour off the vinegar. Add fresh vinegar that has been boiled with salt and cooled; seal the jars. Allow the cherries to stand for at least 15 days before using.

Shopper's Guide

After a considerable amount of correspondence with specialty food shops all over the United States, I have succeeded in locating several that carry many of the hard-to-find items necessary for Persian cuisine that do not ordinarily appear on the shelves of the American supermarket. All of the shops listed do a mail-order business. In order to facilitate the shopper's mail-order purchases I requested lists from the shops of the specific items that they do ordinarily carry, and hope this list will be of assistance to the shopper. The complete addresses are listed on pp. 277–79.

ITEM	AVAILABLE AT:
Coriander leaf *(geshniz)*	Victoria Importing Co., Conn. Skenderis Greek Imports, D.C. Columbus Food Market, Ill. Cardullo's Gourmet Shop, Mass. Imported Foods, Inc., Md. Model Food Importers & Distributors, Maine Karnig Tashjian, N.Y. Trinacria Import Co., N.Y.
Cherries, dried sour *(albaloo khoshk)*	Bezjian's Grocery, Calif. Haig's Delicacies, Calif. Model Food Importers & Distributors, Maine Aphrodisia, N.Y. Karnig Tashjian, N.Y. Trinacria Import Co., N.Y. Near East Market, R.I.

ITEM	AVAILABLE AT:
Fenugreek leaf (*shambalileh*)	Bezjian's Grocery, Calif. Haig's Delicacies, Calif. Victoria Importing Co., Conn. Skenderis Greek Imports, D.C. Columbus Food Market, Ill. Cardullo's Gourmet Shop, Mass. Imported Foods, Inc., Md. Model Food Importers & Distributors, Maine Aphrodisia, N.Y. Kalustyan Orient Export Trading Corp., N.Y. Karnig Tashjian, N.Y.
Fava beans, dried green (*baghali sabz*)	Victoria Importing Co., Conn. Skenderis Greek Imports, D.C. Columbus Food Market, Ill. Model Food Importers & Distributors, Maine Trinacria Import Co., N.Y.
Fava beans, yellow dried (*baghali zard*)	Bezjian's Grocery, Calif. Haig's Delicacies, Calif. Victoria Importing Co., Conn. Skenderis Greek Imports, D.C. Angel's Market, Fla. Columbus Food Market, Ill. Imported Foods, Inc., Md. Model Food Importers & Distributors, Maine Sahadi Importing Co., N.Y. Trinacria Import Co., N.Y. Near East Market, R.I.
Persian currants (*zereshk*)	Skenderis Greek Imports, D.C. Model Food Importers & Distributors, Maine Trinacria Import Co., N.Y. Near East Market, Rhode Island
Persian lime (*limoo amani*)	Bezjian's Grocery, Calif. Haig's Delicacies, Calif. Model Food Importers & Distributors, Maine Kalustyan Orient Export Trading Corp., N.Y. Karnig Tashjian, N.Y.
Persian oregano (*golpar*)	Bezjian's Grocery, Calif. Model Food Importers & Distributors, Maine

ITEM   AVAILABLE AT:

Persian rice   Bezjian's Grocery, Calif.
(domsiah)   Haig's Delicacies, Calif.
                              Columbus Food Market, Ill.
                              Model Food Importers & Distributors, Maine
                              Kalustyan Orient Export Trading Corp., N.Y.
                              Karnig Tashjian, N.Y.
                              Trinacria Import Co., N.Y.

Pistachios, shelled   Bezjian's Grocery, Calif.
(pesteh)   Haig's Delicacies, Calif.
                              Dimyan's Market, Conn.
                              Victoria Importing Co., Conn.
                              Skenderis Greek Imports, D.C.
                              Near East Bakery, Fla.
                              Columbus Food Market, Ill.
                              Imported Foods, Inc., Md.
                              Ellis Bakery, Ohio
                              Model Food Importers & Distributors, Maine
                              Sahadi Importing Co., N.Y.
                              Sammy's Imported & Domestic Foods, N.Y.
                              Trinacria Import Co., N.Y.
                              Near East Market, R.I.

Pomegranate sirup   Bezjian's Grocery, Calif.
(rob-e anar)   Haig's Delicacies, Calif.
                              Dimyan's Market, Conn.
                              Skenderis Imports, D.C.
                              Near East Bakery, Fla.
                              Columbus Food Market, Ill.
                              Cardullo's Gourmet Shop, Mass.
                              Imported Foods, Inc., Md.
                              Ellis Bakery, Ohio
                              Model Food Importers & Distributors, Maine
                              Kalustyan Orient Export Trading Corp., N.Y.
                              Karnig Tashjian, N.Y.
                              Trinacria Import Co., N.Y.
                              Near East Market, R.I.

Rose water   Bezjian's Grocery, Calif.
(golab)   Haig's Delicacies, Calif.
                              Dimyan's Market, Conn.
                              Skenderis Greek Imports, D.C.
                              Near East Bakery, Fla.

ITEM	AVAILABLE AT:
	Angel's Market, Fla.
	Columbus Food Market, Ill.
	Cardullo's Gourmet Shop, Mass.
	Imported Foods, Inc., Md.
	Ellis Bakery, Ohio
	Model Food Importers & Distributors, Maine
	Sahadi Importing Co., N.Y.
	Sammy's Imported & Domestic Foods, N.Y.
	Aphrodisia, N.Y.
	Kalustyan Orient Express Trading Corp., N.Y.
	Trinacria Import Co., N.Y.
	Near East Market, R.I.
Saffron *(zaafaron)*	Haig's Delicacies, Calif.
	Dimyan's Market, Conn.
	Victoria Importing Co., Inc., Conn.
	Skenderis Greek Imports, D.C.
	Near East Bakery, Fla.
	Columbus Food Market, Ill.
	Cardullo's Gourmet Shop, Mass.
	Imported Foods, Inc., Md.
	Ellis Bakery, Ohio
	Model Food Importers & Distributors, Maine
	Sahadi Importing Co., N.Y.
	Sammy's Imported & Domestic Foods, N.Y.
	Aphrodisia, N.Y.
	Kalustyan Orient Export Trading Corp., N.Y.
	Trinacria Import Co., N.Y.
	Near East Market, R.I.
Siyah-daneh (a pungent black seed used in pickling)	Bezjian's Grocery, Inc., Calif.
	Model Food Importers & Distributors, Maine
Sour-grape juice *(ab ghooreh)*	Bezjian's Grocery, Calif.
	Skenderis Greek Imports, D.C.
	Columbus Food Market, Ill.
	Model Food Importers & Distributors, Maine
Split peas, yellow *(lapeh)*	Haig's Delicacies, Calif.
	Model Food Importers & Distributors, Maine
	Karnig Tashjian Corp., N.Y.
	Trinacria Import Co., N.Y.

ITEM   AVAILABLE AT:

Sumac   Bezjian's Grocery, Calif.
(somagh)   Haig's Delicacies, Calif.
                               Dimyan's Market, Conn.
                               Skenderis Greek Imports, D.C.
                               Near East Bakery, Fla.
                               Columbus Food Market, Ill.
                               Imported Foods, Inc., Md.
                               Ellis Bakery, Ohio
                               Model Food Importers & Distributors, Maine
                               Sahadi Importing Co., N.Y.
                               Aphrodisia, N.Y.
                               Near East Market, R.I.

Whey, dried   Bezjian's Grocery, Calif.
(kashk)   Skenderis Greek Imports, D.C.
                               Near East Bakery, Fla.
                               Columbus Food Market, Ill.
                               Ellis Bakery, Ohio
                               Model Food Importers & Distributors, Maine
                               Near East Market, R.I.

Addresses of Specialty Food Shops Doing Mail Order Business

CALIFORNIA

Bezjian's Grocery
4725 Santa Monica Blvd.
Hollywood, California 90029

Haig's Delicacies
642 Clement Street
San Francisco, California 94118

CONNECTICUT

Dimyan's Market
116 Elm St.
Danbury, Connecticut

Victoria Importing Co.
Route #10-958 Queen St.
Southington, Connecticut

DISTRICT OF COLUMBIA

Skenderis Greek Imports
1612 Twentieth Street, N. W.
Washington, D. C. 20009

FLORIDA

Near East Bakery
878 S.W. Eighth St.
Miami, Florida 33130

Angel's Market
455 Athens Street
Tarpon Springs, Florida 33589

ILLINOIS

Columbus Food Market
1651 and Road
Des Plaines, Illinois 60030

MASSACHUSETTS

Cardullo's Gourmet Shop
Six Brattle Street
Cambridge, Massachusetts 02138

MARYLAND

Imported Foods, Inc.
409 West Lexington Street
Baltimore, Maryland 21201

MAINE

Model Food Importers and Distributors
113–115 Middle Street
Portland, Maine 04111

NEW YORK

Sahadi Importing Co.
187–189 Atlantic Avenue
Brooklyn, New York 11201

Sammy's Imported & Domestic Foods
1348–54 Hertel Avenue
Buffalo, N. Y. 14216

Aphrodisia
28 Carmine Street
New York, N. Y. 10014

Kalustyan Orient Export Trading Corporation
123 Lexington Avenue
New York, N. Y. 10016

Karnig Tashjian Corporation
380 Third Avenue
New York, N. Y. 10016

Trinacria Import Co.
415 Third Avenue
New York, N.Y. 10016

RHODE ISLAND

Near East Market
602 Reservoir Avenue
Cranston, Rhode Island 02910

Glossary of Persian-English Foods

Ab ghooreh — sour grape juice
Ab goosht — a thick soup with a meat base
Ab limoo — lemon juice
Adas — lentils
Albaloo — sour cherries
Aloo — a small, yellow prune
Anar — pomegranate
Angoor — grapes
Anjir — figs
Ard — flour
Ash — a thick soup, usually with a vegetable base

Babooneh — camomile
Badam —almond
Badban-e roomi — anise (sweet cumin)
Bad-e ranjbooyeh — balm leaf
Bademjan — eggplant
Baghali — fava beans
Baklava —a sweet pastry made with filo dough, nuts, butter, and honey
Bamieh — okra
Bareh — lamb
Barg-e boo — bay leaf

Barg-e kazerooni — aniseed (wild)
Bareg- mo — grape leaves
Beh — quince
Berenj — rice
Borani — a mixture of various cooked or raw vegetables with yogurt

Chaghaleh-badam — fresh young almonds
Chai — tea
Choghondar — turnips
Compot — stewed fruits

Dig — large copper pot
Dolmeh — vegetables stuffed with a rice-meat mixture
Donbalan — lamb fries
Donbalan-e koohi — truffles

Esfenaj — spinach
Eslamboli pollo — a rice dish that contains tomatoes and lamb

Fandogh — hazelnuts
Felfel — pepper
Felfel sabz — green pepper
Fer — oven
Fesenjan — chicken, lamb, or duck stewed in promegranate syrup

Gandom — wheat
Gerdoo — walnuts
Geshniz — coriander (Chinese parsley)
Ghahveh — coffee
Ghalebi — molded
Gharch — mushrooms
Gharghavol — pheasant
Gholveh — kidney
Ghooreh — sour grape (grows wild in certain parts of the United States)
Ghormeh sabzi — stewed meat flavored with fresh green herbs
Gilas — cherries
Gojeh — plums
Gojeh farangi — tomatoes
Gol kalam — cauliflower
Golpar — a seasoning used in making pickles
Goosht — meat

Halim — porridge
Halvah — a sweet dessert or spread

Havij — carrots
Hendooneh — watermelon

Ja'fari — parsley
Jegar — liver
Jo — barley
Joojeh — chicken
Jowz-e hendi — nutmeg

Kabab — meat or fowl cooked over a charcoal fire
Kabk — partridge
Kabootar — pigeon
Kadoo — squash (or pumpkin)
Kahoo — lettuce
Kalam — cabbage
Kangar — cardoons (prickly artichokes)
Karafs — celery
Kareh — butter
Kashk — whey
Kasti — chicory
Kateh — rice cooked without rinsing or draining, so that it becomes somewhat sticky
Khameh — cream
Khiar — cucumber
Khiar-shoor — dill pickles
Khoresht — a stewed meat or fowl that is served with rice
Khorma — dates
Koofteh — a meatball made from meat, rice, herbs, and yellow split peas
Kookoo — an egg and vegetable dish that somewhat resembles a soufflé
Kotlet — cutlet

Lapeh — yellow split peas
Limoo — lemon
Limoo amani — Persian lime
Loobia chiti — cranberry October beans
Loobia ghermez — kidney beans
Loobia sabz — green beans

Maghz — brains
Mahi — fish
Mash — mung beans
Mikhak — cloves
Miveh — fruit
Moraba — jam, preserves
Morgh — chicken

Nan — bread
Na'na — mint
Narengi — tangerine
Nargil — coconut
Nokhod — chick-peas (or peas)

Ordak — duck

Piaz — onion
Piazcheh — scallion
Pesteh — pistachios
Pollo — rice
Porteghal — orange

Reshteh — noodles
Rob — syrup
Rob-e anar — pomegranate syrup
Rivas — rhubarb

Sabzi — green herbs
Sekanjebin — mint sauce
Shahi-ye abi — watercress
Shambalileh — fenugreek
Sharbat — a sweet drink made from a fruit syrup and cold water
Shebet (also Shevid) — dill weed
Shir — milk
Shir berenj — rice pudding
Shirini — cookies and small cakes
Sib — apple
Sib-zamini — potatoes
Siyah-daneh — a small, black, pungent seed used in pickling
Somagh — sumac

Talebi — cantaloupe
Tameshk — raspberries
Tarkhoon — tarragon
Toot — mulberries
Toot-farangi — strawberries

Zaban — tongue
Za'faran — saffron
Zanjabil — ginger
Zarchoobeh — turmeric
Zardaloo — apricots
Zeereh — cumin
Zereshk — a tiny red currant

Index

Ab doogh khiar, 77
  ba goosht-e morgh, 77–78
Ab goosht, 11, 12
  -dizi, 12–13
Ab-goosht-e
  ab-ghooreh, 14
  bademjan va adas, 15–16
  beh, 14, 15
  boz bash, 17
  gandom, 19
  lapeh, 18
  limoo amani, 14
  loobia chiti, 13
  na'na va ja'fari, 18–19
  sib va albaloo, 16
Adas pollo, 108–109
  ba morgh, 109
Agriculture, Iranian, *xvi, xviii*
Albaloo pollo, 119–120
Alcoholic beverages, *xix–xx*, 3
Almond(s)
  baklava and pistachios with, 221
  cookies, 225–226
  -filled cakes, 233–234
  stewed lamb with, 152–153
Animal slaughter, 205
Appetizers, 3–7
  cardoon hors d'oeuvre, 5–6
  caviar, 6
  drained yogurt with herbs, 3–4
  eggplant hors d'oeuvre, 5
  feta cheese, 4
  lentil puree, 7
  stuffed grape leaves, 6

  yogurt and cucumbers, 7
  zucchini hors d'oeuvre, 4–5
Apple(s)
  cobbler, 243
  stewed lamb with, 148–149
Arnold, Arthur, *x*
Ash, 11, 21
Ash-e
  aloo, 24
  anar, 25
  gojeh farangi, 25–26
  kadoo, 26
  jo, 27
  reshteh, 29
  sak, 23
  shol ghalamcar, 28
  zereshk, 26
Ashe-e
  gooshti, 22
  mash, 28
  mast, 22

Bademjan-e shirazi, 85
Bademjan pollo, 126
Baghala ba kahoo, 82–83
Baghali pollo, 112–113
Baghali-e sabz, 83–84
Baghlava ba pesteh, 221
Baked lamb, 182–183
Baked squash boats, 89
Baklava
  with almonds and pistachios, 221
  with pistachios, 221
  with walnuts, 220

Bamieh, 231–232
Bareh-ye shekam por, 181–182
Barley soup, 27
Bean soup
  cranberry October, 13
  with meat, 22
Beans. *See* Fava beans; Green beans;
    Lima beans; Navy beans; String
    beans
Beef, ground. *See* Ground beef
    tongue, with lemon sauce, 171–
    172
Beet(s)
  -endive salad, 96
  pickled, 263
Bell, Gertrude, *xv*, 197
Bereshtook nokhochi, 230
Beryooni, 177–178
Beverages
  carbonated yogurt refresher, 78
  yogurt refresher, 78
  See also Alcoholic beverages; Sher-
    bets
Black-eyed peas, stewed lamb with,
    144–145
Blossom cookies, 224
Boghchehs, *xviii*
Boniyeh-ye sib, 243
Borani-ye
  bademjan, 74; ba goosht, 72–73
  esfenaj, 71–72
  gharch, 75
  goosht, 74–75
  kangar, 73
Boz ghormeh, 165–166
Brain(s)
  kookoo, 65
  lamb, 175
Braised lamb
  shanks, 161–162
  with yogurt, 163
Braised partridges with cream, 206–
    207
Breads, 213–215
Breast of Lamb, 165–166

Cabbage
  pickled, 261

rice with meatballs and, 117–118
  stuffed, 44–45
Calf's tongue, 173–174
Candy(ies)
  coconut, 231
  honey-almond, 232
Persian marzipan, 234–235
  sweetfingers, 231–232
Cantaloupe gelatin, 241
Caramel syrup, 236
Carbonated yogurt refresher, 78
Cardoon(s)
  hors d'oeuvre, 5–6
  kookoo, 63
  rice with, 125
  salad, 101
  soup, 35
  stewed lamb with, 147; and herbs,
    148
  yogurt with, 73
Carrots, 81–82
  rice and lamb with, 118–119
  salad, 94, 95
  stewed lamb with, 142
Casseroles
  eggplant, 85, 168, 169
  fava bean and lettuce, 82–83
  kidney, 172; liver and heart, 176
  lamb liver, 174
  leek, 179
  lentil-squash, 88
  mashed lamb and rice, 178
  mixed vegetable, 86–87
  okra and lamb, 171
  vegetable with meatballs, 87
Cauliflower
  kookoo, 61
  pickled, 261–262
  soup, 36–37
Caviar appetizers, 6
Celery, stewed lamb with, 143–144
Chardin, Sir John, *xix, xx*, 106
Cheese, feta cheese appetizers, 4
Chef's salad, 101
Cherries
  glazed, 235
  pickled, 271
  See also Sour cherries

Cherry tomatoes, pickled, 260
Chick-pea(s)
    and herb soup, 28, 185–186
    patties, 185
    flour: cookies, 226–227; meatballs,
        192–193; squares, 230
Chicken
    baked rice with, 122–123; and
        spinach, 123
    cold yogurt soup with, 77–78
    croquettes, 166
    kabab, 199
    kookoo, 63–64
    molded rice with dried fruit and,
        130–131
    molded shirazi rice with, 120–121
    okra with, 181
    in orange sauce, 177
    in pomegranate sauce, 139–140
    -potato croquettes, 167
    rice with, 110; and carrots, 118–
        119; and lentils, 109
    soup, 38–39
    sour, 156
    sour cherry rice with, 119–120
    stewed: curry, 150–151; with tan-
        gerines, 154; with yogurt, 149
    in walnut-lemon sauce, 141
Chilau, 105
Coconut
    candies, 231
    cookies, 225
Cold soup, 30
Cold yogurt soup, 77
    with chicken, 77–78
Compot-e aloo, 243
Cookies
    almond, 225–226
    almond filled, 233–234
    blossom, 224
    chick-pea flour, 226–227
    coconut, 225
    cornstarch, 204
    flour, 222
    flourless walnut, 224–225
    Persian, 221, 223–224
    rice flour, 227–228
    spicy nut-date balls, 226

sunshine pills, 228
tea, 223
walnut, 222
"window," 232–233
Cornstarch
    cookies, 234
    pudding, 247
"Coy" soup, 37–38
Crab apple syrup, 253–254
Cranberry October bean soup, 13
Croquettes
    chicken, 166; -potato, 167
Cucumbers
    pickled, 264
    and yogurt, 7, 71
Currant soup, 26
Curry(ies)
    meatballs, 191
    stewed chicken, 150–151
Curzon, Lord, 105

Dami
    eslamboli, 128–129
    ghalebi ba morgh, 130–131
Dampokht, 128
Dates
    noodle-rice with meat and, 126–
        127
    pickled, 268
    yogurt and walnuts with, 75–76
Desser-e
    gele-ye gilas, 239–240
    miveh, 242
    talebi ba gelatin, 241
    toot farangi, 236
Desserts
    apple cobbler, 243
    cantaloupe gelatin, 241
    cornstarch pudding, 247
    fruit medley, 242
    halvah, 245–246
    honeymoon pudding, 245
    ice in paradise, 246
    layered cherry gelatin, 239–240
    marbled cherry gelatin, 240–241
    orange delight, 242
    prune compote, 243
    rice pudding, 247

rosewater pudding, 248
saffron pudding, 244
strawberry gelatin with cream, 240
See also Cookies; Pastries
Dill pickles, 263–264
  salad, 98
Dill weed
  and fava bean meatballs, 192
  rice with fava beans and lamb,
    112–113
Dolmeh kalam, 44–45
Dolmeh-ye
  bademjan, 50–51
  barg-e mo, 6, 45–46
  felfel sabz, 48–49
  gojeh farangi, 46–47
  kadoo, 49–50
  sib zamini, 47, 48
Doogh-e ab-ali, 78
Douglas, William, 69–70
Drained yogurt with herbs, 3–4
Dried fruit
  molded rice with chicken and, 130
  pickled peaches, 270
Duck, duckling
  a la Perse, 209
  in pomegranate-walnut sauce, 155

Eftar, 245
Eggplant(s)
  casseroles, 85, 168, 169
  hors d'oeuvre, 5
  kookoos, 59–60
  and lentil soup, 15–16
  pickled, 259–260; Italian, 258
  rice with, 126
  Shiraz, 85–86
  soup, 20–21
  stewed lamb with, 138–139; and
    yellow split peas, 139
  stuffed, 50–51
  tomato rice with, 128–129
  yogurt with, 74
Eggs, spinach with, 82
Elephant's ears, 229–230
Endive-beet salad, 96
Eshgeneh-ye
  albaloo, 34

gojeh, 33–34
Eslamboli pollo, 114

Fava beans
  and dill weed meatballs, 192
  dill weed rice and lamb with, 112–
    113
  kookoo, 58
  and lettuce casserole, 82–83
  in the pod, 83–84
  stewed lamb with, 149–150
  in tomato sauce, 83
  yellow rice with, 128
Fesenjan-e ordak, 155
Feta cheese appetizers, 4
Fillet of lamb kabab, 197–198
Fish
  in herbs, 157
  kookoo, 64–65
  white, pan-fried fillet of, 183
Flat bread, 215
Flour cookies, 222
Flourless walnut cookies, 224–225
Fraser, James Baillie, Esq., *xiv*, 252
Fruit(s)
  of Iran, *xvi, xviii*
  medley, 242
  pickled mixed, 267; and vegetables,
    266–267
  storage of, *xix*
See also Dried fruit; *and under individual names of*
Fryer, John, *xviii, xix*, 55, 93, 105,
  197, 251

Gelatin
  cantaloupe, 241
  layered cherry, 239–240
  marbled cherry, 240–241
  strawberry with cream, 240
Gele-ye
  gilas, 240–241
  toot farangi, 240
Germek, *xix*
Ghalieh esfenaj, 88
Ghalieh-ye
  esfenaj, 87
  kadoo, 88

Gharghavol ba khameh, 208–209
Gharghavol-e shekam por, 207–208
Gheimeh pollo, 116–117
Ghoorabeh, 177
Ghormeh sabzi-ba mahi, 157
Ghormeh-sabzi pollo, 115–116
Ghors-e khorshid, 228
Ghotab, 233–234
Glazed cherries, 235
Goosh-e fil, 229–230
Goosht-e bareh, 179–180
Grape leaves, stuffed, 45–46
Grapes
  Iranian, xix
  pickled, 269
  sour, stewed lamp with, 146
Green beans
  lamb stew with, 164
  tomato rice with lamb and, 115
Green herb kookoo, 55–56
Green herb rice, 121–122
Green pea(s)
  kookoo, 59
  salad with yogurt, 94
Green pepper salad, 99
Green plum(s)
  soup, 33–34; with meat and herbs,
    35–36
  stewed lamb with, 142–143
Green rice with peas and lamb, 124
Green salad, 97
Ground beef
  cutlets, 186–187
  kabab, 200
  okra with, 180
  patties, tart, 187
Ground meat
  chick-pea patties, 185–186
  split pea patties, 184–185
  See also Ground beef

Halim bademjan, 20–21
Halvah, 245–246
Hamam, xviii
Havij pollo, 118–119
Heart, kidney, and lamb liver casse-
  role, 176
Herbert, Sir Thomas, xv, xviii, 106

Honey-almond sweets, 232
Honeymoon pudding, 245
Hors d'oeuvre-e
  bademjan, 5
  kadoo, 4–5
  kangar, 5–6
  panir, 4
Hospitality, in Iran, xiii-xv

Ice in paradise, 246
Iran, description of, xvi, xviii–xix
Irrigation systems, Iranian, xvi

Jewel-studded rice, 110–111

Kabab-e
  barg, 197–198
  gharghavol, 201–202
  joojeh, 199
  koobideh, 200
  ran-e bareh, 200–201
Kababs
  chicken, 199
  fillet of lamb, 197–198
  ground beef, 200
  leg of lamb, 200–201
  pheasant, 202–202
  shish kabab, 199
Kabk, 206–207
  ba sos-e gojeh-farangi, 207
Kachi, 245
Kalampeh, 226
Kalam pollo, 117–118
Kaleh-joosh, 75–76
Kanali, 179–180
Kangar-pollo, 125
Kashk-e kadoo, 76–77
Kateh, 129
  ghalebi, 129–130
Khayyam, Omar, xx
Khiar torshi, 264
Khorak-e
  bademjan, 169
  baghala, 83
  bamieh ba gheimeh, 180
  ba goosht, 171
  ba morgh, 181
  bareh, 162

boz ghormeh, 170
del-o gholveh-o jegar, 176
donbalan, 176
gholveh, 172
goosht ba mast, 163
jegar, 174
jegar va gholveh, 173
kadoo, 89
kadoo va ja'fari, 84
kashk-e bademjan, 168
loobia, 163–164
maghz, 174–175
mahicheh, 161–162
mahi sefid, 183
nokhod farangi, 165
zaban, 173–174
Khoresht-e
aloo, 138
bademjan, 138–139
bamieh, 153–154
beh, 146–147
chaghaleh-badoom, 152–153
esfenaj va aloo, 141
fesenjan, 139–140
gharch, 152
gheimeh, 137–138
ghooreh, 146
ghormeh sabzi, 144–145
gojeh, 142–143
gol dar chaman-baghala ghatogh, 149–150
havij, 142
kadoo, 151
kangar, 147; ba sabzi, 148
karafs, 143–144
kari, 150–151
loobia, 136–137
mast, 149
morgh-e torsh, 156
na'na-ja'fari va gojeh, 143
narengi, 154
rivas, 145
sib-e derakhti, 148–149
Kidney casserole(s), 172
with liver, 173
with liver and heart, 176
Kisel-e porteghal, 242

Koofteh
berenji, 190
shebet-baghala, 192
Tabrizi, 189
Koofteh-ye
ard-e nokhochi, 192–193
kari, 191
sabzi, 188
Kookoo-ye
bademjan, 59–60
gol kalam, 61
kadoo, 61
kangar, 63
loobia sabz, 56–57; ba goosht, 57–58
maghz, 65
mahi, 64–65
morgh-choghortmeh, 63–64
nokhod farangi, 59
sabzi, 55–56
shebet baghala, 58
tareh, 62; ba gerdoo, 62–63
Kotlet-e
goosht, 186–187
morgh, 166
morgh-o sib zamini, 167

Lamb
baked, 182–183
baked rice with, 122–123; and spinach, 123
brains, 174–175
braised, with yogurt, 163
breast of, 165–166
casserole, 170
dill weed rice with fava beans and, 112–113
fillet of, kabab, 197–198
fries, Persian, 176
green rice with peas and, 124
leg of, kabab, 200–201
liver: casserole, 174; kidney, and heart casserole, 176
mashed, and rice casserole, 178
noodle-rice and dates with, 126
and okra casserole, 171
in pomegranate sauce, 139–140

red rice and peas with, 115
and rice: with carrots, 118–119; with herbs, 115–116; with yellow split peas, 116–117
shank(s): braised, 161–162; soup, 12–13; soup with Persian limes, 14; soup with sour grape juice, 14
stew: with apples, 148–149; with black-eyed peas, 144–145; with cardoons, 147; with cardoons and herbs, 148; with carrots, 142; with celery, 143–144; with eggplant, 138–139; with eggplant and yellow split peas, 139; with fava beans, 149–150; with fresh almonds, 152–153; with green beans, 164; with green plums, 142–143; with herbs and plums, 143; with mushrooms, 152; with navy beans, 163–164; with okra, 153–154; with peas, 165; plain, 162; with quince, 146–147; with rhubarb, 145; with sour grapes, 146; with spinach and prunes, 141; with squash, 151; with string beans, 136–137; with yellow split peas, 137–138; with yellow split peas and prunes, 138
stuffed whole, 181–182
tomato rice with, 114; and green beans, 115
Layered cherry gelatin, 239–240
Lebanese mountain bread, 108
Leek(s)
    casserole, 179
    kookoo, 62; with walnuts, 62–63
Leg of lamb kabab, 200–201
Legume and noodle soup, 29
Lemon
    rind, pickled, 268
    sauce, beef tongue with, 171–172
    syrup, 252
Lentil(s)
    puree, 7, 84–85
    rice with, 108–109; and chicken, 109

soup, 32–33
-squash casserole, 88
yogurt and meat with, 74–75
Lettuce
    and fava bean casserole, 82–83
    soup, 38
Lima bean kookoo, 58
Liteh-ye bademjan, 259–260
Liver and kidney casserole, 173
    See also Lamb, liver
Loobia pollo, 115
Loz-e nargil, 231

Mangoes, pickled dried, 270
Marbled cherry gelatin, 240–241
Masghati-e
    borideh shodeh, 234
    kaseh-i, 247
Mashed lamb and rice casserole, 178
Mast, 70
Mast-e-kisei, 3–4
Mast-o-khiar, 7, 71
Meat, yogurt and lentils with, 74–75
    See also Beef; Chicken; Ground beef; Ground meat; Lamb; Meatballs
Meatballs
    chick-pea flour, 192–193
    curry, 191
    fava bean and dill weed, 192
    parsley, 188
    and rice, 190; with cabbage, 117–118
    soup, 23
    Tabriz, 189
    vegetable casserole with, 87
Meshkoofi, 248
Mint
    cucumber sauce, 102
    and parsley soup with green plums, 18–19
    sauce, 102
Mirza ghassemi, 85
Mixed pickles, 258
Mixed vegetable casserole, 86–87
Molded rice, 129–130
    with chicken and dried fruit, 130–131

Shirazi, with chicken, 120–121
Morasah pollo, 110–111
Morier, James J., *xiii–xiv*, 55, 135
Morgh pollo, 110
Mung bean soup, 28
Mushrooms
    stewed lamb with, 152
    yogurt with, 75

Nan-e
    ard-e gerdooi, 222
    ardi, 222
    badami, 225–226
    barbari, 214
    berenji, 227–228
    chai, 223
    gerdooi, 224–225
    lavash, 215
    nargili, 225
    nokhochi, 226–227
    panjarei, 232–233
    shirini, 221
    shirini-ye khoshk, 223–224
    shokoofeh, 224
Narenjak, 235–236
Nargessi esfenaj, 82
Navy beans, lamb stew with, 163–164

Okra
    with chicken, 181
    with ground beef, 180
    and lamb casserole, 171
    stewed lamb with, 153–154
Onions, pickled, 265
Orange
    delight, 242
    rind, pickled, 268–269
    sauce, chicken in, 177
    syrup, 252
Ordak, 209

Pan fried white fish fillet, 183
Parsley
    meatballs, 188
    squash with, 84
Partridges
    braised, with cream, 206–207
    roast, with cream, 206
    in tomato sauce, 207
Pastries
    baklava, 220–221
    chick-pea flour squares, 230
    elephant's ears, 229
    syrup-dipped cakes, 235–236
Peaches, pickled dried, 270
Peas
    green rice and lamb with, 124
    lamb stew with, 165
    red rice with lamb and, 115
Persian bread, 214
Persian cookies, 221, 223–224
Persian lamb fries, 176
Persian marzipan, 234–235
Persian "ravioli," 179–180
Persian "Sloppy Joe," 177–178
Persian soup, 17
Pheasant
    with cream, 208–209
    kabab, 201–202
    stuffed, 207–208
Pickled foods
    beets, 263
    cabbage, 261
    cauliflower, 261–262
    cherries, 271
    cherry tomatoes, 260
    cucumbers, 264
    dates, 268
    dried mangoes, 270
    dried peaches, 270
    eggplant, 259–260
    Italian eggplant, 258
    grapes, 269
    lemon rind, 268
    mixed fruits, 267; and vegetables, 266–267
    mixed vegetables, 265–266
    onions, 265
    orange rind, 268–269
    quince, 269
    shallots, 264
    turnips, 263
    See also Pickles
Pickles
    dill, 263–264

mixed, 258
seven-tone, 262–263
See also Pickled foods
Pinto bean salad, 97–98
Pistachios
baklava with, 221; almonds and, 221
Plain lamb stew, 162
Plain rice, 129
Plums, stewed lamb with herbs and, 143
See also Green plums
Pomegranate(s), *xvi*
sauce, chicken or lamb in, 139–140
soup, 25
syrup, spinach in, 88
-walnut sauce, duckling in, 155
Pooreh-ye adas, 7, 84–85
Pork, *xix*
Potato(es)
salad with yogurt, 100–101
stuffed, 47–48
Prune(s)
compote, 243
soup, 24
stewed lamb with spinach and, 141
Puddings
cornstarch, 247
honeymoon, 245
rice, 247
rosewater, 248
saffron, 244
Pullow, 105

Quince
-lemon syrup, 252–253
pickled, 269
soup, 14, 15
stewed lamb with, 146–147

Raspberry syrup, 254
Red rice with lamb and peas, 115
Reshteh pollo, 126–127
Restaurants, in Iran, *xv–xvi*
Rhubarb, stewed lamb with, 145
Rice
with baked lamb, 122–123; and spinach, 123

with cabbage and meatballs, 117–118
with cardoons, 125
with carrots and lamb, 118–119
with chicken, 110
cooking method, 107–108
dill weed, with fava beans and lamb, 112–113
with eggplant, 126
flour cookies, 227–228
flour soup, 36
green herb, 121–122
green, with peas and lamb, 124
with herbs and lamb, 115–116
jewel-studded, 110–111
with lentils, 108–109; and chicken, 109
and mashed lamb casserole, 178
meatballs, 190
molded, 129–130; with chicken and dried fruit, 130–131; Shirazi, with chicken, 120–121
noodle-, with meat and dates, 126–127
plain, 129
pudding, 247
red, with lamb and peas, 115
sour cherry, with chicken, 119–120
and spinach soup, 21
sweet, 111–112
tomato: with eggplant, 128–129; with lamb, 114; with lamb and green beans, 115
with yellow fava beans, 128
with yellow split peas and lamb, 116–117
Roast partridges with cream, 206
Rosewater pudding, 248
Royal salad, 99
Russian salad, 100

Sabzi pollo, 121–122
Saffron pudding, 244
Salad(s)
cardoon, 101
carrot, 94, 95
chef's, 101
dill pickle, 98

endive-beet, 96
green, 97
green pea with yogurt, 94
green pepper, 99
pinto bean, 97–98
potato with yogurt, 100–101
royal, 99
Russian, 100
spinach, 95–96
watercress, 97
yogurt, 71
Salad dressings
mint-cucumber sauce, 102
mint sauce, 102
Salad-e
ashpaz, 101
esfenaj, 95–96
felfel sabz, 99
havij, 94, 95
kangar, 101
khiar shoor, 98
laboo, 96
loobia chiti, 97–98
nokhod ba mast, 94
sahrai, 97
saltanati, 99
sib zamini ba mast, 100–101
Salad russe, 100
Scallion soup, 31
Sekanjebin, 102
Sekanjebin-e khiar, 102
Seven-tone pickles, 262–263
Shallots, pickled, 264
Shami-e
ard-e nokhochi, 185
nokhochi, 185–186
pook, 184–185
Sharbat-e
ab-limoo, 252
albaloo, 253
beh-limoo, 252–253
porteghal, 252
tameshk, 254
toot-farangi, 254
zoghal-akhteh, 253–254
Sheep, in Iran, xviii–xix
Sherbets, syrups for, 252–254
Shesh-andaz-e havij, 81–82

Shiraz eggplants, 85
Shirazi pollo-ye ghalebi, 120–121
Shir berenj, 247
Shirin pollo, 111–112
Shish kabab, 199
Shol-e
beryooni, 178
zard, 244
Sohan asali, 232
Soufflé. See Kookoo
Soup(s)
barley, 27
bean with meat, 22
cardoon, 35
cauliflower, 36–37
chick-pea and herb, 28
chicken, 38–39
cold, 30
cold yogurt, 77; with chicken, 77–78
"coy," 37
cranberry October bean, 13
currant, 26
eggplant, 20–21; and lentil, 15–16
green plum, 33–34; with meat and herbs, 35–36
lamb shank, 12–13; with Persian limes, 14; with sour grape juice, 14
legume and noodle, 29
lentil, 32–33
lettuce, 38
meatball, 23
mint and parsley, with green plums, 18–19
mung bean, 28
Persian, 17
pomegranate, 25
prune, 24
quince, 14, 15
rice flour, 36
rice and spinach, 21
scallion, 31
sour cherry, 34; and apple, 16
spinach with Chinese parsley, 31–32
squash, 26
tomato, 25–26

wedding, 30
wheat, 19, 20
yellow split pea, 18
yogurt, 22
Soup-e
  adas, 32–33
  ard-e berenji, 36
  aroosi, 30
  gojeh, 35–36
  gol kalem, 36–37
  kahoo, 38
  kangar, 35
  morgh, 38–39
  naz, 37–38
  piazcheh, 31
  sak, 31–32
  sard, 30
Sour cherry(ies)
  and apple soup, 16
  rice with chicken, 119–120
  soup, 34
  syrup, 253
Sour chicken, 156
Spicy nut-date balls, 226
Spinach
  in pomegranate syrup, 88
  rice with baked lamb and, 123
  salad, 95–96
  soup with Chinese parsley, 31–32
  stewed lamb with prunes and, 141
  yogurt with, 71–72
Split pea patties, 184–185
Squash
  baked boats, 89
  -lentil casserole, 88
  with parsley, 84
  soup, 26
  stewed lamb with, 151
  stuffed, 49–50
  yogurt with, 76–77
Strawberry
  delight, 236
  gelatin with cream, 240
  syrup, 254
String bean(s)
  kookoo, 56–57; with ground beef,
    57–58
  stewed lamb with, 136–137

Stuffed foods
  cabbage leaves, 44–45
  eggplants, 50–51
  grape leaves, 6, 45–46
  green peppers, 48–49
  pheasant, 207–208
  potatoes, 47, 48
  tomatoes, 46–47
  whole lamb, 181–182
  yellow summer squash, 49–50
Stuffing
  for pheasant, 208
  for whole lamb, 181–182
  See also Stuffed foods
Sweet rice, 111–112
Syrup(s)
  crab apple, 253–254
  -dipped cakes, 235–236
  orange, 252
  lemon, 252
  quince-lemon, 252–253
  raspberry, 254
  sour cherry, 253
  strawberry, 254
Sunshine pills, 228
Sweetfingers, 231–232

Ta'arof, 219–220
Table manners, in Iran, xv
Tabriz meatballs, 189
Tah-chin, 122–123
  esfenaj, 123
Tala-kooleh, 177
Tangerines, stewed chicken with, 154
Tart ground beef patties, 187
Tas kabab, 182–183
Tea cookies, 223
Tomato rice
  with eggplant, 128–129
  with lamb, 114; and green beans,
    115
Tomato sauce
  fava beans in, 83
  partridges in, 207
Tomato soup, 25–26
Tomatoes
  pickled cherry, 260
  stuffed, 46–47

Tongue
  beef, with lemon sauce, 171–172
  calf's, 173–174
Toot, 234–235
Torsh-e tareh, 86–87, 179
Torshi shami, 187
Torshi-ye
  anbeh, 270
  angoor, 269
  bademjan, 259, 260
  bademjan-e riz, 258
  barg-e holoo, 270
  beh, 269
  gilas, 271
  gojeh farangi, 260
  hafte-bijar, 262–263
  kalem, 261
  kalam-gol, 261–262
  khiar shoor, 263–264
  khorma, 268
  laboo, 263
  makhloot, 258
  miveh, 267
  miveh-ye makhloot, 266–267
  moosir, 264
  piaz, 265
  poost-e limoo torsh, 268
  poost-e porteghal, 268–269
  sabzi-ye makhloot, 265–266
  shalgham, 263
Turnips, pickled, 263

Vegetables
  casserole, with meatballs, 87
  pickled mixed, 265–266; fruits and,
    266–267
  stuffed. See Dolmeh
  See also under individual names of

Walnut (s)
  baklava with, 220–221
  cookies, 222
  leek kookoo with, 62–63

-lemon sauce, chicken in, 141
  yogurt and dates with, 75–76
Watercress salad, 97
Wedding soup, 30
Wheat soup, 19, 20
"Window" cookies, 232–233
Wine-making, xix-xx

Yakh dar behesht, 246
Yellow split pea(s)
  patties, 184–185
  rice and lamb with, 116–117
  soup, 18
  stewed lamb with, 137–138; and
    eggplant, 139; and prunes, 138
Yogurt, xix, 70
  braised lamb with, 163
  carbonated refresher, 78
  with cardoons, 73
  cold soup, 77; with chicken, 77–78
  and cucumbers, 7, 71
  with dates and walnuts, 75–76
  drained with herbs, 3–4
  with eggplants, 74; and meatballs,
    72–73
  green pea salad with, 94
  with meat and lentils, 74–75
  with mushrooms, 75
  potato salad with, 100–101
  refresher, 78
  salad, 71
  soup, 22
  with spinach, 71–72
  with squash, 76–77
  stewed chicken with, 149

Zaban-e gav ba sauce-e limoo, 171–
  172
Zoroastrians, xix
Zucchini
  hors d'oeuvre, 4–5
  squash kookoo, 61